NO MORE TEAMS!

NO MORE TEAMS!

MASTERING THE DYNAMICS OF CREATIVE COLLABORATION

MICHAEL SCHRAGE

CURRENCY · DOUBLEDAY

NEW YORK · LONDON · TORONTO · SYDNEY · AUCKLAND

A CURRENCY PAPERBACK
PUBLISHED BY DOUBLEDAY
a division of Bantam Doubleday Dell Publishing Group, Inc.
1540 Broadway, New York, New York 10036

CURRENCY and DOUBLEDAY are trademarks of Doubleday,
a division of Bantam Doubleday Dell Publishing Group, Inc.

Permissions are listed on pages 240–41.

No More Teams! was originally published in hardcover as *Shared Minds* by Random
House, Inc., in 1990. This Currency Doubleday edition reprinted by special
arrangement with Random House, Inc., New York.

Design by Julie Duquet

Library of Congress Cataloging-in-Publication Data

Schrage, Michael.
No more teams! : mastering the dynamics of creative collaboration
/ Michael Schrage.
p.   cm.
Rev., updated ed. of: Shared minds.
Includes bibliographical references.
1. Communication—Philosophy.   2. Communication in organizations.
I. Schrage, Michael.   Shared minds.   II. Title.
P90.S3628   1995
302.2'01—dc20   95-11542
                                                        CIP

ISBN 0-385-47603-5
Copyright © 1989 by Michael Schrage
New Introduction and User's Guide © 1995 by Michael Schrage
All Rights Reserved
Printed in the United States of America
First Currency Paperback Edition: May 1995
10 9 8 7 6 5 4

For my parents . . .

Contents

Preface

THIS BOOK BEGAN AS ANOTHER BOOK AND THEN TURNED INTO several other books until it finally ended up as this book.

Originally, it was going to be about meetings and how people could take advantage of new technologies to improve meetings' quality and effectiveness. Barely four months into this project, I realized I had completely missed the real questions—the questions that matter.

I discovered that meetings are the awkward social rituals that organizations put their people through in the hope that they might productively collaborate. I recognized then that the vital relationship to study, learn about, and understand was collaboration.

As I talked with doctors, artists, Nobel laureate scientists, inventors, movie directors, and other creative collaborators, I realized that one could easily write a book about collaboration in the visual arts or in physics or in literature or Fortune 500 companies. Why not a chapter on each? I could examine the differences between mentor/protégé collaboration and the peer/peer collaboration. A delightful treatise could be done on the differences in collaborative temperaments, and Francis Crick strongly suggested I consider a chapter on age differences of collaborators. A helpful Paris-born source warned me that the word *collaborators* would be the kiss of death in any French translation of this book because it still conjures up the images of traitors in World War II France.

The more I spoke with people the more it became clear that collaboration was a topic that excited them even as they struggled to explain what it meant. In the meantime, my research forced me to learn something about social psychology, impressionism, quantum physics, hermeneutics, linguistics, cubism, and the history of management theory.

But the most important thing it forced me to do was watch: viewing relationships in the context of collaboration forced me to examine how people related to one another in a way I had never done before. I became extremely sensitive to how airplane crews work with one another; how surgical teams collaborated; how industrial designers and architects explored alternatives with their clients.

This is not an academic or rigorously comprehensive book. It's a book written with a journalist's sensibility: that is, it's intended to be accessible, insightful, and provocative. It is filled with examples and observations that people of diverse backgrounds and professions can relate to and, most important, will find useful to (or can incorporate into) their lives. It is designed to make people aware both of the dynamics and the new tools of collaboration in a way that should enable them to improve the quality of their own relationships.

There are no panaceas or quick fixes here; there are only perspectives and ideas about a very powerful—and empowering—aspect of human relationships. As the typically egomaniacal journalist, I can only say that what I have discovered, learned, and internalized about collaboration has made my professional relationships far more productive and far more enjoyable for everyone concerned. My ego remains intact; my mania has gone into remission.

The reader might keep in mind that this book doesn't tell a story so much as it explores a theme. The beginning, middle, and end are really arbitrary—much in the way that most relationships are.

My advice to the reader before reading on is to remember the most bitter and frustrating working relationship you've ever had with someone you thought was bright and talented—and then ask yourself why it was so difficult.

Then you should remember the most productive and successful working relationship you've ever had with a colleague or a client— and ask yourself why that can't happen more often. I think this book will show you how it can.

Introduction
No More Teams!—An Organizational Manifesto

WHY DON'T TEAMS MAKE SENSE? WHAT COULD POSSIBLY BE wrong with more and better teamwork? In an ideal world, absolutely nothing. But we don't live in an ideal world: we live in this one.

At a job interview, a friend was asked if he was a "team player." "Yes," he replied, "team captain." That story—which happens to be true—invariably gets a good laugh. But it is a cynical and knowing laugh. Everyone in the room understands precisely what most organizations mean by "team players."

Quite simply, the word *team* has been so politicized, so ensnared in the pathology of the organization, that we don't really know what it means anymore. Is a team a medium to manage value? Or a mechanism to play politics? It's easy to answer "Both." Of course, in that case, a team means whatever the organization wants it to mean. Which means, of course, that it has no real meaning at all. It is, however, the popular management metaphor of the moment. But is it the right metaphor? Is it a metaphor we should be building— and rebuilding—our organizations around? Does this metaphor create more understanding than confusion?

The answer to all these questions, unfortunately, is no. The concept of teams obscures, rather than reveals, the real relationship challenges our organizations face. Teams are a fiction, a verbal convenience, rather than a useful description of how people in a firm cooperate and collaborate to create value. Even worse, teams make it too easy for organizations to lie, cheat, and kid themselves about the way they work. More often than not, a "team" is as much a political entity as a value-creating one. The word is a little too flexible, too malleable, too manipulable.

Are you on the team? . . . Or not? Is that a question centered on creating value for customers and clients or is it meant to satisfy the insecurities of a manager checking on the loyalty of his people?

The answers reveal an awful lot about what "teamwork" and "team players" really mean in today's organizations—and tomorrow's. *No More Teams!* is a book that insists that organizations literally can't afford to design themselves around words that are dangerously ambiguous. The issue isn't teams; it's what kind of relationships organizations need to create and maintain if they want to deliver unique value to their customers and clients. That's what this book is about.

No More Teams! is the revised, updated, and improved version of *Shared Minds: The New Technologies of Collaboration.* The change of title is only the most obvious difference. In fact, this is a fundamentally different and better book than its predecessor. It's crisper, smarter, and more relevant for managers. The book's ideas have been sharpened and honed by a marketplace that cares far more for results than for academic cleverness. The essential themes of shared creation, collaborative tools, and productive relationships have become even more significant. Organizations whose futures depend on intelligent innovation will find the messages here just as provocative but even more practical.

To be sure, I had learned and observed a great deal about collaboration and collaborative media. Yes, I had studied successful collaboration in a variety of fields and had invested months in the people who had made them work. But I hadn't really brought the collaborative concepts and techniques I had identified to business organizations struggling for better ways to create value. I had observed more than I had participated.

Since the book was published, I have had the opportunity to participate as well as observe. At one global professional services firm, we helped build networks that were really more like worknets

—a medium for collaboration, not just communication; a virtual environment where shared creation is more valued than mere information exchange. At another professional services firm, we turned an on-line information service into a medium to better manage client relationships. At a financial services firm, we crafted software that made it easier for financial advisers and their clients to collaboratively craft their investment portfolios. In each case, my book offered a design sensibility that sparked the kinds of conversations that got people to experiment with innovation. I had the opportunity to help turn those experiments into everyday practice. The book brought me to organizations around the country and around the world. People inspired by the notion that managing creative relationships could matter more than managing creative individuals wanted to talk about their concerns.

Shared Minds did rather well in Japan—a country and culture that cares desperately about group creativity. The book's title there was *Mind Networks*. Japanese companies were fascinated by the idea of using technology to better leverage their community work ethic. That required a completely different view of the internal computer networks they were building. But the book also brought me into contact with Europe's industrial design community and the need for companies to design their new product teams as rigorously as they design their products. They also needed to use models and prototypes to be drivers of the innovation process instead of just derivatives of it.

In America, many organizations (intriguingly, mostly professional services firms) saw *Shared Minds* as a manifesto to create new kinds of relationships between colleagues and clients. They wanted to know—and they wanted to know *now!*—how best to implement the collaborative tools described here. They wanted to understand what made collaborative relationships different from other kinds of organizational relationships.

Needless to say, several of these companies are valued clients. Sure, it's wonderful that they like the ideas and that their checks clear. But their real value came from the wonderful opportunities to learn what ideas worked and what ideas didn't in the real world.

They gave me the chance to ground these concepts in practice. They were—and are—superb collaborators who care as much about people as they do results.

So what has been learned? What are a few of the key differences between *Shared Minds* and *No More Teams!* There are several answers to that, and you will find them weaving through the book as critical themes.

The single most important thing I learned was that organizations must recognize and reward collaboration as clearly and unambiguously as they have traditionally celebrated individual achievement. Organizations that don't design and implement their collaborative incentives as carefully as they design and implement their collaborative tools guarantee a nightmare of cultural resistance and interpersonal conflicts. If you want collaboration, reward it. Remember, it wasn't Watson or Crick who won the Nobel Prize for discovering the double helix—it was Watson and Crick (and, for that matter, Maurice Wilkins, who provided the vital X-ray crystallography data).

Similarly, managers and leaders must take the time and care to issue challenges that actually encourage people to collaborate. Creating the right challenges enormously improves the chances of creating the right collaborations. The idea that people will enthusiastically collaborate around the challenge of cutting 20 percent of their budgets is idiotic on its face. Perhaps the challenge of eliminating 40 percent of waste might be more inviting . . . or introducing a new material into a key production process. The point is simple: far too many organizations are so intellectually lazy that they don't define their problems and opportunities in ways that can seduce their people into enthusiastic, unrestrained collaborative efforts. They'd rather manage things the old-fashioned way: divvy up the problem and delegate it. It's motivation by delegation. If an organization wants to reap the synergies of collaboration, motivation by delegation represents a failure of leadership.

Another fundamental difference is the issue of creating collaborative teams. Organizations need to be more aware of how they assemble or grow their collaborations. Do they just pick the people and make them collaborators? Do they define a challenge and let people enlist? Or do they pick a core leader or two and then get them to build the collaborative group? Each approach has its benefits and drawbacks—and reveals an awful lot about an organization's culture. But the issue of how to collaborate to create collaboration in the organization is essential to its success. There can be a world of difference between top-down, bottom-up, and middle-driven collaborative teams. Leadership from the top, middle, or the bottom is similarly a different task.

Collaboration isn't necessarily teamwork; and teamwork certainly isn't collaboration. That distinction deeply matters. That's why I changed the title of the book. Sadly, organizations that confuse collaboration and teamwork are destined to fail at both. *No More Teams!* stands as much for the creation of effective collaborations as it does against the misbegotten metaphors of teams and teamwork.

No More Teams! is certainly a book filled with ideas but it is also a book offering pragmatic approaches to collaborative creativity and productive relationships. *Shared Minds* might be likened to a business plan that's been updated and revised in the face of market results. What's worked there's more of; what hasn't is either appropriately modified or gone. You might think you've finished a book when it's finally published, but you really haven't. It turns out that you learn far more from the way people react to your book—their comments, their criticisms, the ideas they embrace, the problems they had, their stubborn efforts to bring the techniques to their organizations—than you do from the process of actually writing the book.

In other words, if you are as lucky as I was, publishing a book isn't the end of a text but the beginning of a conversation. *No More Teams!* continues that conversation.

Acknowledgments

DON'T THINK I'VE MISSED THE IRONY OF A BOOK ABOUT COLLABO-
ration being authored by a single person. . . .

This book really is the product of several collaborations—lots of
them, in fact—and I would like to gratefully acknowledge as many
of them as I can. Many extraordinarily bright and busy people were
extremely generous with their time and insights. What I found most
gratifying was how curious and enthusiastic most people were about
this topic. The intersection of media technology, relationships, and
creativity is a great area to explore with others.

My friend Rob Fulop is most responsible for introducing me
to the concept of collaborative technologies. Our arguments about
collaboration and this book have been both entertaining and even
useful.

Peter Keen and Martha Ruh of the International Center for Information Technology were very supportive of this effort along several dimensions. The people at Xerox's Palo Alto Research Center
—including its director, John Seely Brown, Mark Stefik, Lucy
Suchman, Daniel Bobrow, Gregg Foster, and Carlin DeCato—provided me with more help than I had any right to expect. My discussions at PARC renew my belief that it's always a good idea to spend
time with people who are smarter than you are.

Similarly, I want to thank Nicholas Negroponte for inviting me
to spend a year at the Media Lab at MIT as a visiting scholar. MIT
and the people at the Media Lab provided a terrific environment in
which to finish this book. It's a tossup as to whether Michael

Hawley, my housemate at MIT, was a better critic or friend. His comments improved both my thinking and my type fonts.

Kris Olson, an Apple Computer consultant, was responsible for setting up an interesting electronic roundtable on collaboration. Joyce Massey and Ashby Woolf of the Center for Machine Intelligence's Capture Lab, and Lotus Development Corp.'s Irene Greif were also quite forthcoming. Jane Anderson of Regis McKenna was kind enough to lend me her Macintosh for a summer.

I am also grateful to Bernie DeKoven, David Braunschvig, Michael Doyle, and other "facilitators" for taking the time to describe not just their techniques but their impressions of how collaborative tools shape the way people interact.

I learned more than he suspects from my collaboration with Lotus Development Corp. founder Mitch Kapor. My friends—old and new including Curt Pesman, John Markoff, Katie Hafner, Robbie Myers, Jacqueline Deval, Suzanna Andrews, my brother Elliot, George Anders, Betsy Corcoran, Chris and Jill Hall, Terry and Katrina Garnet—were nothing less than extraordinarily tolerant and very encouraging. I'd also like to acknowledge my former colleagues at the *Washington Post* and *Manhattan, inc.* magazine, and my current colleagues at the *Los Angeles Times* for what I learned from them. Esther Dyson and Harriet Rubin also provided insights and support.

Only when you have finished a book can you understand why people write things like "What's terrific in this book is primarily due to the time and talents of other people—any and all mistakes are mine and mine alone" but it turns out to be true. I think writing a book is the closest a male can come to giving birth: The moments of conception are wonderful and then comes the morning sickness and waking up feeling like something else is living inside of you and running your life. Then people start asking you when you are going to finally deliver. Then come the labor pains. Finally, out pops this thing that's screaming for attention and you don't know whether to feel more happiness or relief.

I feel both—and I wouldn't have missed it for anything.

————

FOR THIS PAPERBACK edition of *No More Teams!* special thanks are due to Harriet Rubin, the editor-in-chief of Currency Doubleday, for recognizing that the themes and ideas of *Shared Minds* had become even more business-relevant over time. To a very large extent, this book is an experiment to see if individuals and organizations are now more interested in reshaping their relationships rather than merely reengineering themselves.

Special thanks are also due to Rob Earp and Lynn Fenwick for helping edit this book and shepherding it through the production process.

I am grateful to acknowledge the support I've received from friends and colleagues at the MIT Sloan School of Management and the MIT Media Lab—notably Tom Malone, Bob Halperin, Michael Hawley, and Nicholas Negroponte.

David Braunschvig, now of Lazard Frères, has been a patient friend as well as a source of ideas and encouragement; Tom Peters has been extremely kind and supportive in his notes and writing; and Keiko Satoh has been generous with her insights into Japanese business culture and her personal friendship.

Hiroshii Ishii of Japan's NTT, Brook Manville and Leif Knutsen of McKinsey & Co., and David Kelley of IDEO have all been terrific to work with as people who like to play with ideas. Many of the better ideas in this revised and enhanced version of *Shared Minds*—now titled *No More Teams!*—are the direct result of their comments, criticisms, questions, and active implementation of our own collaborations.

NO MORE TEAMS!

1

Why Collaboration Now?

DURING THE SECOND HOUR OF AN OTHERWISE ROUTINE TRIPLE bypass procedure, the vital signs of the patient—a slightly overweight fifty-two-year-old male Caucasian ex-chain smoker with a very mild case of diabetes—change. For a few moments, respiration becomes shallower and the EKG patterns shift markedly. While the patient appears to be holding up very well under the surgery, the anesthesiologist and the surgeon agree to increase the flow of oxygen to the patient slightly.

Less than seven minutes later, the patient's temperature is slowly rising, respiration is dramatically deeper, and the EKG patterns are growing more jagged. The surgeon is at a particularly delicate point in the operation, but the operation is no longer routine. Neither the surgeon nor the anesthesiologist understands why the patient is responding in this way. Is this a temporary phase change? A minor reaction? Or a precursor to a serious problem that could leave the patient dead on the operating table? Is it best to continue the procedure, alter it, or terminate it?

The surgeon and the anesthesiologist hurriedly discuss what should be done next.

THREE QUARTERS OF the way through a transcontinental flight, the copilot of a passenger jet notices a panel light signaling that the fuel level for one of the starboard engines is unusually low. The light flickers for a moment and then goes out. A few moments later, the copilot finds that the temperature of both the plane's starboard engines is rising significantly. There are no changes in any other of the panel indicators. He notifies the captain.

Early in the flight, the plane had been struck not once, but twice by lightning. The plane seemed unaffected, but it is unclear whether these panel warnings reflect the real situation or are merely an electrical artifact of the lightning. The captain, who has flown this type of plane for more than twelve years, radios his airline to talk with ground engineers about the situation. He and the copilot can come up with several scenarios to explain the panel behavior, but he wants additional guidance. The talk is tense. This flight is no longer routine. The pilot, copilot, and ground crew discuss their options: Is the current situation manageable? Should the flight be terminated immediately? Are there other ways to test the validity of the panel lights? Should one of the engines be shut down?

A SMALL TEAM of creatives and account executives are planning their presentation for a new campaign to a potential client with an annual advertising budget in excess of $40 million. The client, tops in its field, has a history of being difficult and willing to take a chance on unusual ideas if they can be executed well. While this client has a great deal of respect for the creative side of advertising, it insists upon campaigns that produce measurable sales as well as memorable images. The client also has a reputation for being a bit of a penny-pincher—although if it really likes an idea, it is prepared to go all out. Moreover, the client prefers to view its advertising agency as a partner rather than a subcontractor. While it will not directly interfere in the creative evolution of a campaign, this client will not hesitate to make its feelings known and offer "insights" into its preferences.

The creatives at the agency have spent months studying this client and have developed three extremely intriguing campaign approaches but nothing, unfortunately, that can be described as spectacular. They're also kicking around some new ideas. The account executives have several ideas about what campaigns might be most appealing and how best to package the pitch. The formal client presentation is scheduled in seven working days. The group has to decide whether to develop one or all of these campaigns or scrap them and crash for a new idea that has a shot at the spectacular, and they have to figure out how best to make their pitch. They've all gone through this before, but everyone in the room has decided their agency really wants this client, both for the money and the prestige. What do they do next?

THESE TEAMS OF professionals—in the operating room, the cockpit, and the conference room—each have a genuine problem and a limited amount of time to deal with it. There may be no one right answer, but there are certainly wrong answers. For the advertising agency, the wrong answers will be costly and possibly embarrassing. For the doctors and the pilots, the wrong answers could be tragic.

None of these possible answers will be routine because none of these problems is routine. Going by the book is meaningless here because this is a book they have to write as they go along.

This can be literally true. When the tail engine exploded on United Airlines flight 232 from Denver to Chicago in July 1989, Captain Alfred C. Haynes shut it down while his second officer Dudley Dvorak got out the procedure book. The plane had lost all its hydraulic systems and thus its ability to maneuver. "When I asked Dudley what the procedure was for that he said, "There isn't one," Haynes recalled. "So we made it up as we went along."

An off-duty pilot came up to the cockpit to help operate the engine throttles. "We became a four-man crew instead of a three-man crew," said Haynes. "Everyone either helped in running the airplane or flying the airplane or doing the many, many radio reports that were required. Everybody kicked in. . . . Everybody agreed as a group to agree among ourselves before anything was done. And that was, I think, an important part of our survival."

By alternating power and thrusts from the two remaining engines —a technique known as porpoising—Haynes managed to crash-land the crippled DC-10 by the Sioux City, Iowa, airport. One hundred eleven people died, but 185 survived the fiery crash. Aviation experts said it was practically a miracle that the plane could be brought in at all with any survivors.

Although one person in our examples may ultimately make the critical decision, no one individual is in a position to come up with the answer on his own. The cardiac surgeon and the anesthesiologist are completely dependent upon each other to see the patient through; the pilots and the ground crew must work together to figure out what's wrong; the client can't be won over by either the creatives or the account executives alone. To make the decision on one's own would be unprofessional at best and criminally negligent at worst. There is no escaping the interdependence.

To have any chance at all of succeeding, these people can't rely on what we commonly refer to as communication. The dictionary defines communication as "transmitting information," but just exchanging information won't work because there has to be a useful context to put it in. These people have to use words, symbols, images, models—whatever they can lay their hands and minds on—to construct relevant meanings from both the available information and their individual expertise. Don't forget that the linguistic root of communication is the Latin verb *communicare*—which doesn't mean "to communicate" but "to share." Collaboration takes communication back to its roots.

The act of collaboration is an act of shared creation and/or shared discovery. Not all professional situations require collaboration. Some tasks are simply a matter of giving orders or following them or whispering the right word in the right ear at the right time with the right tone. The authoritarian military model will always have a place in organizational relationships as, of course, will personal charisma. You don't need collaboration to get someone to turn the lights out at the end of the day.

But collaboration is called for when an individual's charm, charisma, authority, or expertise just isn't enough to get the job done. Real challenges rarely lend themselves to routine dispatch. If they did, they wouldn't be real challenges. Indeed, bureaucracies are designed to handle the routine patterns of everyday events—it's the different and the new that give them the headaches.

So why collaboration now? Because we no longer have much of a choice. The trends are painfully apparent. On one hand, problems, opportunities, and the environments in which they appear are becoming more complex. On the other hand, to survive this explosion of complexity, people cultivate specialties. They want to be experts at something. Organizations increasingly hire and train experts to deal with the daily plethora of problems and opportunities. In society, academe, the sciences, and business, the age of complexity confronts the era of specialization.

The new reality is that it will take the collaborative efforts of people with different skills to create innovative solutions and innovative products. "Complex situations put a real premium on group processes, division of labor, trust, reaffirmation of what we respect and what we question in each other," management theorist Karl Weick has commented. "In that way, we can act more like a single organism and cover more." Savvy organizations and managers already know this and craft their internal networks accordingly.

Organizations that attempt to substitute increased communication for increased collaboration will learn the hard way that there is a tremendous difference. Flooding someone with more information doesn't necessarily make him a better thinker. Creating a shared understanding is simply a different task than exchanging information. It's the difference between being deeply involved in a conversation and lecturing to a group. The words are different, the tone is different, the attitude is different, and the tools are different.

Collaboration has always been a fundamental force in the arts, the sciences, and commerce; today's technologies have not. Thus, the way we collaborate is evolving along with both the technologies and the demands of the times. This ongoing coevolution of collaborative tools and the need to innovate will completely reshape the way organizations create value.

Why collaboration now? Not only because we don't really have a choice—but because it's the best choice we've got.

2

Shaping Interactions: Technological Imperialism

THIS IS A BOOK ABOUT RELATIONSHIPS. MORE PRECISELY, THIS IS A book about a new medium for relationships, both personal and professional. As surely as the clock imposed a new concept of time and the telephone breached the barriers of conversational distance, new technologies of collaboration are emerging that will radically transform the way people share their thoughts.

At a time when industries worry about global competitiveness and the challenge of managing change, at a time when people are frustrated with professional relationships trussed up by ambiguity and meetings that create little but ennui, this book offers a radically different way for people to become more effective. It's radical because it overturns some very fundamental assumptions about the way things get done.

It's easy to ignore the obvious, so we do. We're too quick to take too many things for granted. By treating the obvious with a dash of skepticism and putting a twist in what we take for granted, professionals and managers will have the opportunity to amplify their productivity dramatically. Success frequently depends on how effectively people draw on the resources of their working environments.

The key is to remember that even as we use technology to shape our environments, technology is shaping us. Technology, like gravity, has its own imperative. New technology rearranges our perceptual world and subtly redefines our relationship with our environment.

APPRECIATING THE OBVIOUS

Most telephone connections are models of clarity. But, as any international caller knows, intercontinental calls can be expensively annoying experiences even if the line is perfectly clear. Unlike most other calls, something feels wrong. Callers can't help interrupting each other, stepping on the other's voice in a clumsy verbal dance. Eerie gaps haunt the line as the callers desperately try to figure out whose turn it is to speak. They start to be more concerned with who speaks next than what's going to be said. Frustration sets in. The conversation decays. They hurry off the line.

The reason? In its quest for cost-effectiveness, the phone company is trying to cram as many calls as it can on its intercontinental lines (something that's almost never needed for local and ordinary long-distance calls). That makes sense for the phone company because it can get the maximum use out of a scarce resource. Using a technique called TASI—time-assigned speech interpolation—the phone company can pipe numerous conversations across a single line simply by clipping out the gaps and pauses in those conversations.

But people use gaps in their conversations as nonverbal cues; it's natural to pause. Breaks in our speech are often as significant as what we actually say. What's more, we use these pauses as signals to let the other person know that it's their turn to speak. Optimizing a resource through TASI is achieved at the conversational expense of people who rely on that resource to communicate clearly. It doesn't matter what a sparkling conversationalist you are; the TASI algorithm doesn't care. TASI can clip-job a pleasant chat into an uncomfortable sequence of interruptions.

OUTSIDE, IT'S TWENTY degrees below zero with the wind chill. Inside, the conference room is hotter than the third circle in Dante's *Inferno*. It's the second hour of a morning-long meeting, but the heat has sucked the energy right out of the room. People are listlessly watching the slide-show presentation of multicolored charts and graphs. It's even money that the participants are more concerned about the quality of their antiperspirants than the actual substance of the meeting. Every five minutes, someone mutters about the heat. People have started to wipe the sweat off their faces.

The thermostat is broken. A lone fan futilely pushes against the thick air. There are no other appropriately sized conference rooms with the right audiovisual equipment in the building. A preliminary decision from the group needs to be made by three P.M. What technology has had the biggest impact on the decision-making process of this group?

COLLEGE DAYS. YOU'RE working late into the night with a fellow student in an empty classroom. You're both scribbling equations on the blackboard, trying to figure out how to solve a new type of problem. Armed with chalk, the two of you work back and forth— plugging in a formula here, erasing a variable there. It's a genuine collaboration. You're rapidly filling up the board with all these quantitative concatenations, and you really think that the two of you are on the verge of cracking this thing. It's just a matter of getting a new variable to fit. You backtrack to check on an earlier calculation just to be sure.

You and your partner turn to each other and grimace. You can't check on it: you've already erased that section of the problem. You have to start over.

THESE THREE EXAMPLES illustrate how a technology or technique that's normally taken for granted can pollute personal interactions. Yet each of these failures to communicate has its own distinct pathology.

In the case of intercontinental communications, long distance isn't the next best thing to being there because it's not designed to be. TASI precludes the relaxed conversational intimacies that people have come to expect from their telephone calls. From the telephone company's perspective, TASI is a rational trade-off—the callers get most of what they want when they want it and the phone company saves money by exploiting network efficiencies. But TASI doesn't have to be part of intercontinental calling; it's a design decision.

The busted thermostat example is simpler. Things break. For want of a nail, the shoe was lost; for want of the shoe, the horse was lost; and so on. Some breakdowns are more predictable than others —thermostats rarely malfunction during major business meetings— yet because people tend to take technology for granted, breakdowns tend to have a disproportionately painful impact on the way people interact. You can't call someone if the phone lines are down; meetings are different if the thermostat fails; you miss the meeting if the rental car breaks down on the way there. Interactions fall apart when the technologies that support them fall apart.

Blackboards are marvelously versatile display devices. They're terrific when two or three people need to get together to represent a problem graphically or discuss a design. But blackboards have a finite physical space: they cannot expand or contract according to the users' needs. People can and do run out of space. When that happens, an even more unfortunate problem surfaces. Blackboards don't have memory. When something is erased, it is gone forever.

These three variables—design, breakdown, and constraints—are the cornerstones of technological imperialism. For better and worse, they shape the way people interact.

COCKPIT CATASTROPHES

Nowhere are the limitations of these three variables more tragically evident than in the sophisticated high-tech environment of a large-body passenger jet cockpit. Typically, a three-person crew—a pilot, copilot, and navigator—monitor over 160 different instrument settings over the course of a six-hour flight. Most of the flight is handled routinely through the autopilot—the technological linchpin of the system—but when problems appear, the crew is supposed to interact smoothly with one another and their technology to resolve them. There are chilling examples of when that didn't happen.

In 1978, a United Airlines DC-8 carrying 189 passengers ran out of fuel six miles outside Portland, Oregon, and crashed. The plane had spent half an hour circling outside the airport while the three members of the crew struggled with a landing gear problem. The cockpit voice recorder (recovered after the crash) revealed that the copilot and flight engineer were both aware that the fuel shortage was becoming critical. But they never directly alerted the captain, who was preoccupied with the landing gear. The cockpit systems didn't alert the captain that the fuel was getting low. The tanks ran dry, the engine quit, and the plane went down. Ten people were killed. The captain survived.

According to a *New York Times* account, this accident so shocked United (which is widely considered to have one of the best pilot training programs in commercial aviation) that the airline required all its pilots to attend a training session where the cockpit tape was played along with a visual simulation of the airplane's location in relation to the airport.

"They were wrenching, emotional sessions," recalls Rick Brown, flight manager for the airline's fleet of Boeing 767s. "Pilots would cry out in pain and disbelief when the captain asked the flight engineer how much fuel they had and the flight engineer said several minutes and the captain still didn't comprehend the significance of the information."

Would United flight 771 to Portland have crashed if the cockpit crew—particularly the captain—could have actually seen the fuel gauge slowly dropping to empty? What if the low fuel level had triggered a loud acoustic alarm that couldn't be ignored? Clearly, the designers of the DC-8 did not anticipate that this sequence of failed interactions between instruments, captain, and crew could lead to such a tragedy.

Though rare, this catastrophic chain of events is not atypical. The increasing sophistication of airplane technology and the high stakes involved have prompted extensive studies of the ways airline crews interact in flight by both federal agencies and the airlines. Using a flight simulator, volunteer Boeing 747 crews flew a simulated flight from Washington to New York, where they simulated a stop to refuel and board passengers for Europe.

The first part of the flight was routine, but the departure from Kennedy Airport was not. The air traffic was heavy, the weather was deteriorating, and, as the crew prepared to head out over the Atlantic, a series of small things began to go wrong. A warning light came on; eventually, the pilots had to shut down an engine and return to New York. The emergency landing required that fuel be dumped, which meant that the flight engineer would have to perform a critical set of calculations.

"I think everyone was shocked when we saw the variability in the performance of the pilots in those simulator flights," Dr. John K. Lauber, a psychologist with the National Transportation Safety Board, told the *Times*. "Some of the crews handled them well. More of them, however, committed serious errors, sometimes compounding them to the point where, in a couple of instances, the safe outcome of the flight was seriously in question."

Although they often do well when dealing with potentially catastrophic situations—such as coping with the explosive decompression caused by a bomb blast—pilots frequently have problems when a series of minor problems emerge. Advances in aviation technology have added layers of complexity that can spark these initially trivial events.

"Some recent incidents and accidents have convinced me," says Dr. Lauber, "that rather than eliminating human error, some of the new technology has resulted in the creation of new opportunities for entirely new categories of human error.

"It's only been relatively recently that people have focused on the design questions," he adds. "People are just beginning to talk about the interaction of cockpit teams and the design of highly automated cockpits."

Indeed, Dr. Earl Wiener, an aeronautical engineering professor at the University of Miami, says that these new automated environments create a "breakdown in the clear-cut role definition of who does what at any given time. . . . [The new systems] sometimes clear up small errors while creating opportunities for huge blunders."

For example, Wiener's research indicates that the division of roles between the cockpit crew members tends to break down in a highly automated aircraft. Reprogramming a computer in flight is an intellectually demanding and time-consuming task, and crews have to guard against the tendency of one pilot to look over the shoulder of the other who is keying data into the computer. The technology touches every important facet of the plane's operation.

For the benefit of passengers and crew, the cockpit should be an environment that both fosters and reinforces the values of readiness, cooperation, and control. Yet in the wake of a rash of incidents involving Delta Airlines in the summer of 1987, the Federal Aviation Administration (FAA) concluded, "There is no evidence that Delta's crews are . . . either unprofessional or purposefully negligent. Rather, it was observed that crew members are frequently acting as individuals rather than as members of a smoothly functioning team."

That can be a formula for disaster.

"We think, we're worried, we're beginning to suspect that we're on tenuous ground here," says H. Clayton Foushee, a psychologist formerly with NASA's Ames Research Center who was the FAA's chief scientific and technical adviser on human factors. "By paying too much attention to who does what in the cockpit, we're programming more to individual tasks, not team tasks. We have done studies of intracockpit communications and the conclusion is that more communication was correlated with better performance."

Foushee goes further and acknowledges that the issue isn't just the quantity of cockpit communication but its quality as well. The FAA wants to learn a lot more about the way cockpit crews collaborate with one another and the ground crews.

The possibility that new technology can lead to better communication and collaboration is now being explored, says Foushee. But we can't ignore the fact that technology can serve either as a tool or a barrier to collaboration. The right cockpit technology can literally save hundreds of lives in an instant. Technology misplaced can lead to disaster.

The cockpit is thus a microcosm—albeit an unusually dramatic one—of the technological environments we all inhabit. It's a model that raises the fundamental questions individuals and organizations must face to cope with the unexpected. To what extent do our environments enhance performance? To what extent do they mire us more deeply in our problems? The design, breakdowns, and constraints of our environments help determine the design, break-downs, and constraints of our relationships.

EPOCHS OF INTERACTION

When we're with other people, our surroundings can't help but influence us. We behave differently depending on where we are. Discussions over dinner are qualitatively different from discussions over desks. Inflight conversations in the cockpit are different from conversations on the ground. While personality matters, environment often determines which part of the personality is revealed. Privacy, intimacy, and accessibility are as often imposed by where we are and what technologies surround us as they are by the way we may feel at any given moment. Are the lights on? Who can see us? Who can hear us? Can you hear me? Are we being (audio/video) taped? What does that monitor say? Should I take the call? What time is it, anyway? These are all questions imposed on us by an escalating arsenal of technology. We can choose to answer them or ignore them, but they often serve as an unspoken context for our behavior. The web of technology tacitly or overtly complicates our relationships with others. If technology isn't busy framing our inter-actions, it's busy mediating them. To a very real extent, the quality of technology determines the quality of our interactions.

Just as critically, media technology creates the metaphors that govern our models for relationships. As media ecologist Neil Postman notes, "The introduction into a culture of a technique such as writing or a clock is not merely an extension of man's power to bind time but a transformation of his way of thinking—and, of course, the content of his culture. And that is what I mean by calling a medium a metaphor. . . . Indeed, our tools for thought suggest to us what our bodies are like, as when someone refers to the 'biological clock' or when we talk of our 'genetic codes' or when we read someone's face like a book or when our facial expressions telegraph our intentions."

In the past, architecture, design, and the clock carved up the dimensions of time and space. The rise of photography, radio, the telephone, and television redefined time and made distance irrelevant. Computers completely transformed our concept of information and our ability to interact and manipulate it; indeed, computer networks have emerged as a powerful new medium for communication with both other computers and with people (and have given us the eighties' metaphor of networking as a cultivated euphemism for either social climbing or professional connection making).

Each new medium builds upon its predecessors and redefines them in the process. Each new medium offers up its own metaphors to reshape the context of our culture. In the past, these media have all spun metaphors around the concept of communication. What's now emerging is a new hybrid of text, video, sound, image, and computation that frames a different mode of human interaction: collaboration.

New tools for thought will generate new metaphors. Collaborative tools will give us collaborative metaphors. As they have in the past, these new metaphors will give us a better way both to express ourselves and understand our relationships. They will be metaphors that matter.

3

Transmission Failures and Media Mythunderstandings

I am in the position of Louis Pasteur telling doctors that the greatest enemy was quite invisible, and quite unrecognized by them. Our conventional response to all media, namely that it is how they are used that counts, is the numb stance of the technological idiot. For the "content" of a medium is like the juicy piece of meat carried by the burglar to distract the watchdog of the mind.

MARSHALL McLUHAN • UNDERSTANDING MEDIA

AS MOVIE MOGUL SAM GOLDWYN MIGHT HAVE PUT IT, "IF MAR-shall McLuhan were alive today, he'd be spinning in his grave." The sage of Aquarius would need to whip up a new brew of pith and vinegar epigrams for a generation that's completely media saturated. "The medium is the message" is the message on the medium, so don't touch that dial (unless, of course, you want to pick up the newspaper for a story on how television covers media coverage of media coverage).

Media have become the reigning myths and metaphors of our time—which is, depending on which magazine you read, the Information Age or the Computer Age. Broadcast, cable, and fiber-optic networks carry high-bandwidth images as easily as alphabets. Scholars gnash their teeth and bewail the decay of the printed word in public life. Self-described media ecologist and McLuhan disciple

Neil Postman smoothly argues in *Amusing Ourselves to Death* that, thanks to television, public discourse has degenerated into a pea-brained brand of show business. Photo ops and sound bites have nibbled away the substance of meaningful policy debate. In *No Sense of Place*, Joshua Meyrowitz explains how electronic media have destroyed traditional notions of privacy and blurred the lines between childhood and adulthood. Central banks fear global telecommunications networks because they subvert economic policy by changing money from a medium of exchange into a free-floating set of electronic blips that cycle endlessly around the world seeking safe, profitable (but temporary) harbor in computers offering the best returns. Nearly every aspect of social concern from national security policy to AIDS research is viewed through this metaphor of media. Even molecular biology and genetic engineering are information sciences: DNA's double helix is but a blueprint for geneticists to refer to as they rewrite, edit, and "publish" new life forms.

The media paradigm is so powerful and so pervasive that it's become the grand unified field theory of the West. The media are to culture what particle physics is to cosmic design. (Don't think of muons, gluons, charms, and quarks as elementary particles; think of them as God's media.)

But grand metaphors are subject to grand misinterpretations. The media may define and shape our perceptual biases and cognitive environments, but media philosophers have historically ignored fundamental aspects of communication. Only a foolish physicist would construct a theory of natural phenomena that ignored, say, electricity. Yes, a lot could still be explained—gravity, optics, kinematics, and so on—but there would be huge gaps in our understanding of fundamental forces. Our gaps in understanding media make our awareness of their influence dangerously inadequate.

These gaps are painfully evident in the work of the two most brilliant and controversial media philosophers: Harold Adam Innis and Marshall McLuhan. Their theories (perspectives, really) are rich, sweeping, and studded with provocative insights. The ferocity and scope of their arguments is nothing short of breathtaking. History becomes an astonishing succession of new media toppling old empires by repatterning perceptions of time and space. Culture becomes a dizzying kaleidoscope of hot and cold running media. And yet both men display a curious blindness to fundamental aspects of human relationships—particularly collaboration—that blunts the edges of their perspectives. But just as the writings of Adam Smith and John Maynard Keynes define economic discussion to this day, so do the elaborately dense musings of Innis and McLuhan define media.

A University of Chicago–trained political economist, Innis takes the concept of economic monopolies and superimposes it on the study of information monopolies. In *Empire and Communications* and *The Bias of Communications*, Innis rewrites the history of civilization as a history of media. He begins with the cradles of civilization in Mesopotamia and Egypt and ends with the British Empire and the Nazis.

He sees control over communication media (such as a complex writing system controlled by a special class of priests) as a means through which social and political power is wielded. New media technology, however, can break old monopolies. The medieval Church's monopoly over religious information (and therefore over salvation), argues Innis, was broken by the printing press. The printing press bypassed the Church's scribes and made the Bible and other religious material widely available. The same content, the Bible, therefore had different effects in different media.

Innis argues that different media offer different opportunities for power and control. A medium that is scarce or that requires special encoding or decoding skill is likely to be exploited by an elite class that has the time and resources to gain access to it. Conversely, a medium that is very accessible to the common person tends to democratize a culture.

Innis also claims that every medium has a bias either toward lasting for a long time or traveling easily across distances. Time and space are a culture's seesaw. Innis suggests that the bias of a culture's dominant medium affects both the culture's stability and its potential to extend its sovereignty. "Time-biased" media such as stone hieroglyphics, he argues, lead to relatively small, stable societies. Stone carvings, after all, are difficult to edit and rewrite, and their weight makes them a poor medium to distribute over great distances. In contrast, messages on "space-biased" media like papyrus enabled the Romans to cultivate and maintain a large empire.

Before he died in 1952, Innis's work enjoyed cult status in select academic circles, and he had attracted a most flamboyant acolyte: Marshall McLuhan. McLuhan (who once commented that his work was nothing but an "extended footnote" to Innis) takes Innis's model of world history and makes it into his own medium. To Innis's information monopolies and media biases, McLuhan adds the notion of "sensory balance." He analyzes media as an extension of man's senses and argues that different technologies alter the ratios of the human sensorium. McLuhan divides history into three major periods—oral, written/printed, and electronic. Each period, says McLuhan, is characterized by its own interplay of the senses and therefore by its own forms of thinking and communicating.

"Oral societies live in an 'ear culture' of simultaneity and circularity," says McLuhan scholar Joshua Meyrowitz. "The oral 'tribal' world of the ear is a closed society" of high interdependence that lacks individuality. McLuhan asserts that writing—and to a greater degree print—cracks this tribal balance and substitutes the "eye for an ear," making the sense of sight dominant and thus shifting the sensorium away from sound, touch, and direct response. The break from total reliance on oral communication allows people to become more introspective, rational, and individual. Abstract thought develops. From the circular world of sound with its round huts and round villages, people move over time toward a linear, cause-and-effect, one-thing-follows-another world that mimics the linear lines of writing and type. (In *Understanding Media*, McLuhan refers to the myth of Cadmus, the king who reputedly introduced phonetic letters into Greece. When Cadmus sowed the dragon's teeth, "They sprang up as armed men. . . . The alphabet meant power and authority and control of military structures at a distance.")

The concept of the global village is the logical byproduct of McLuhan's assertion that electronic technology creates a media web that ensnares the world—the instantaneous, simultaneous nature of electronic communications recreates the tribal village on a global scale.

A few paragraphs in a quick summary can't capture the tremendous impact that McLuhan's quirky epigrams and insights had on pop-cultural sensibilities. His books and essays launched intellectual firestorms of debate from Oxford to Berkeley. Madison Avenue executives and network big shots listened with mouths agape to McLuhan's Olympian pronouncements on The Future of The Media. *Playboy* interviewed him; NBC gave him a prime-time hour; Tom Wolfe (no slouch when it comes to media pyrotechnics) asked in an article "What If He's Right!!???" and wondered amid the exclamation points if this Canadian professor might not be "the most important thinker since Newton, Darwin, Freud, Einstein, and Pavlov." The media celebrate those who celebrate them: the eye-patched messenger of "The medium is the message" even made a cameo appearance as himself in a Woody Allen film.

But McLuhan's ascholarly style and media hype shouldn't obscure the penetrating truths he and Innis exposed. That our senses and thoughts are molded and distorted by shifts in media environments was a mind-snaring insight a generation ago and remains compelling today. The majesty of media over cultural patterns and social styles is now a cliché. McLuhan planted the insistent itch of media self-awareness in the body politic, and pundits have been scratching at it ever since. America, soaking itself daily in a whirlpool of text, images, and sound released by thousands of high-pressure media nozzles, is the most media self-conscious nation on earth. We know this because the media tell us so.

But as brilliant as these insights might be, they aren't very useful. They create awareness more than understanding. They don't quite mesh with the real problems of communication that people are forced to deal with in everyday life.

In one respect, the theories of Innis and McLuhan are like macroeconomics: they are extraordinarily broad and general. Just as macroeconomic theory describes a national economy by the aggregate interplay of fiscal and monetary policy, the pervasive societal influences of media technologies are explained by phrases like "global village" and "empire and communications" and "perceptual bias"—the interplay of media and man. (McLuhan even goes into light-year overdrive by calling his book on the printing press *The Gutenberg Galaxy.*) The individual is just another statistical blip resonating furiously in a multimedia field that lies just beyond perception and control.

Macroeconomics is designed to explain such macrophenomena as national consumption and investment. It's useless for capturing such phenomena as entrepreneurialism or consumerism or innovation. Macroeconomics offers nothing more and nothing less than The Big Picture. If there is one thing you can say for McLuhan and Innis, it's that they offer a full color-and-sound Big Picture. In contrast, economists developed microeconomic theory to explain the economics of the company; how wealth and value are created in the society; how supply and demand intersect; how new companies grow and old companies die. This is where the media philosophers are conspicuous by their absence. There is no comparable microeconomics of media. The nuances of human language and interaction are scarcely addressed. The way new media technologies actually shape human relationships is left unexplained. McLuhan is rendered practically epiphanyless.

Part of the problem is that Innis, McLuhan, and their disciples view media technology in a way that captures mechanisms instead of meanings. McLuhan and Innis are so intent on proving that technology shapes content that they shackle themselves to a disturbingly limited model of communication. They basically describe only two modes of communication: physical *distribution* for print and electronic *transmission* for telecommunications. In effect, communication is something (maybe a message) that is packaged and fit into a medium's format and subsequently sent off in either physical or electronic form. The recipient is almost irrelevant to this process; the presentation is what matters. Monograph, radio program, movie, Xerox copy—they are all bundles of symbols distributed or transmitted to people who may or may not get the message.

To conjure up a McLuhanesque metaphor, this model of media treats communication as an infectious disease—as something you may catch depending upon the perceptual bias of your personal sensorium. Some people are particularly susceptible to print, others to television. Some individuals are naturally immune to certain forms of information; they resist perceptual infection by a new media technology. Cultural transformation, according to McLuhan, is thus nothing more than media epidemiology—the spread of a new medium throughout a society. The symptoms are radical differences in the patterns of perception and thought. For some societies, as Innis and McLuhan show, such a disease can be fatal. For others, new media bring forth new life-styles and aesthetics.

THE PROBLEM IS that the idea of actually *understanding* a message has no place in this model. That symbols can be spread by media from one mind to another is undeniable. Whether these symbols are actually understood by the receiver is less certain. No matter how gross the perceptual bias, no matter how skewed the personal sensorium, understanding the message—sharing the thought—remains at the heart of communication.

One way to illustrate this is to think of media and the messages they contain as a smorgasbord of different cuisines. Take McLuhanism and transform it into a technique for gastronomic analysis. The analogy is startlingly apt. Some foods are hot, spicy, and exciting; others are cool and bland. There are all kinds of flavors and textures —crunchy, prickly, moist, juicy, dry, crumbly, flaky, sharp, tangy. There are natural foods and synthetic concoctions that require you to add water, stir, and pop into the microwave. Some cuisines are stick-to-your-ribs heavy; others will leave you hungry in an hour. These options all shape the way we perceive the experience of eating. People who grow up in Paris have a different concept of snacking than suburban mall hoppers who love McDonald's french fries. People who like microwave cooking see food differently from gourmet chefs who insist on fresh ingredients. People who constantly eat out view dining differently than do people who cook their own meals. Of course, some people can't abide certain cuisines. Some people eat the same things over and over again. It's a matter of different tastes.

Despite this incredibly rich array of offerings and an equally rich vocabulary to describe them, many people are dissatisfied. The food doesn't always taste quite right; they get indigestion. An hour after eating, they're hungry again. They eat food with little nutritional value. Yes, food technology does shape perceptual biases: different foods appeal to different senses.

The same holds for the media diet. The media table holds a rich feast, but the meal is larded with cheap data calories and informational cholesterol. It's frequently filling but often unsatisfying. It can make you fat or sick. It isn't as good for you as it should be. Too much of one medium or not enough of another causes cognitive malnutrition. Information that is consumed isn't necessarily digested. In reality, many media dishes are recipes for misunderstanding and confusion no matter how prettily they're served. McLuhan is like a food critic obsessed with taste, texture, and presentation. He doesn't care about calories or cholesterol or whether or not it's good for you. Yet to divorce media from the act of creating understanding is like divorcing food from its role of providing nutrition: it can be done (and often is), but it's unhealthy.

Instead of focusing on perceptual bias and media monopolies, we need to pay closer attention to the distribution/transmission bias that underlies media analysis. Obviously, the mode of distribution or transmission shapes the perceptual bias. But what motives underlie the means of distribution and transmission? Historically, the driving ethic of a new medium in the marketplace is the opportunity to "express yourself"—but technology that enables you to express yourself doesn't mean that other people understand you any better. Media technologies work to reinforce the bias of media as the transmission of individual expression rather than a mechanism to create understanding between sender and receiver.

Ever since the creation of the written word, new media technologies encourage communication at the expense of collaboration; in fact, "writing tools tend to work against collaboration," says Xerox's John Seely Brown. How many hands can grasp a pencil? How many people can huddle around a legal pad? How does one collaborate with a televised image? That's why we're drowning in torrents of information and data.

While the telephone, the radio, the fax machine, the video camera, and so on are superb communications media, there's nothing in them that inherently fosters collaboration. Media technology encourages generation, creation, distribution, transmission, duplication, replication, and proliferation of symbols, sounds, and imagery. Collaboration is a derivative effect rather than a primary focus of these technologies. Media technology is designe[d] [for com]munication—not collaboration.

Why? Because no matter how comfortable this [tech]nologies looks, the distribution/transmission bias [is a] Procrustean bed, lopping off the incentives to cre[ate under]standings. Each successive generation of technology has fragmented shared understandings further by putting more power in the distribution/transmission process. People are more concerned with presenting their messages within the constraints of the medium than assuring that the recipient actually understands the message. As Philip Schlesinger put it in his fine study of the BBC news-gathering department, "You do not find people wandering around in a state of existential *angst* wondering whether they are 'communicating' or not. You do, on the other hand, find an intense obsession with the packaging of the broadcast and comparative evaluation of others' goods."

We've used new media technology to engage and capture attention while we've worried less about engaging and capturing the mind. Media have become tools for individual transmission rather than tools for collaborative action. We use media technology to *share an experience* rather than *create a shared experience*. The difference is not subtle. It's the difference between passivity and participation, talking and conversation. It's also the reason so many people feel so lonely despite their technical links to so many media networks. The ability to express oneself is not enough.

A NEW EPOCH

There are dozens if not hundreds of these efforts to characterize the evolution of media influences upon culture. Certainly, McLuhan's "global village" metaphor remains popular. Joshua Meyrowitz argues convincingly that telecommunications technology helps make physical distance between people irrelevant. Neil Postman argues eloquently that America's shift from a typographic culture to an image-drunk video culture erodes the society's ability to reason with rigor and self-discipline:

To be confronted by the cold abstraction of printed sentences is to look upon language bare, without the assistance of either beauty or community. Thus reading is by its nature a serious business. It is also, of course, an essentially rational activity. From Erasmus in the sixteenth century to Elizabeth Eisenstein in the twentieth, almost every scholar who has grappled with the question of what reading does to one's habits of mind has concluded that the process encourages rationality; and that the sequential, propositional character of the written word fosters what Walter Ong calls the "analytic management of knowledge." To engage the written word means to follow a line of thought, which requires considerable powers of classifying, inference-making, and reasoning. It means to uncover lies, confusions, and overgeneralizations, to detect abuses of logic and common sense. It also means to weigh ideas, to compare and contrast assertions, to connect one generalization to another.

This shift from print culture to video culture has occurred without our paying enough attention to its impact on personal interactions, and collaboration.

As computer scientist Alan Kay likes to ask, "What does a medium ask you to become in order to use it?" In the case of print, the answer is a rational creature. For television, a passive observer. For the telephone, a conversationalist. For the personal computer, a creature that is prepared to manipulate, play with, and program information.

The well-crafted collaborative environment integrates the intellectual virtues of print, the video appeal of television, and the information-manipulating powers of the personal computer. Carefully calibrated collaborative media are self-contained but able to work productively with a larger network. That's how great ideas are born and get the chance to grow.

Media environments can indeed be collaborative environments that spark fundamental changes in science, the arts, and technology. As prescient as McLuhan may have been, he could not have foreseen the emergence of a new generation of collaborative media precisely because of his own perceptual biases about what media do. Collaborative tools and technologies will have as profound an impact on the way people create as the television set has had on the way people see. The architecture of collaborative media has yet to find its community of philosophers and artisans, but that is simply a matter of time. The medium may still be the message, but collaborative media will redefine the meaning of both.

But the first step in grasping the potential of collaborative media is to understand collaboration. To understand collaboration, you have to appreciate the things it's not.

4

Collaboration

*Fads will come and go. The fundamental fact of man's
capacity to collaborate with his fellows in the face-to-face
group will survive the fads and one day be recognized.
Then, and only then, will management discover how
seriously it has underestimated the true potential of its
human resources.*

DOUGLAS MCGREGOR • THE HUMAN SIDE OF ENTERPRISE

*Attentiveness to context, not to self-expression, is the skill
we have to foster, to encourage, to share. . . . The
context, not the boss, has to become the manager of what
is done, and how.*

JOHN CHRIS JONES • SOFTECNICA

TRUE STORY: A PROFESSOR FROM A WELL-KNOWN EASTERN UNIVER-
sity had come to MIT to present a few of her most recent findings
on how work groups make decisions. In passing, she pointed to her
research with university students revealing that collaborative efforts
to solve problems were consistently less successful than individual
efforts. That created a bit of a stir.

Without batting an eyelash, the professor continued, "My colleague, Professor Smith, and I will shortly publish a paper that examines the implications of those findings."

Such foolish ironies confirm that collaboration is one of the most poorly understood and least appreciated human behaviors. It also happens to be one of the most important. George Bernard Shaw once noted that "Success comes from taking the path of maximum advantage instead of the path of least resistance." Too often, our willingness to believe conventional wisdom takes us down the wrong path. The road of working alone may be easier, but the view isn't necessarily as good and we don't necessarily end up where we'd like to be.

The conventional wisdom that creativity and innovation are kingdoms ruled by supremely gifted individuals is the path of least resistance, a poor approximation of reality. Truly successful creativity and innovation—the type that transforms a discipline or a marketplace—is as much a social act as an individual affair. More often than not, collaboration proves to be the path of maximum advantage.

James Watson, who won a Nobel Prize with Francis Crick for their discovery of the double helix, puts it simply: "Nothing new that is really interesting comes without collaboration."

If there is a core theme to this book, it's that people must understand that real value in the sciences, the arts, commerce, and, indeed, one's personal and professional lives, comes largely from the process of collaboration. What's more, the quality and quantity of meaningful collaboration often depends upon the tools used to create it.

WHAT IS COLLABORATION?

As a young editor at Charles Scribner's Sons, Maxwell Perkins transformed American literature with his unerring knack for finding fresh talent. Perkins discovered and launched F. Scott Fitzgerald and Thomas Wolfe—bracing voices for a new American era. Both his literary and commercial judgments were astute. His biographer noted that "he was famous for his ability to inspire an author to produce the best that was in him or her. More a friend to his authors than a taskmaster, he aided them in every way. He helped them structure their books, if help was needed; thought up titles, invented plots; he served as psychoanalyst, adviser to the lovelorn, marriage counselor, career manager, moneylender. Few editors before him had done so much work on manuscripts, yet he was always faithful to his credo, 'The book belongs to the author.' "

Perkins didn't coauthor his writers' books, but he was indispensable in shaping *The Great Gatsby* and *Look Homeward, Angel*. Not merely a catalyst, Perkins offered a compelling intellect and sure counsel that sculpted and refined his authors' prose. No, not a coauthor—but just an editor? Or was Perkins more accurately a necessary partner, a collaborator, in these literary efforts?

Consider Ezra Pound's intimate working relationship with T. S. Eliot, arguably the finest English-language poet of the century. Pound relentlessly pushed and prodded Eliot. "Pound persuaded his fellow-poet that his future lay in literature, not philosophy; in London, not the United States—a future to which Eliot then and there committed himself," one critic writes. "And the poem that afterward brought him fame and fortune, *The Waste Land*, was—as we have known for fifteen years—almost as much Pound's work as it was Eliot's." There's no concealing the lyrical brilliance of a *Waste Land* or *Four Quartets*, but could Eliot have been quite so much the genius without Pound? Or does the real genius of the poetry lie within the collaborative intersection of Eliot's writing and Pound's editing? What does genius mean if it takes two?

"Look," argues playwright and film director David Mamet, "does a bricklayer 'collaborate' with the architect when he builds a wall?" Mamet defines collaboration as a creative process of equals. An editor is no more a collaborator than the bricklayer. The primary creator generates the compelling vision; the creator is the magnet that brings all the filings into neat symmetrical patterns.

But where does one draw the line? The bricklayer is implementing a vision, not adding to it. But if no one doubts that, with a few vicious strokes, an editor can cripple a manuscript or a movie, why is it so hard to accept that an editor can elevate one? At what point in the creative process does an editor add enough value to call the relationship a collaboration? As far as a Wolfe novel is concerned, does it really matter that Perkins is called an editor and not a coauthor? Or are these labels more of convenience than substance? Do words like *editor* or *director* or *designer* adequately capture the essence of a professional relationship?

In that sense, collaboration is like romance; it's difficult to define the precise boundaries of the relationship. (The edges of those boundaries haunted Perkins, Fitzgerald, and Wolfe in both their personal and professional lives.) Is a one-night stand a relationship? Well, yes. . . . For some people, it can be a life-changing experience. For others, it's just another evening. An unrequited love can often be the most powerful and enduring. Romance embraces a continuum of interaction from the simple flirtation to a deep and abiding love (and every possible permutation in between).

Similarly, the collaborative continuum stretches over vast possibilities of interaction: from the serendipitous stranger saying the right thing at the right time to the decades-long mutual obsession of two scientists to tap the secrets of molecular biology. Collaborations have their own brand of simple flirtations and deep and abiding commitments. No passivity here; like a romantic couple, collaborators are constantly reacting and responding to each other. Frequency of contact becomes almost as important as the nature of the contact. The collaboration becomes an entity unto itself.

The critical difference, however, is that unlike romance, a collaboration is supposed to produce something. Collaboration is a *purposive* relationship. At the very heart of collaboration is a desire or need to

- solve a problem,
- create, or
- discover something

within a set of constraints. These constraints include

- expertise—one person alone doesn't know enough to deal with the situation;
- time—collaboration is a real-time effort in an airplane cockpit or an operating theater, a more leisurely process in the arts and sciences;
- money—budgets matter in both business and top-flight scientific research;
- competition—in science or business, others may threaten to

beat a collaborative team to publication or to the market-place;

- conventional wisdom—the prejudices of the day (for example, the impressionists had to launch their own gallery to exhibit their work to challenge the French Academy).

Given these constraints, collaboration is anything but an assembly-line process. It can't be routine and predictable. People collaborate precisely because they don't know how to—or can't—deal effectively with the challenges that face them as individuals. There's uncertainty because they genuinely don't know how they will get from here to there. In that respect, collaboration becomes a necessary technique to master the unknown.

Because a collaboration has an overarching purpose, the success of a collaboration can be measured by its results. The collaborators either solve the problem or they've failed. Artists fail when their visions are incoherent; scientists fail when their experiments explode their hypotheses; new-product teams fail when their creations can't find a market. But when these collaborations succeed, they redefine their fields.

John Dykstra has redefined the field of movie special effects through his pioneering work in computer-controlled camera shots in such films as *Star Wars*. His job is, quite literally, to create things that people have never seen before. His intergalactic images of hyperspace and exobiological fauna are products of an intensely collaborative environment. By linking technologies in unanticipated ways, the images on-screen create a new set of realities that both the eye and mind find completely believable. With Dykstra's camerawork, traveling faster than the speed of light is a supraliminal event that the viewer quickly takes for granted.

When he talks about the creative process, Dykstra could be describing collaboration at a top-notch research lab, an advertising agency, a law firm, or any organization confronting a new challenge.

"In an ordinary communication," says Dykstra, "you're trying to tell someone something you know: apples are apples and oranges are oranges. But when you say 'Let's make something you've never seen before,' then apples and oranges take on a completely different significance. Now, you're both trying to create something you *don't* know. So you try to get a communal mind going; you want to get people's minds to interact as components of a larger mind—one person's logical sense, one person's visual sense, another person's acoustic sense. You get a communal brain. What matters is not just the individual talents but the ability to integrate them."

Some collaborations—notably in the arts and sciences—feature compatible people with compatible interests: mathematicians working with mathematicians, comedians working together on a sketch. These collaborations don't necessarily fuse radically different perspectives; they serve primarily to prevent people from getting stuck in their own mental ruts on the way to discovery. Other collaborations bring wildly divergent skills together: Apple Computer's origin in the visionary talents of Steve Jobs and the technical brilliance of Steve Wozniak comes to mind, as do the musical and lyrical talents of Gilbert and Sullivan. These complementary skills produce the friction that generates creative sparks as well as emotional heat. Lotus Development Corporation founder Mitchell Kapor points to the labor pains associated with birthing the internationally bestselling Lotus 1-2-3 spreadsheet software as an example:

> One of the most salient features of the product design process was that there were two people involved in it, myself and [programmer] Jonathan Sachs. We came from very different backgrounds and had very different perspectives. He had a great deal of experience in technical design and the implementation of spreadsheets and computer products. I was not technically as sophisticated but I did have a very good design sense and also a sense of what users wanted in terms of specific features. We had a lot of arguments, and I would say that the argumentation process contributed materially to it being a better product.

Kapor's idea of argumentation isn't pushy contrariness or a macho challenging of assumptions. It's really more a craft of explicitness. The arguments are a technique not just to flush out assumptions and underlying thoughts but to force the participants to express their ideas so explicitly that they can be represented in a variety of ways, both tangible and intangible. The notion of "winning" an argument is completely irrelevant—if not counterproductive—to the primary goal of clearly articulating ideas.

At these levels of effective creativity and innovation, collaboration isn't what people conveniently describe as "communication" or what positive-thinking managers call "working together."

Collaboration is not, as some managers believe, the craft of treating people like jigsaw puzzle pieces to be fitted together to achieve The Grand Vision. The reality is that the vision is never static—it's dynamic, always shifting as whim and circumstances change. Those human pieces of the puzzle are likewise dynamic, and they can frequently add color, depth, and texture to the grand vision if they have the opportunity. People aren't preengineered patterns designed to be plugged into a preconceived whole.

Collaboration is certainly not the bastardized American notion of teamwork and its Grantland Rice grab bag of tired sports metaphors —handing off, touching all the bases, striking out, and so on. (During an interview for a job on a crash software project, a Silicon Valley friend of mine was asked if he was a team player. "Yes," he replied, "team captain!") People substitute easy familiarity for penetrating insight. Sports metaphors imply that people should be seen as performing specialized functions: pitcher, catcher, quarterback, power forward. Your job is to perform your task; to fit in.

In practice, collaboration is a far richer process than teamwork's handing off on an idea or blocking and tackling for a new-product rollout or attempting a slam-dunk marketing maneuver. The issue isn't communication or teamwork—it's the creation of value. Collaboration describes a process of value creation that our traditional structures of communication and teamwork can't achieve.

"I've noticed that it is extraordinarily difficult after a really good idea has emerged to recall exactly what was the project that gave birth to it," remarks John Cleese, the gifted comic writer and actor who has done everything from perform as a member of the Monty Python comedy troupe to produce corporate training videos. "Certainly, it is never the case that one person suddenly had a brilliant idea, which is then accepted by everyone in that original, untouched form. The really good idea is always traceable back quite a long way, often to a not very good idea which sparked off another idea that was only slightly better, which somebody else misunderstood in such a way that they then said something which was really rather interesting. . . . [That's] actually why I have always worked with a writing partner, because I'm convinced that I get to better ideas than I'd ever do on my own."

For the purposes of this book, collaboration is the process of *shared creation:* two or more individuals with complementary skills interacting to create a shared understanding that none had previously possessed or could have come to on their own. Collaboration creates a shared meaning about a process, a product, or an event. In this sense, there is nothing routine about it. Something is there that wasn't there before. Collaboration can occur by mail, over the phone lines, and in person. But the true medium of collaboration is other people. Real innovation comes from this social matrix.

We know this intuitively even if it's hard to measure. There are so many levels to conversations, interactions, and communications that it's difficult to parse the collaborative process logically. Collaboration is a state of grace we switch into and out of as the moment and the task demand. We do it informally when we pick up the phone to ask for help solving a problem, and we try to do it formally when we all jam into a conference room to brainstorm our way out of a crisis.

Formal collaborations can involve structures and processes (like meetings and new-product reviews); informal collaborations can involve instances and episodes (like scribbling on a napkin over lunch at the cafeteria). The thing these collaborations have in common is people who realize that they can't do it all by themselves. They need insights, comments, questions, and ideas from others. They accept and respect the fact that other perspectives can add value to their own.

Such collaborations are governed by design, circumstance, serendipity, and need. An ordinary chat by the watercooler can be transformed into an intensely creative collaboration; the right questions can spark a dialogue that gives the parties the glimmer of an idea that neither could have seen individually. Collaboration occurs when ideas just rub up against one another in person or on paper.

Sometimes ideas spring from the well of a creative misunderstanding, from the right words taken out of the wrong context. Harlan Ellison, the brilliant writer of speculative fiction, once overheard a snatch of conversation at a party: "Jeffy is five . . . he's always five." That sparked Ellison to write one of his best and most chilling stories about a little boy who can't grow up. Creativity often builds upon the shards and fragments of different understandings. The trick is how best to share those understandings.

Not all conversations carry seeds of collaboration, but not all collaborations are conversations, either. A snatch of music, a lyric, an intriguing diagram, a provocative paper can provide the cornerstone of a collaborative effort. We don't just collaborate with people; we also collaborate with the patterns and symbols people create. Artists, writers, and musicians are influenced by the work of peers and predecessors. Scientists are guided by the theories and experiments of their colleagues. Science historian Bruno Latour observes, "I was struck in a study of a biology laboratory by the way in which many aspects of laboratory practice could be ordered by looking not at the scientists' brains (I was forbidden access), at the new cognitive structures (nothing special), not at the paradigms (the same for thirty years), but at the transformation of rats and chemicals into paper."

In science, paper is as much a medium of collaboration as personality. The most successful collaborations in science, business, and the arts blend personality with these patterns of expression. Determining where one ends and the other begins becomes impossible. Which is precisely the point: collaboration is a relationship with a dynamic fundamentally different from ordinary communication.

There's an alchemical, almost mystical quality to the best of these collaborations; a sense of creation that transcends individual talent and skill. You can hear it in a Rodgers and Hart musical or a Lennon and McCartney song. Yet there's nothing inherently fragile about the process: some of the most productive collaborations occur at the top of the participants' lungs.

"When the immovable object of his unwillingness to change came up against the irresistible force of my own drive for perfection," Richard Rodgers recalls about his work with lyricist Larry Hart, "the noise could be heard all over the city. Our fights over words were furious, blasphemous, and frequent, but even in their hottest moments we both knew that we were arguing academically and not personally."

Double helix codiscoverer Francis Crick observes a similar phenomenon in his memoir. "Our . . . advantage was that we had evolved unstated but fruitful methods of collaboration. . . . If either of us suggested a new idea, the other, while taking it seriously, would attempt to demolish it in a candid but nonhostile manner." (In fact, Crick once told a BBC interviewer at the time he got the Nobel that "Politeness is the poison of all good collaboration in science." Candor—if not rudeness—is at the heart of most successful collaborative relationships.) To be successful, a collaboration can't afford the risk of substituting euphemisms for clarity. Collaborative relationships aren't built on rudeness; it's just that they won't let good manners get in the way of a good argument.

Collaboration as this dialectical process of "depersonalized argumentation," as Xerox's Mark Stefik puts it, makes for great entertainment. With science in particular, there is a delicious tension between people passionately proclaiming their dispassionate analyses. Francis Crick enjoyed the rhetorical ruthlessness with which he and Watson demolished each other's errant hypotheses. In contrast, collaboration in the arts more readily indulges individual eccentricities. Medical doctor and Old Vic theater director Jonathan Miller (who has enjoyed successful collaborations as a comedian, scientist, and director) notes that butchering sacred cows and serving them up as hamburger is part of the theater tradition. "When I work with a designer to create a set," says Miller, "and we have no explicit ideas —we simply provoke one another. We gradually enlarge each other's understanding until we reach a new understanding about how best to proceed."

The same process holds when Miller tries to tease new meaning out of an old play. "Occasionally, I work with a historian to discuss what a text might mean," says Miller. "Those inner meanings would be opaque to me without those discussions." Collaboration is a natural and indispensable part of this artistic process: the director's vision can't be realized without it.

At the risk of sounding maudlin, collaboration also forges the bonds of the most personal relationships. At friendship's heart is a continuous act of collaboration. Two individuals create a set of shared experiences and understandings that are unique to them. Their interactions revolve around sharing ideas and feelings that give new depth to the relationship. They build contexts. That people have "nothing in common" is a meaningless phrase—friends constantly create things in common. The same holds true for lovers. A couple creates a world of intimacy and shared secrets to which only they are privy. The relationship deepens as life is experienced as a couple rather than as just a pair of individuals.

When a friendship dissolves or a couple breaks up, people shake their heads and blithely talk about how one partner outgrew the other. Euphemisms aside, that usually means that the process of collaboration has withered. As a result, nothing new comes from the relationship. Without the desire and ability to create new understandings, a relationship can't grow—it can only be maintained.

Of course, personality matters. But what's so striking about the range of collaborations in the arts, the sciences, and in business is the way that the collaborative relationship seems to transcend age, gender, temperament, energy level, nationality, and the thousands of idiosyncratic quirks to which humans are heir. Being a jerk, a blowhard, or a patient, sweet-tempered soul is frequently irrelevant to the quality of the collaboration. The thing that matters most is that the collaborators possess a modicum of mutual trust, the belief that they are each adding value, and a genuine desire to solve the problem at hand or create something new.

Remember, collaborations aren't designed to last forever—they are designed for a specific purpose. Once that purpose is attained, the collaboration frequently dissolves. The real issue may be whether personalities define the collaboration or whether the collaborative task defines the personalities. Either way, it seems as if personality is *a* factor in determining the collaborative relationship, not *the* factor. If a challenge warrants it, it appears that people *want* to collaborate to meet it. Collaboration is as much the offspring of necessity as desire.

"There is a natural drive to collaborate," asserts anthropologist Edward T. Hall, the author of *Beyond Culture*. "It may be one of the basic principles of living in substance."

Professional collaborations can be as intense, demanding, frustrating, and as emotionally rewarding as personal ones—and just as poorly understood.

The fundamental point is that people are locked into patterns that hide the real importance of collaboration. They're viewing the world through lenses that obscure as much as they reveal. The Western tradition of intellectual thought doesn't embrace collaboration as a vital creative behavior. You don't find collaboration as part of Aristotelian or Platonic thought (which is ironic, given the role of dialogue in creating enlightenment). Nor is collaboration a part of the Judeo-Christian ethic of community. Adam Smith talked about the "division of labor," not collaboration; Marx heralded the "labor theory of value," yet left the collaborative processes that yield this value virtually unexamined.

Similarly, the nascent sciences of human thought and behavior give collaboration short shrift. Pavlov, John B. Watson, B. F. Skinner, and the behaviorist school scarcely touch collaboration as a social process. Freud brilliantly explored and described the inner beyonds of the human psyche, but not in the context of the way people create shared understandings.

Cognitive scientists probe deeply into the mechanisms of the mind—memory, perception, learning, thought—but rarely into their social contexts. There's a certain solipsistic quality to cognitive psychology, as if the mind is all that matters.

As a result of disillusionment and the limited success of these paradigms, some psychologists argue along with Michael Argyle that "the social situation, rather than the individual, may develop into a new unit of psychological research."

Far too slowly, the formal academic world is exploring the building blocks of collaborative interaction. For now, real life remains the best laboratory to observe the influence of collaborative work. There are rich veins of anecdote and observation to draw upon.

While the levels of collaborative complexity may be different, the process itself transcends disciplinary boundaries.

"Creative people must use their skills to devise environments that foster their work," says psychologist Howard Gruber. As a result, "they invent new peer groups appropriate to their projects. Being creative means striking out in new directions and not accepting ready-made relationships. . . . Each creator therefore invents new forms of collaboration."

Such collaborative forms emerge with one's colleagues, mentors, and subordinates. Creative effectiveness depends as much on managing the collaboration as it does on individual effort. That means focusing on the areas where the collaborative interaction is essential to success. James Watson stresses that his double helix hunt with Crick went so well because the two men "regarded each other as equals. . . . I think the best collaborations are done between equals." The journey to discovery almost always demands good traveling companions. In their excellent history of quantum physics, *The Second Creation*, Robert Crease and Charles Mann describe the work style of Niels Bohr, one of the conceptual godfathers of the New Physics:

Bohr talked. He discovered his ideas in the act of enunciating them, shaping thoughts as they came out of his mouth. Friends, colleagues, graduate students, all had Bohr gently entice them into long walks in the countryside around Copenhagen, the heavy clouds scudding overhead as Bohr thrust his hands in his overcoat pockets and settled into an endless, hesitant, recondite, barely audible monologue. While he spoke, he watched his listeners' reactions, eager to establish a bond in a shared effort to articulate. Whispered phrases would be pronounced, only to be adjusted as Bohr struggled to express *exactly* what he meant; words were puzzled over, repeated, then tossed aside, and he was always ready to add a qualification, to modify a remark, to go back to the beginning, to start the explanation over again. . . .

His articles were composed with such care and precision that they sometimes verged on incomprehensibility, and were always late. He asked friends to read preliminary versions, and weighed their comments so thoughtfully that he would often begin over again; a frustrated collaborator once snarled to a colleague who had given Bohr a minor suggestion on a draft, prompting a seventh rewrite, that when the new version was produced, if "you don't tell him it is excellent, I'll wring your neck."

Consider the intrinsically collaborative nature of the mentor-protégé relationship. On a purely political level, mentors and protégés can pleasantly exploit one another for mutual gain. In business and the arts, the protégé benefits from his association with the mentor, while the mentor gets a boost from the youthful vitality and hustle of his protégé.

On a practical level—where collaboration sparks creativity—the tensions of such a relationship are profound. In science, which has had a long tradition of such top-down collaboration, the tensions can be particularly acute. The senior scientist, usually a professor, provides a conceptual vision and a research scheme to be pursued by his graduate students. Inevitably, if the problem is challenging enough and the students clever enough, the students take over the problem. The professor may have had the original vision, but it is the students who have the commanding grasp of the experimental details and their implications for the hypothesis. The result is either a fruitful collaboration where the scientist and students are peers in every way but title or a mutual resentment that combusts into public acrimony. Robert Kanigel's excellent *Apprentice to Genius* details four generations of mentor-protégé relationships in the field of neurochemistry. Nobel laureate Julius Axelrod's relationship with his protégé and likely future Nobel laureate Solomon Snyder was filled with mutual admiration and extraordinary professional success. In contrast, Snyder's collaboration with protégé Candace Pert led to profound new vistas in explaining the chemistry of the brain but gradually degenerated into a public feud over priority.

The ubiquitous frictions of ambition, pride, and ego can't be ignored no matter how the collaborative relationship is structured. But even when they are present to excess, collaboration is still a powerful engine of creation. After interviewing and examining the work of some forty-one Nobel laureates, sociologist Harriet Zuckerman concluded, "Nobel laureates in science publish more and are more apt to collaborate than a matched sample of scientists. . . . Comparison of their research output with the output of the matched sample indicate that these patterns hold at every stage of the life-work-cycle."

Thus, individual genius is not enough. This is particularly true, says psychologist Vera John-Steiner, when people are struggling to establish a new paradigm for their field. Like the birth of a new galaxy, a disparate group of individuals gradually swirl and coalesce into a collaborative community. The impressionists banded together to challenge the Academy and to teach one another about how best to paint the world through seeing with a new eye. In the summer of 1869, Monet and Renoir literally set their easels side by side at La Grenouillère along the banks of the Seine. They talked—and they weren't just talking about the weather. Through both proximity and dialogue, they collaborated so intensely that many of their paintings from that period are indistinguishable.

Van Gogh biographer Richard Brower notes that, even during his period of solitude, the artist maintained "a complex network of correspondence with significant collaborators." Van Gogh went so far as to live for several weeks with primitivist Paul Gauguin, and the two worked together, visited museums, and exploded into arguments about the nature of art. "Though short-lived and poorly ended," Brower writes, "the experiment nonetheless helped van Gogh crystallize his vision."

Some twenty years later, collaborative communities were again redefining the arts and sciences. The French cubist Georges Braque wrote of the powerful connections between the painters as they struggled to express their emerging notions. "The things Picasso and I said to one another during those years will never be said again, and even if they were, no one would understand them anymore. It was like being roped together on a mountain."

"Almost every evening, either I went to Braque's studio or Braque came to mine," wrote Picasso in a letter to Françoise Gilot.

"Each of them *had* to see what the other had done during the day. We criticized each other's work. A canvas wasn't finished unless both of us felt it was."

In fact, around this time the two artists didn't sign their names to their paintings because, as Braque explained, "Picasso and I were engaged in what we felt was a search for the anonymous personality. We were prepared to efface our personalities in order to find originality."

Similarly, the quantum physicists who displaced Newton's models of nature with their own concepts of fields, forces, and particles created a community that went far beyond the notions of traditional collegiality. They traveled together, played together, worked together, argued together, and lived in one another's homes. (Werner Heisenberg's absorbing memoir, *Physics and Beyond: Encounters and Conversations* and George Gamow's *Birth of the New Physics* superbly recreate the spirit of the new science.) Their rich theories were forged in the crucible of collaborative work.

Collaboration occurs here on two distinct but inseparable levels: conceptual and technical. Braque did not wield Picasso's brush, but he certainly challenged and sharpened Picasso's nascent intuitions about cubism. Braque and Picasso helped frame each other's new perspectives of cubism by creating conversations and techniques that forced them to critically reexamine their works. The quantum physicists wrote, analyzed, and rewrote one another's equations to explain the probabilistic eccentricities of fields and particles. Blackboards and correspondence were smeared with annotations, comments, and corrections. The new physics demanded both conceptual collaboration and technical collaboration. Interactions of both personality and knowledge were essential to the discipline's advance. The conceptual collaborations yielded the vocabulary; the technical collaborations yielded the specific expressions and results. The collaborative community made it possible for gifted individuals to articulate their visions.

The notion of great art (and great science) as the product of intensely personal visions passionately conveyed through a medium isn't wrong—it's just not right. There is a value chain of collaboration that enables the individual artist to express that vision with grace and technical skill. The paints of the palette that color a new paradigm are mixed in a collaborative pot.

The thing that distinguishes collaborative communities from most other communities is this desire to construct new meanings about the world through interaction with others. The collaborative community becomes a medium for both self-knowledge and self-expression.

With rare exceptions—Charles Darwin and natural selection, Sigmund Freud and his new model of the mind—that generalization applies with equal vigor to basic science. (Even Einstein—popularly regarded as the paragon of scientific genius—had a long and rich collaborative friendship with mathematician Marcel Grossman. That collaboration, dating back to Einstein's Gymnasium days in Zurich, ultimately provided the physicist with key mathematical tools he used for his gravitational theory.) Individual genius may spot fertile ground, but it takes a collaborative community to cultivate and harvest it.

"All work in art and science is the extending of unfinished business," says Jonathan Miller. "People who write history as a succession of great men underestimate the importance of the network. The new expressions of science and art occur in a context." And so collaboration is really part of a tradition that spans generations rather than an unusual function of circumstance.

This tapestry of collective genius is all very grand, but it shouldn't obscure the everyday quality of collaboration. Creation of shared meaning isn't something confined to the genius of Braque/Picassos and Watson/Cricks. The point is that these collaborations can and should serve as models for people who are working together to create innovations or solutions to problems.

The collaborative context appears wherever people are working together to add value. For example, an ethnographer studying a group of machine technicians came to a blunt rethinking of what expertise means in the context of the workplace. His analysis was that expert knowledge among technicians is less a matter of what each individual knows than of their joint ability to produce the right information when and where it's needed. Anecdote, example, analogy, and encounter are the essence of collaborative expertise here. There is a fusion of both conceptual and technical collaboration. In other words, expertise is a social affair. The organizational tools, technologies, and training should all reflect that.

Every day some of the most important collaborations occur in hospitals and doctors' offices around the world. Unfortunately, it's too often a perfunctory collaboration. When people who feel ill or in pain come in for a checkup, the physician examines them and asks a battery of questions. For many doctors, these questions are nothing more than a rote checklist to match against the patient's complaints and symptoms. The interview is a diagnostic pop quiz.

In the hands of a master diagnostician, however, the interview becomes far more. The questions elicit answers that enable the physician to create a shared understanding with the patient of what's happening and what might be wrong. The excellent physician doesn't just want to know if there's pain—he wants to know what kind of pain it is: the shape, the intensity, the focal points. Simply articulating the symptoms isn't enough; the physician has to be able to put them into the right context. Similarly, the patient has to express himself in a meaningful way. The doctor and patient have a conversation where each improves the understanding of the other. This ongoing dialogue is often crucial to a successful diagnosis.

Without these efforts to create a shared understanding, the doctor might just as well be a veterinarian tapping and probing an ailing dog. (In fact, some doctors treat their patients in just that fashion. The patient is seen as not being able to help or really understand what's going on.) A real collaboration between doctor and patient can play a critical role in determining the patient's physical and mental well-being. The best doctors know this and treat their patients accordingly.

The operating theater is the setting for another crucial collaboration. For any significant surgical procedure, there are two essential players: the surgeon and the anesthesiologist. Normally, the surgeon runs the operation and the anesthesiologist monitors the patient's vital signs to let the surgeon know how the patient is doing. In a well-run surgical team handling a delicate operation, the surgeon and anesthesiologist constantly work to create a shared understanding about the patient's status. The surgeon is not in a position to know the vital signs of his patient; conversely, the anesthesiologist doesn't know the intricacies of the surgical procedure. A truly collaborative effort is required to see the patient through the operation without unnecessary trauma.

(In stark contrast, there are situations where the surgeon and anesthesiologist argue about how the patient is doing during a delicate operation—how much time a procedure should take; how deeply a patient is under anesthesia; what levels of blood pressure are acceptable, and so on. Sometimes the surgeon and anesthesiologist are locked in a power struggle over who should have control over how the operation should be handled. Whatever the reasons, the surgery is not a collaborative effort. Sometimes, the patient suffers for it.)

While most everyday collaborations don't occur on these life-and-death planes, even the most ordinary transactions can have collaborative qualities. Anyone who's gone shopping for a suit knows that the salesperson can be either an obnoxious pitchman of marginal value or a collaborator providing enormous help. The pitchman trots out the suits by the armload, fawningly admires the cut, color, and fit of each, and asks whether this will be cash or charge. The collaborative salesperson solicits information, discusses what you've worn in the past and enjoyed wearing. The salesperson doesn't know you and you don't know the store's selection, so there has to be the creation of a shared understanding if you're going to get the suit you want. This holds the potential to be a win-win situation.

The collaborative salesperson makes the sale, has possibly created a repeat customer, and has learned more about the sort of people he sells to. You come away with a suit you like, a sense of rapport with a salesperson who seems to understand your concerns, and a sense of satisfaction about the process.

The idea that selling can be a creative act of collaboration shouldn't be dismissed. Too often, buyers and sellers in the marketplace choose to collide rather than collaborate. The most painful collisions frequently occur when multiple disciplines meet in the marketplace of ideas.

New technologies are often the most demanding when it comes to multidisciplinary collaboration. Microsoft chairman Bill Gates, who runs the most powerful computer software company in the world, points out that the nature of technology in his industry forces disparate technical disciplines either to collaborate or fail in the marketplace.

Gates's Microsoft designs the operating-systems software for IBM's personal computers. This software is the crucial link between the actual computer hardware and all the other software. The most critical component of the personal computer is a chip called a microprocessor, which actually runs the operating system. Intel, a Silicon Valley semiconductor company, designs and builds the microprocessor that runs the IBM PC. This technological collaboration between Microsoft and Intel has made these two companies the dominant firms in their industries.

Technically, the microprocessor is just a piece of hardware—a sliver of silicon etched with the circuits that run the computer's internal network of inputs, outputs, and memory. But when Intel wants to design a next-generation chip, it wants to know how its design will fit into Microsoft's operating-systems architecture. Depending on the design, the Intel chip will allow Microsoft's software to course smoothly down its microscopic pathways—or be a digital Rube Goldberg contraption that gets the job done but treats the software like Charlie Chaplin's character in *Modern Times*—a poor creature who ricochets like a human pinball through the factory to keep everything running smoothly. Effectiveness without efficiency.

"There is an intensive collaboration" between Microsoft and Intel, Gates observed, because "Intel doesn't understand systems software and Microsoft doesn't understand silicon."

Without that collaboration, without the creation of a shared understanding between Intel's hardware jocks and Microsoft's software designers, the power and versatility of Intel's microprocessor and Microsoft's operating system would be emasculated. The technology wouldn't run—it would limp. An ongoing collaborative relationship is essential if Intel and Microsoft want to maintain their preeminence, asserts Gates. The new alchemy of microprocessor development demands it. Neither Intel nor Microsoft could succeed on its own. The cost of *not* collaborating is too high. Collaboration becomes an act of managing risk as well as managing innovation.

Inventor Raymond Kurzweil, a pioneer in optical character recognition technology, notes that this trend transcends specific technologies. Emerging fields exert forces that supersede individual talents. "Inventing today is very much a team effort and its success is a function of the quality of individual members of the team as well as the quality of its communication," he comments. "As Norbert Wiener pointed out in *Cybernetics*, scientists and engineers with different areas of expertise often use entirely different technical vocabularies to refer to the same phenomena. Creating an environment in which a team of linguists, speech scientists, signal processing experts, VLSI designers, and other specialists can understand each other's terminology and work effectively . . . is at least as challenging as the development of the technology itself."

Mapping out an urban landscape is no different from etching bold new patterns onto silicon. Architecture demands a balance of aesthetics and functionality, and that requires collaboration. Behavioral psychologist Robert Sommer has extensively studied and worked with architects and concluded that "The days of Frank Lloyd Wright and *The Fountainhead* are finished. . . . Unless you're designing a fifth vacation home for someone, architecture is collaboration. Collaboration is the *sine qua non*. . . . When you're working on a major project, you have to work with a transportation consultant, an acoustic consultant, an interior design consultant."

Ayn Rand's brand of solipsistic arrogance may capture the imagination, but it's a lousy formula for great buildings. Collaboration doesn't curtail the architect's overarching vision. As much as black glass and steel, collaboration becomes a medium that makes the vision possible.

People are also a medium for the design of art. A stage play combines the differing and not necessarily complementary talents of playwright, actors, director, designer, and lighting crew. Success requires collaboration if the play isn't to degenerate into prima donna posturing, an autocratic director pulling the strings of living-puppet actors, or scenery that distracts from the work's meaning.

(Jonathan Miller complains that American actors, schooled in the

Method acting approach of deeply relating to their roles, are more difficult to direct because they are frequently more interested in their characters than in the play as a whole. "There is a selfish self-indulgence there," he remarks.)

This collaborative complexity reaches another order of magnitude in the realm of film. Increased technical sophistication and the unforgivingly expensive demands of the medium turns the making of a movie into a village industry. Forget the auteur-theory propaganda spewed by chain-smoking French intellectuals and well-fed members of the Directors Guild: filmmaking at its finest is a truly collaborative enterprise.

In his delightful autobiography *When the Shooting Stops . . . The Cutting Begins*, film editor and director Ralph Rosenblum (whose editing credits include *Annie Hall, The Pawnbroker, The Producers,* and *Goodbye Columbus)* says:

Having spent so many years in the back rooms, I would naturally like to see filmmaking emerge from its hero myths and be recognized as a collective enterprise. I believe in collaboration, in the excitement of team effort, and in every man's right to credit for his work. As a director, I'm too mindful of the odds and the challenges to want to surround myself with slaves or yes-men who will push me and my blunders into permanent embrace. . . .

Of course, anyone who's made a career in filmmaking, unless he's been hopelessly brainwashed by the director mystique, knows how things really stand—how petrified a director is of failure, how keenly he hunts down each member of his team, and how grateful he is (whether he acknowledges it or not) for any original ideas or sparks of inspiration his teammates may contribute. . . . Yes, the director is still the key man on the team. But as Casey Stengel said after winning his ninth American League pennant in ten years, "I couldn't have done it without the boys."

TIME FOR A CHANGE

If collaboration is such a vibrant and necessary part of the creative process in the arts and sciences, why is it the Rodney Dangerfield of interpersonal relationships, getting no respect or formal recognition in business and professional life?

Part of the reason is that even the most ardent collaborators don't necessarily think of themselves that way. Nobel laureate Francis Crick, for example, has enjoyed at least two astonishingly successful collaborations: one with James Watson in their quest for the double helix; the other, a twenty-year partnership with molecular biologist Sydney Brenner. "The fact is," he confides, "that both those collaborations began spontaneously and I haven't given them much thought . . . the idiom of collaboration wasn't the one we used. It never struck me as a collaboration." Although, upon reflection, that is precisely the way Crick now views those relationships.

If Crick, who has an international reputation as a gifted collaborator, takes such a cavalier attitude toward the relationship, then it should be no surprise that collaboration is both undervalued and misunderstood.

Despite the fact that the world is a more complex and volatile place, despite the fact that the workplace has grown more demanding and diverse, despite the fact that management throws together specialists from different disciplines for crash projects in the hope they can be innovative and creative, there is astonishingly little discussion of collaboration in the business world. *Collaboration* is a word that scarcely appears even in popular discussions of the workplace (people are more comfortable discussing words like *teamwork).*

Peter Drucker, for example, is one of the most influential management thinkers of this century. His books—ranging from *Concept of the Corporation* to *The Effective Executive* to *Innovation and Entrepreneurship*—have been translated into innumerable languages and are regarded as intellectual touchstones by managers around the world. He's a champion of rational, effective, and pragmatic management.

The word *collaboration* doesn't appear in any index of his work. (In contrast, *communication* gets top billing.)

Similarly, one doesn't find *collaboration* in the index of *In Search of Excellence, The One Minute Manager,* and most other best-selling management books. When it does appear, it's usually undefined— tossed into the verbal stew to add spice to much juicier words like *leadership* and *innovation.*

As in philosophy and psychology, the intellectual tradition of Western management has been to ignore or obscure the process of collaboration. Frederick W. Taylor, the father of so-called scientific management at the turn of the century, dismissed collaboration altogether. His guiding axiom was "the rationalization of the workplace"—the imposition of a set of structures and procedures that would assure maximum productivity. "Every single act of the workman can be reduced to a science," he insisted. From that base, management could scientifically determine the optimum workplace standards.

> It is only through ENFORCED standardization of methods, ENFORCED adoption of the best implements and working conditions, and ENFORCED cooperation that his faster work can be assured. And the duty of enforcing the adoption of standards and of enforcing this cooperation rests with the MANAGEMENT alone.

This passage from his *Principles of Scientific Management* underscores the fact that Taylor wasn't interested in collaboration as a process to create shared understanding. In fact, collaboration was irrelevant to his management model. Management's task was solely to create standards to boost output, not create an environment to generate innovation. In a Tayloresque world, people wouldn't even have to talk with one another on the shop floor to get the job done. Taylor's legacy of scientific management lives on in many American organizations.

In contrast, Harvard's Elton Mayo offered a far more humanistic management model. Mayo was responsible for perhaps the most famous and influential studies of organizational behavior ever done:

the Hawthorne Studies. This project, done in the late twenties and early thirties at a Western Electric plant in Illinois, employed over thirty full-time researchers and surveyed over twenty-one thousand employees. The findings supported the antithesis of scientific management: people could not be treated as bits of human piecework to be molded on the lathes of Taylorism. The workplace was a rich complex of individuals and social groups that needed to be treated with respect and concern. Mayo's work ushered in the human relations movement in management.

With such a humanistic emphasis, said Mayo, the workplace wouldn't have to be a battleground between management and labor. Productivity would naturally increase. Mayo foresaw a workplace characterized by spontaneous cooperation where everybody would work together harmoniously.

Mayo's beliefs are simultaneously naive and astonishing. This is less of a vision than a hallucination. It's sociology's counterpart to the popular but wrongheaded "scientific" arguments for spontaneous generation, the eighteenth-century notion that inanimate chunks of matter can spontaneously burst into life. Actually, it's more like the joke about how to become a millionaire without paying any taxes. *First: Get a million dollars. Then: Don't pay taxes.* Such academic romanticism may be endearing, but it doesn't bear any resemblance to real life.

Nevertheless, the human-relations movement spawned a multitude of splinter groups. Kurt Lewin, a German-trained social psychologist, launched the T-groups (for training groups) often known as sensitivity-training groups. People would get together with their trainers to talk and explore and receive feedback on their discussions. The meetings were little experiments in group dynamics designed to heighten individual sensibilities about working together. "Sensitivity training," wrote psychologist Carl Rogers a little too enthusiastically, "is perhaps the most significant social invention of the century." Practically, it proved to be a fad. T-groups didn't necessarily lead to greater innovation, productivity, or creativity.

Douglas McGregor, management consultant turned university president, went back to basic assumptions. Scientific management as articulated by Taylor was Theory X—the belief that people are basically lazy, shiftless, and in desperate need of supervision. McGregor proposed Theory Y—that people want to be productive and want the chance to participate in the governance of the workplace. His 1960 book proposing this management theory, *The Human Side of Enterprise*, was well received and quite successful. Participatory management has now become a workplace theme. But there is a fundamental difference between participation and collaboration. The former relates to how the workplace is governed; the latter often determines how well the task is performed. The two are often confused. While McGregor does mention the importance of collaboration, he doesn't mention how to achieve it.

Other influential management thinkers have been more concerned with management as management, rather than just a theory of organizations. Chester Barnard, a former New Jersey Bell Telephone executive, authored *The Functions of the Executive*, an influential work that stressed the coordinating functions of management and its limitations. Peter Drucker is perhaps best known for the phrase "management by objectives," which represents his philosophy that what you get is more important than how you get there. Delegation becomes the form of collaborative interaction between manager and subordinate. Of course, the gap between delegation and autocracy is vanishingly small.

While virtually all of the leading management philosophers emphasize the need for effective communication in the workplace, collaboration seems to be a conceptual afterthought. Leaders are supposed to communicate their vision of the organization to their followers, but there's little mention, short of following orders, of how these followers need to interact to create value. The assembly line model of management, courtesy of Frederick Taylor and Henry Ford, still prevails; it seems best designed to discourage collaboration rather than tap into it. Management theorists seem more interested and concerned about coordinated actions than shared creation.

"People don't think too much about collaboration," says anthropologist Edward T. Hall, "maybe because it's so complex a phenomenon. As a culture, we're ambivalent about turning anything over to anyone else. We're highly individualistic; there's positive reinforcement for not collaborating. Where talent is centered on making a personal reputation, collaboration will get the back of the hand."

A more provocative explanation comes from Robert Reich, a lecturer at the Kennedy School of Government at Harvard University and Clinton Administration Secretary of Labor who likes to puncture popular management myths. In a 1987 *Harvard Business Review* article titled "Entrepreneurship Reconsidered: the Team as Hero," Reich lashes into the uniquely American myths of "entrepreneurial heroes and industrial drones—the inspired and the perspired."

"In this myth," Reich writes, "entrepreneurial heroes personify freedom and creativity. They come up with the Big Ideas and build the organizations—the Big Machines—that turn them into reality. They take the initiative, come up with organizational innovations, devise new solutions to old problems. They are the men and women who start vibrant new companies, turn around failing companies, and shake up staid ones. To all endeavors, they apply daring and imagination. . . . Prosperity for all depends on the entrepreneurial vision of a few rugged individuals."

In contrast, Reich notes, "the rest of the vast work force plays a supporting role—supporting and unheralded. Average workers in this myth are drones—cogs in the Big Machine, so many interchangeable parts, unable to perform without direction from above. They are put to work for their hands, not for their minds or imagination. . . . They have little opportunity to use judgment and creativity. To the entrepreneurial hero belongs all the inspiration; the drones are governed by the rules and valued for their reliability and pliability."

These myths, Reich argues, undermine America's economic strength and cripple its productivity: we are victims of this mythology. "Which will we celebrate," he challenges, "individuals or teams?" We need a new mythology, a new set of stories, for the workplace.

Reich calls for a new paradigm of "collective entrepreneurship." "In this paradigm," he says, "entrepreneurship isn't the sole province of the company's founder or its top managers. Rather, it is a capability and attitude that is diffused throughout the company. Experimentation and development go on all the time as the company searches for new ways to capture and build on the knowledge already accumulated by its workers. . . . "In collective entrepreneurship, individual skills are integrated into a group; this collective capacity to innovate becomes greater than the sum of its parts."

Reich's notion of collective entrepreneurship is virtually indistinguishable from the idea of a collaborative community. His article is a tough, eloquent plea for a new model of organizational collaboration to create marketplace value.

Japan, with its more collectivist society, is culturally predisposed toward collaborative organizations. Even Germany, despite its cultural predisposition toward hierarchical corporate structures, enjoys a rich collaborative tradition in engineering and design, Walter Gropius's Bauhaus collective being just one example. The point is not to emulate what works in Japan or Germany; America has its own unique cultural strengths to be enhanced. The real issue is to decide what collaboration *should* mean within the organization. Effective collaboration—indeed, effective cross-cultural collaboration —is a global phenomenon. It exists and persists because it works.

But changing attitudes, exchanging one set of mythologies for another, is obviously not enough. Organizations are too quick to jury-rig social structures like quality circles or new product skunk works in the hope they'll coalesce into productive collaborations. There is a bias toward organizational restructuring as the best recipe for attaining change.

Futurists like Alvin Toffler and management theorists like Henry Mintzberg enthusiastically describe "ad-hocracies," fluid, organic, and selectively decentralized structures that spring up to smother problems or pry open opportunities. They're seen as a natural response to the turbulent challenges of the marketplace—and as a way of cracking stodgy bureaucracies into highly effective teams.

Unfortunately, the harsh reality remains that tossing a few people into a room and nailing them to a deadline does not an ad-hocratic collaboration make. Ad-hocracies involve purely human structures that are reconfigured in interesting ways.

While flexible, versatile social structures are important, so are technical infrastructures. In fact, technical infrastructures are indispensable. No matter how novel, organizational structures aren't enough. You need rooms to meet in; lights to see by; computers to link to; telephones to talk through. These tools unquestionably shape the social structures of organizations.

So where are the tools to encourage collaboration? How does one create an infrastructure that supports productive collaboration?

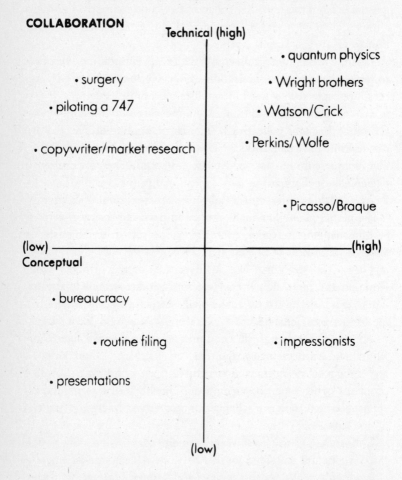

COLLABORATION

Technical (high)

- quantum physics
- surgery
- Wright brothers
- piloting a 747
- Watson/Crick
- copywriter/market research
- Perkins/Wolfe

- Picasso/Braque

(low) ——————————————————————— (high)
Conceptual

- bureaucracy

- routine filing
- impressionists

- presentations

(low)

All economic enterprises that seek to innovate and understand their customers' needs must have collaborative infrastructures. It's not enough to try to change people's perceptions and attitudes through friendly persuasion or hard-knuckled threats. The best way to build those infrastructures is to make sure that people can easily grasp and use tools for collaboration. As surely as people rely on language, paper, post, and telephones to communicate, they will come to rely on new sets of tools to collaborate.

"Tools that encourage collaboration and that enable creation of community knowledge bases may function to pull organizations toward a more open sharing of ideas," asserts Xerox's John Seely Brown.

These tools for collaboration will help unlock the innovative, creative, and productive abilities of workers at all levels of the organization—if that's what the organization really wants.

Each of the four quadrants in this matrix represents different levels of collaborative interaction. The horizontal axis represents the level of *conceptual* collaboration. The vertical axis represents the level of *technical* collaboration.

Conceptual collaboration occurs when people work together to devise concepts, ideas, themes, metaphors, analogies, and so on that frame the overarching goal of the collaboration. Examples of this would include

- a film director and a cinematographer discussing what visual effect they hope to achieve with a shot;
- Lennon and McCartney deciding on a subject for a song;
- an art director and a copywriter trying to devise a theme for an advertising campaign;
- Picasso and Braque discussing the role of light in cubism;
- a market researcher and an engineer discussing what kind of product innovation might appeal to an emerging market segment.

Conceptual collaboration yields insights into fundamental notions of the problem, innovation, or discovery that is the focus of the collaboration.

Conversely, technical collaboration is not unlike the key that fits into the lock; it's the way people physically represent the conceptual aspects of the task at hand. Technical collaborations are the attempts to solve the problems the conceptual collaborations identify. Examples of technical collaboration include

- Watson and Crick reconfiguring their metal helices when new data came in;
- Maxwell Perkins editing Thomas Wolfe's copy and sending it back for revision;
- an architect and contractor deciding what ventilation scheme is best for an office building;
- a surgeon and an internist determining a patient's treatment options;
- a group of managers allocating a budget to launch a new product.

Technical collaboration involves people with complementary skills bringing them to bear on a specific task. People of similar skills can also collaborate on a technical level, but that's usually done for the sake of speed rather than innovation or creativity. For example, two accountants collaborate on an audit less for complementary expertise than because it gets the job done faster.

The upper right-hand quadrant of the matrix depicts collaborations that require high levels of both conceptual and technical collaboration, a constant reshuffling of ideas and tinkering with models to achieve success. The Watson-Crick double-helix collaboration is a classic example, as is the collaboration that occurred within the community of quantum physicists. Directors and actors constructing a character also require both a conceptual appreciation and a technical mastery of performance.

The lower right-hand quadrant features collaborations that are high in conceptual value but fairly low in technical content. One example is the impressionist school of art. While impressionists such as Monet, Pissarro, and Renoir often did discuss questions of technique, the bulk of their professional relationships was consumed in discussions about color, light, art, ambition, society, and other themes that created a context for their work. Similarly, mentors and "blue-sky" friends with oddball perspectives often make excellent conceptual collaborators. They succeed in reframing old perspectives into new paradigms.

The upper left-hand quadrant focuses on collaborations that are highly technical and less conceptual. These are the collaborations where one requires an expert. A design engineer needs to know the stress tolerance of a material and seeks a mechanical engineer for the answer. A software programmer consults a mathematician on how best to write a certain segment of an algorithm. An advertising copywriter goes over the polls with the agency expert on market research. In these instances, the collaboration creates a shared understanding about the solution to a very narrowly defined problem.

The lower left-hand quadrant features collaborations that require little technical or conceptual effort. This is better known as "routine," and that's what bureaucracies were designed for. The issue here isn't creating shared conceptual or technical understanding but rather simply coordinating the implementation of a well-defined task.

This matrix can give you a crude metric to evaluate collaborative relationships. Sometimes, collaborators see themselves working in different quadrants. Some people may feel that their collaborations should be highly conceptual and highly technical when, in practice, the collaboration need only be technical. Similarly, some people only want to indulge in conceptual collaboration and not get their fingernails dirty with technical implementation. Though simple to the point of simplistic, the real value of this matrix is that it gives people another way to view their own collaborative aspirations.

5

Appropriate Tools: Ones That Work

If we could rid ourselves of all pride, if to define our species, we kept strictly to what the historic and prehistoric periods show us to be the constant characteristics of man and intelligence, we should not say Homo sapiens *but* Homo faber. *In short, intelligence, considered in what seems to be its original feature, is the faculty of making artificial objects, especially tools to make tools, and of indefinitely varying the manufacture.*

HENRI BERGSON • CREATIVE EVOLUTION

IT WOULD BE STUPID TO GIVE A BAND OF BRIGHT, INDUSTRIOUS people access to a lumberyard and blueprints for a house but deny them the tools to build it. Without hammers, saws, and nails, the group faces little but frustration, impotence, and rotting wood.

Unless one's tastes ran to purely a cappella performances, it would be similarly pointless to insist a talented jazz band jam without their instruments. Only a corporate jester would send interoffice memos via smoke signals, and only a fool would want to be diagnosed for treatment in a hospital with no X-ray machines, CT scanners, or MRI scanners.

The right tools are essential to doing a job well, and yet every day, people are asked to accomplish their tasks with tools that are ill conceived, ill designed, and inadequate. Too frequently, some of the brightest and most talented people in an organization are asked to create and build value using no tools at all, as if some sort of organizational alchemy will magically yield something from nothing.

When, despite good intentions and hard work, those efforts fail, these people are called incompetent and unproductive, an accusation that is both wrong and cruel. The cliché may be that a bad craftsman always blames his tools, yet no one can be a good craftsman without the appropriate tools. You don't cut your steak with scissors. Tools must fit the task.

There's a tremendous irony here: most pop management and self-help books and videotapes offer a cornucopia of suggestions on how the individual can become a better manager or a better person, enjoy more intimate or more professional relationships. This advice ranges from right-brain holistic *Zen and the Art of Motorcycle Maintenance* counseling to "go-with-the-flow" to left-brain personal development "management by objectives." Many of these books and tapes sell staggeringly well to masses of people hungering to improve themselves. They tap people's incredible yearning to better their lives.

All you have to do to achieve your ambitions, these programs promise, is become more

- intuitive,
- compassionate,
- sensitive,
- rigorous,
- biased for action,
- willing to fail,
- adventurous,
- open-minded,
- and so on,
- *ad nauseam.*

You "unlock your hidden potential" by doing things you have never done before. Just get an emotional bypass or personality transplant and everything will be fine. The fundamental message is cruelly specific: *You'd be a much better person if only you were someone else.*

This is a monstrously cynical view. It goes a long way toward explaining the angst and self-consciousness people feel as they struggle to do the best they can in often trying circumstances. The message preys on people's fears and self-doubts. We are being told that we're inadequate, that we need to become something else to be something better. The advice may be well meaning, but then the road to hell is paved with good intentions. Do people want to improve themselves by becoming someone else? Or do they want to improve themselves by improving who they are? The right tools can help.

The virtue of good tools is that they don't ask you to become someone else. They invite you to create an extension of yourself that, with a little time and skill, lets you be more than what you are. Tools are a medium for self-expression.

At the same time, an appreciation of good tools offers another way to appreciate and influence the world. A musician's ear listens differently; a photographer's eye sees differently; a carpenter views craftsmanship and detail with a different sense of proportion. A good tool expands the boundaries of perception.

Unfortunately, most people and organizations understand neither the importance nor the power of tools. Tools are, literally and figuratively, the way people come to grips with their work. Too often, organizations apply a perverse calculus of counterproductivity by asserting that technology equals machines equals tools. These organizations try to substitute technology for blue-collar labor and white-collar thought. Or, if they consider themselves enlightened, they position new technology as an amplifier, a complementary prosthetic for boosting managerial and work-force productivity. Technology is their capital investment to improve the organization, the department, and the individual.

But in an era of increasing organizational complexity and competitiveness, those approaches are lethal. They will slowly and surely poison the organization's productivity because neither approach addresses the fundamental ways organizations create and maintain value. To see technology primarily as a way either to reduce costs or accelerate output is simplistic: *technology is really a medium for creating productive environments*. As an organizational medium, technology is at its most expressive and powerful in the form of tools—tools that build these productive environments.

The only tools worth having are those that create and enhance value. Directly and indirectly, the tools people use—and organizations choose—reflect the sort of value they wish to create. Automation, robotics, artificial intelligence are technobabble buzzwords with all the semantic content of a presidential campaign slogan. These technologies are geared toward reducing costs and increasing output; they don't deal with the reality of the organization as a place where people interact to create value.

The technology now exists to transform and harden these new ideals into organizational reality. Ironically, but appropriately, these new ideals are modeled on past traditions of excellence, innovation, and craft. They demand that people reexamine the way they look at tools—and themselves.

WHAT TOOLS REALLY MEAN

In the universe of natural laws, the symbiosis of scientist and instrument is essential to discovery. It is our instruments, the artificial extensions of the senses and the mind, that let us explore new dimensions and new worlds. Pick any scientific field of the last three hundred years—physics, biology, chemistry, medicine—and it's immediately clear that instrumental innovations have reengineered their structures of knowledge. While it is true that ingenious theories and hypotheses often provide the intellectual impetus for scientific advances, those theories and hypotheses frequently feed at the table of data generated by new tools and technologies. Of course, the instruments themselves can be modified as data-rich theories signal new paths to explore.

Indeed, there is an ongoing dispute among science historians as to whether theories or instruments are more important in advancing knowledge. Such chicken-and-egg philosophizing is best left to professional epistemologists. The crucial point to remember is that new instruments are an indispensable part of the vocabulary, grammar, and metaphor of a science. Scientific instruments are the machine tools of knowledge, yielding the symbols, indices, and measures that frame theoretical debates.

The history of astronomy perfectly tracks the evolution of astronomical instruments. Lens crafting and mirror grinding—the nascent science and technology of optics—led to Galileo's telescope and Newton's reflecting telescope, which allowed the human eye to examine details of the heavens in ways the ancients only imagined. The discovery of radio waves inevitably led to the invention of the radio telescope, which revealed a new dimension in scanning the stars. Satellites and sophisticated multispectral systems have sampled the soil and atmosphere of other planets; they've looked into the red eye of Jupiter and scanned Saturn's rings. All in all, astronomers have enjoyed a very impressive technological arsenal. Who can say which has been more important to the search: the minds that conceived the instruments or the minds that used the instruments to build new theories of the universe?

The same holds true for the other natural sciences. Leeuwenhoek's microscope transformed naturalist biology just as surely as restriction enzymes and other tools of the genetic engineer revolutionized molecular biology. The cloud chamber was the first dynamic lens into the world of particle physics; the linear accelerator allowed man to crack the atom and create his own subatomic particles.

These instruments were more than just functional devices; they helped create new models of nature. Scientific disciplines grew up around them. They are as essential to the understanding of natural phenomena as metaphor is to language. Indeed, these tools spawned the metaphors we use to describe and deal with the world.

As Neil Postman argues, "Where do our notions of mind come from if not generated by our tools? . . . It takes some digging to grasp, for example, that a clock recreates time as an independent, mathematically precise sequence; that writing recreates the mind as a tablet upon which experience is written. . . . And yet such digging becomes easier if we start with the assumption that in every tool we create, an idea is embedded that goes far beyond the function of the thing itself. . . . The invention of eyeglasses in the twelfth century not only made it possible to improve defective vision but suggested the idea that human beings need not accept as final either the endowments of nature or the ravages of time."

That strongly suggests that the tools we use define who we are. Chemist and philosopher Michael Polanyi writes that a good tool becomes an extension of ourselves: "We pour ourselves out into them and assimilate them as parts of our own existence." The same holds true for tools of thought. "When we accept a certain set of pre-suppositions and use them as our interpretive framework, we may be said to dwell in them as we do our own body."

In our personal lives, our repertoire of tools frequently defines our leisure-time selves. The elaborate cooking utensils, gardening tools, video camera, darkroom, handyman's belt, piano in the living room are all tools where functionality is intimately entwined with personal satisfaction.

Conversely, the affluent classes—which suffer from the poverty of time—choose tools as time savers and time shifters. The microwave oven and the programmable VCR are two appliance artifacts of urban life. Let's not forget the "tool" that simultaneously confers the twin powers of convenience and control: the hand-held remote control device, which enables its user to wield choice with the merest flick of a finger. These tools of convenience, which demand a somewhat different standard of expertise than, say, a 35-mm camera, also reveal an individual's leisure-time preferences.

This is all, of course, often a matter of individual perception and choice. A wristwatch can be just a way to tell the time, a symbol of affluence, or an indispensable tool for an individual's life-style. If the watch is the trigger that makes sure schedules are kept, it determines that person's behavior as surely as his immediate surroundings or his companions. The watch is the substance—as well as a symbol—of that person's priorities.

Whether they're passive or interactive, we deliberately choose these tools to make our personal lives richer, more meaningful, and more convenient. Tools can create the values that we deem important. Those same choices should exist for making our professional lives richer, more meaningful, and more productive.

CONVIVIAL TOOLS?

In his brief essay about tools, philosopher Ivan Illich eloquently argues against what he sees as technological fascism in favor of "tools for conviviality." Tools should be designed in harmony with human values as opposed to, say, purely marketplace concerns. "Tools foster conviviality to the extent to which they can be easily used, by anybody, as often or as seldom as desired for the accomplishment of a purpose chosen by the user. The use of such tools by one person does not restrain another from using them equally. They do not require previous certification of the user. Their existence does not impose any obligation to use them. They allow the user to express his meaning in *action*." The level of technology is not the real issue here, according to Illich; a telephone can be as convivial a tool as a pair of scissors.

Conviviality is a useful notion. It offers a different context in which to view the design and use of organizational tools. In workaday life, it's clear that few tools are designed for conviviality. Multifunction telephone keypads are many things, but convivial isn't one of them. What's worse, the things that organizations proclaim are tools for productivity are often irrelevant to the task at hand. For professionals, that usually means that their most effective tools are their wits. No disrespect intended, but while cleverness, charisma, and character go a long way, they don't go as far as they used to. Professionals need tools to enhance their effectiveness. The current arsenal of tools is neither rich enough nor powerful enough.

Look at the tools in a typical office. The manager/professional has a desk, a chair, one or more chairs for visitors, a telephone, a calendar, a dictating machine, perhaps, a personal computer and assorted software packages. (A photo of the spouse or significant other sits on the desk as inspiration or morale booster.) There's a file cabinet, in and out baskets, pencils and pens, reams of paper, paper clips, rubber bands, a stapler, and a letter opener. The successful manager/professional has easy access to a secretary and a photocopier and can commandeer a conference room when needed.

To use Peter Drucker's felicitous phrase, this is the office infra-structure of the typical "knowledge worker." Clearly, the bulk of the tools are there to aid in the accumulation, processing, duplica-tion, packaging, transmission, and distribution of information. The telephone is the hub of verbal communication; the in and out bas-kets the nexus for memos and reports; the personal computer may be hooked up to an electronic mail or bulletin board system or a file server so that messages and documents can be transferred at the touch of a button. The photocopier is there to mass-produce the copies spit out by the personal computer's laser printer. The office is a node on a verbal, textual, and computational network.

But look at the underlying design ethic and intended use of those office tools. That desk is designed for individual use. So is the phone. The personal computer is just that: personal. The dictating machine records individual thoughts. The photocopier supports high-speed duplication of all those individually generated memos and reports.

On the surface, there's nothing wrong with that: individuals need tools to support their work. There is nothing in the office, however, explicitly designed to support collaboration.

Quality collaboration—the kind of efforts that have driven break-throughs in science, the arts, and technology—occurs with neither the frequency nor the intensity it should, in part because there are few tools explicitly designed to encourage or support it. As Danish computer scientist Pelle Ehn points out, "[a criticism] of the tool perspective has to do with the focus on individual skill whereas less attention is paid to the collective competence of a group of workers. Typically, work and interaction in the labor processes are performed as co-operation. The individual work is dependent on that of others. . . . Hence the tool perspective as design ideal needs to be supple-mented with ideals that help focus on co-operative aspects."

Insisting that existing office tools are adequate for collaborative work is a bit like insisting that tweezers and a scalpel are perfectly fine as eating utensils. Tools designed to support collaboration will be qualitatively different from tools designed to support individuals. They should be.

Remember that the mere presence of tools can motivate people to behave in certain ways. A telephone on a desk invites verbal communication in a way that the pay phone down the hall does not; easy access to a laser printer and photocopier encourages mass distribution of memos and documents.

Who would argue that the presence of these tools doesn't play a significant role in shaping the way work gets done in the office? Is it unreasonable to believe that tools designed to encourage collaborative work could similarly motivate people?

The notion of collaborative tools raises a fascinating number of design questions, which in turn raise challenges about the nature of collaboration, communication, and creativity. What is the right metaphor for these tools? What's the appropriate trade-off between ease of use and effectiveness?

"Will an artistic environment comprised of tools so powerful, so easy to use, and with techniques so transparent and quickly mastered really stimulate creativity?" asks Xerox's John Seely Brown. "Or is the real struggle for self-expression not just to master a tool but rather to discover what one wants to say through the mastering of the tool itself?"

Learning to paint, learning to play a musical instrument, learning how to express oneself in a medium gives people an inner awareness and a self-consciousness they did not possess before. Painting, music, and craft become tools for discovery as well as creation. Tools for collaborative work should offer no less.

Language can be such a collaborative tool. Indeed, language is at the core of virtually all the tools one finds in the office—the telephone, the photocopier, the dictating machine, the word processor. Without language, these tools are mute. Most people can speak a language fluently, but it takes care, craftsmanship, and sincerity to speak in a way that consistently evokes empathy, understanding, and commitment. Most people aspire to such a high level of expression. They need tools to help them achieve their aspiration.

"A notion that can open major new opportunities for toolmaking," contend software designers Fernando Flores and Chauncey Bell, "is to see the manager as a human being making linguistic commitments, soliciting commitments from others, creating and identifying possibilities, and dealing with breakdowns in the midst of a network of help."

Language under these circumstances isn't just a medium of communication; it can and should be a tool for collaboration. Just as the telephone and dictating machine are tools that enhance individual communication, language can be embodied in technologies that augment collaborative relationships. To understand and appreciate that, one needs to better understand and appreciate the role of language.

6

Language Matters

*A thought may be compared to a cloud shedding a
shower of words.*
L. S. VYGOTSKY

PERHAPS NO IMAGE BETTER CAPTURES THE PAIN AND FRUSTRATION
of writing than a line from Flaubert's *Madame Bovary:* "Language is
a cracked kettle on which we tap out crude rhythms for bears to
dance to while we long to make music that will melt the stars."

That frustration never goes away. Expression and understanding
are hard work. "What did he mean by that?" / "Do you understand
what I'm saying?" are questions always lurking close behind any
conversation. Language may be a natural medium and tool for
thought, but it generates as much ambiguity and confusion as clarity. (In *After Babel*, philosopher George Steiner argues that, instead
of being an open medium of communication, language is used more
often to conceal thought than to reveal it.)

Concealing or revealing, uttered or written, language is so powerful and so fundamental to what makes us human that leading
philosophers and scientists argue that it is at the very core of culture. The right words at the right time can make all the difference
in the world. So can the ill-timed phrase and tired cliché. Language
matters. It's the raw material of collaboration.

In the thirties, Benjamin Lee Whorf, a full-time insurance company fire inspector who held a degree in electrical engineering, de-

cided to make linguistics his hobby. With anthropologist Edward Sapir, he began to explore the influence that language exerts on thought and culture. Whorf was particularly interested in native American languages, in part because they contrasted so sharply with English.

According to legend, Whorf fell into his avocation as a byproduct of his work. He was astonished at how frequently verbal misunderstandings led to fires. While people would be exceptionally careful about smoking around barrels full of gasoline, they were a bit too cavalier around "empty" drums. They'd cheerfully light their cigarettes and toss the matches into the empties without a second thought. Of course, gasoline fumes are highly flammable. In this context, empty did not mean safe. So buildings went up in flames.

The Sapir-Whorf hypothesis, one of the most provocative theories of human culture, essentially says that language molds the form and texture of thought. As Whorf puts it, "We dissect nature along lines laid down by our native tongues. . . . We cut nature up, organize it into concepts, and ascribe significances as we do, largely because we are parties to an agreement to organize it this way—an agreement that holds throughout our speech community and is codified in the patterns of our language."

What's more, differences in these language patterns lead to differences in perception. "We are thus introduced to a new principle of linguistic relativity," says Whorf, "which holds that all observers are not led by the same physical evidence to the same picture of the universe, unless their linguistic backgrounds are similar, or can in some way be calibrated."

There are at least four ways that language shapes thought. The first and most obvious is the words themselves. They're the atoms and molecules of expression—and not all languages have the same table of elements. Virtually all cultures have some proprietary vocabulary. The Eskimos reportedly have twenty-seven different words for snow. Americans invented high technology and most of the vocabulary that goes with it. For years, the esteemed members of the French Academy have oscillated between outrage and disgust at the emergence of Franglais, the half-French/half-English patois of Americanisms that has infiltrated their language. The French believe that foreign words are lexical pollutants. The personal computer has, for example, been transformed to *l'ordonnateur*—"personal organizer."

The Soviet Union, where political dialogue has been limited by Marxist-Leninist terminology since 1917, has imported a new vocabulary to ease the transition to *perestroika*. To wit, a Soviet *menedzher* would do well to launch a *dzhoint venchur* with a Western *partnyori* who has *no-khow* and, preferably, access to *komputeri tekhnologiya*.

As the *New York Times* put it, "Gorbachev's policy of *glasnost*, the tolerance for freer expression, . . . created a demand for words to express things that were not talked about before."

America, a nation of immigrants and proud of it, has no problem assimilating foreign-born words and phrases. In America, necessity is the mother of verbal invention. If the right word to express an interesting new concept doesn't yet exist, it can be in mass media production and into the popular culture by year's end. Conversely, in the tradition of Orwellian Newspeak, a language deliberately designed to control and suppress thought,* groups and subcultures create words to pervert meanings.

At one client company of mine, a top executive never spoke of problems—he insisted that they be called opportunities. At meetings, he and his subordinates would discuss their progress in handling a multitude of opportunities. After a few months of this, the word *opportunity* acquired a distinctly unpleasant odor. When someone talked about opportunities, listeners weren't certain whether it was a real opportunity, a snide reference to the boss, or yet another problem. *Opportunity* was transformed from a word signaling the chance for genuine gain into a cynical euphemism. The word had been corrupted.

All organizations have their little pet words, phrases, and linguistic idiosyncracies. These words shape organizational thought as much as they reflect it.

A second way language molds thought is by insisting that certain kinds of information be included. In Western, Indo-Germanic lan-

---

* Orwell, no doubt, was a Whorfian.

guages, we always indicate when something is happening because all verbs must have tense. The language inherently makes us conscious of time. In contrast, Japanese requires that the speaker denote the relative ranks of the speakers (higher, lower, or equal) in every sentence. Japan is one of the most status-conscious societies in the world.

Language also shapes patterns of thought by its own patterns of expression. English's subject-verb-object sentence structure encourages actor-action-receiver thought patterns and cause-and-effect expression. In Navaho, it is easiest to name something by describing its characteristic behavior: a duck is *naal'eethi*, "that which floats all around." The majority of Navaho nouns are made from verbs in this pattern; as a result, Navaho tends to be much richer in active descriptions than English.

A fourth way language shapes thought is simply by making some things more difficult to say than others. Given the opportunity, most people take the path of least resistance in expressing themselves. These lazy tendencies discriminate against more awkward expressions. In Japanese and Navaho, it is difficult (though not impossible) to specify whether something is singular or plural. The speakers only specify number when it is important to do so.

In English, we normally don't give reportorial status—the source of what we're saying. We usually make this distinction only when asked for it specifically. In contrast, Whorf points out that the Hopi language requires every sentence to contain this distinction. The Hopis, says Whorf, manage attribution with the same facility that English speakers handle time.

The irony of all this is that, even as management texts and pop-management best-sellers spew aphorisms about the importance of *communication* in organizations, they rarely say more than a few words about *language*.

"A commonsense view of the organization makes it obvious that language is the one single currency of every aspect of organizational work," notes Peter Keen, the Oxford- and Harvard-trained organizational-design and information-technology consultant. "Yet there is very little discussion of language in work on communication, teams, authority, etc. It is treated as a given. There is no discussion of language in any of the major writers on organization management who have shaped how we think about and design organizations. This is a huge gap and an intellectual failing. . . . Words like *dasein, ontological, throwness,* and *hermeneutic* to us today seem like abstractions. Tomorrow, they should be a part of the vocabulary we use to talk about organizational function and how to redesign that functioning."

While such epistemological vocabulary boosting may ultimately be as necessary and inevitable as Keen suggests, the real problems run far deeper than the strictures of a limited lexicon. Language may be ubiquitous, but it is also seriously misunderstood. What is the role of language in the organization? How does language determine communication and creation of value in the enterprise? What metaphors does the organizational culture use? What should the role of language be in an organization? These are fundamental questions for any organization—or for any professional relationship. Management theorist Karl Weick argues that managing "eloquence" is critical to shaping the way people interpret what they see: "If leaders can influence what people say to themselves, then they can influence what those same people are thinking."

Sadly, most people honestly think that when they talk with someone or send off a memo or hold a meeting that they are communicating. People grunt affirmation, sign off on memos, and make phone calls to touch base in a delirium of ignorance, thinking that they really understand what's been said or written. Most organizations genuinely believe that their people all speak the same language when, in reality, the enterprise is a tower of Babel where marketing can't talk to accounting can't talk to research can't talk to manufacturing without a translator. This sad state shades into pathos as manager after manager, employee after employee, professional after professional starts whining that "people don't understand what I'm saying. . . . They just don't get it."

There needs to be a new model to describe and explain the role of language in relationships and the organization. Consider Taylorism, Nobel laureate Herb Simon's satisficing, Theories X, Y, and Z, Drucker's management by objectives, and the Peters-Waterman search for excellence. None of these models can exist without language, yet none addresses either the ambiguities or potentials that language creates in organizations. Language is taken for granted.

One important implication of the Sapir-Whorf hypothesis, notes computer writer Birrell Walsh, is that language could be designed to shape thought. Such languages actually exist: they're called computer languages. Different computer languages offer different vocabularies, grammars, and metaphors for thought. To wit, "Forth [can be] used to make a unique factory that will build answers. LISP [will let you see the problem as one of] connection and a network of pipes woven to solve it. In Smalltalk, the answer comes from commerce among objects. In APL, the problem will be seen in terms of latticeworks and matrices."

The metaphors embedded in the computer language largely determine the programmer's thoughts about how best to structure software written in that language. The point—and the promise—is clear: a new approach to language can lead to a better quality of communication and collaboration. No, people don't need to learn a new language. Creating some sort of organizationally engineered Esperanto is exactly the wrong way to go. A better way is to make people a little more conscious of the language they already use—and to provide tools that make that language more effective.

ONE LOOK AT LANGUAGE

Rotating the more traditional models of management on their ears, two scientists (one political, one computer) assert that language is the single most important tool for organizational effectiveness. Managing organizations means managing language.

The model is radical but its sources are credible. Terry Winograd, a computer science professor at Stanford, was one of the young Turks of the artificial-intelligence movement. At one stage, he believed that computers were only a few years away from understanding natural language. He has since recanted, and this new model of language is an outgrowth of his new perspective. His colleague, Fernando Flores, holds a doctorate in philosophy from the University of California at Berkeley and once served as a cabinet minister in Allende's Chile.

The two collaborated to produce a book—*Understanding Computers and Cognition*—and a design philosophy that skewers the conventional wisdoms of computer science and human decision making. The book offers both a powerful challenge and a useful approach to managers and professionals who intuitively understand the importance of language but need a context in which to express it.

Though more polemical and provocative than practical, Winograd and Flores's approach to organizations is still constructive. They dismiss the conventional perception of an organization as a bureaucracy or as clusters of teams and individuals: they see the organization as a "network of conversations" where the design of communication doesn't just link people and places but also coordinates conversations for action. "Nothing happens here without language," the two assert. "If we are to understand this bit or any bit of organizational activity, we must understand the speaking and listening that happens in organizations."

Indeed, Flores believes that "a business (like any organization) is constituted as a network of recurrent conversations" that managers must learn to manage effectively.

Viewed through the prism of language, there are three axioms for organizational design:

- Managerial work about the future happens linguistically.
- The basic unit of communication in work is commitment.
- The basic structure of managerial and office work is the network.

The effective organization, say Winograd and Flores, has a strongly woven web or network of commitments that are made, observed, and honored. The manager's role is to create, coordinate, and enforce those commitments, whether they've been made between employees or with customers or suppliers. "We ask, 'Who makes requests and promises to whom and how are those conversations carried to completion?' At a first level, we treat the company as a unity, examining its conversations with the outside world—customers, suppliers, and providers of services. There are some obvious central conversations with customers and suppliers, opened by a request for (or offer of) [products] in exchange for money. Secondary conversations deal with conditions of satisfaction for the initial ones: conversations about alterations . . . , conversations concerning payment (billing, prepayment, credit, etc.), and conversations for preventing breakdown in the physical setting (janitorial services, display preparation, etc.).

"Taking the business as a composite, we can further examine the conversational network among its constituents: departments and individual workers. There are conversations between clerk and stockroom, clerk and accounting, stockroom and purchasing, and so forth. Each of these conversation types has its own recurrent structure and plays some role in maintaining the basic conversations of the company."

There are misunderstandings, of course, that Winograd and Flores term "breakdowns," but renewing and continually clarifying commitments can repair those mishaps.

It is a fact that conversations determine what will and won't get done. The conversational web becomes a marvelous metaphor to examine the inner workings and interrelationships of the organization. Peter Drucker suggests that managers can become more effective executives by keeping a time log. Perhaps departments would be better off becoming conversational cartographers, drawing maps to represent who said what to whom when—and what the ultimate outcome of those conversations actually was.

In fact, the Winograd-Flores model has been embodied in a piece of network software called Coordinator, which captures the spirit, if not the gritty details, of language-driven management. Conversational cartography it's not, but Coordinator offers a radical departure from traditional business memos, conversations, and calendars.

"The Coordinator works on the premise that most business communications have some underlying purpose," notes Esther Dyson, editor of the newsletter *Release 1.0*, one of the more savvy computer industry analysts. "For example, 'Juan and I are going to be out in Palo Alto next week' might be a request for a meeting; 'Unfortunately I've got a sales call in Redmond' is a denial of that request (especially if the second person doesn't ask what day Juan and partner will be there). Then there are promises: 'I'll have it for you by Wednesday,' 'I'll get back to you tomorrow,' 'The check is in the mail,' 'We'll make it up next quarter.'

"The Coordinator makes these explicitly—or rather, makes the user specify them, along with a related time element. . . . The set of possibilities numbers about 100. . . . A request, for example, triggers these options: promise, decline, counter-offer, or report completion (changing the status of the conversation), acknowledge, open a subconversation, commit to commit, or interim report (status quo). . . . Each commitment or request has some due date —which shows up as a reminder on the schedules of each party to the commitment."

Dyson wryly comments that Coordinator is particularly suited to organizations afflicted with a "cover your ass" corporate culture, though she adds, "It might also encourage people to think more clearly about what they need and what they're promising."

The power of Coordinator as a language tool is that it forces people to crack what they're saying into communicable, manageable, and measurable chunks of commitments. Coordinator forces its users to treat language with a level of care and self-consciousness that is often missing from memos and phone conversations. For better or worse, Coordinator flushes out the very human refuge of ambiguity (*"But I thought you meant . . ."*).

The real issue is language for action, not just description. Flores and Chauncey Bell of Action Technologies (which sells Coordinator) add, "When our subject is productivity in some human enterprise, the representation of action in words is interesting—and necessary for recording history. But the more important question will always be how to bring forth future actions with words and not how actions are best recorded in words. For the most part, Western civilization has lost this distinction as a pivotal question."

But are Coordinator-like tools the best way to deal with language in professional relationships?

MEDIUM OF EXCHANGE OR MEDIUM FOR CREATION?

While Coordinator was the first and most intriguing effort yet to use language to define workplace activity, it has relied on a model of interaction that is both restrictive and misleading. With Coordinator, Winograd and Flores treat language as a medium of information exchange, a linguistic currency to be traded back and forth like greenbacks and pork bellies. The value of language, Winograd and Flores appear to be saying, comes primarily when it is being used to create, confirm, and monitor a commitment.

The Coordinator model consequently distills language into a byte-sized commodity. Communication becomes a transaction to be consummated; conversations are transformed into contracts. The true richness and versatility of language as a collaborative tool goes unrealized. The power of creating metaphors—the ability to conjure up images and analogies that resonate in other people's minds —goes untapped. Indeed, the software is called Coordinator and not Collaborator for good reason. While Coordinator literally lets you make a date, it doesn't help you have a meaningful relationship.

Language must be viewed as a medium to create meaning and shared understanding rather than simply to exchange information. Language should evoke images, impressions, reasons, memories, and thought. There is an art, a craft of conversation. Some conversations should only be verbal transactions; most should be much more.

In economic terms, it's the difference between spending and making an investment. In using language as a tool for collaboration, it's the difference between the ritual incantations of the formal presentation and the informal lowdown at the water cooler; the difference between the professor delivering a lecture from the podium and the kibitzing that goes on with the graduate students at the lab; the difference between a salesman making a pitch and a salesman spending an afternoon with the customer, observing the situation, asking questions, and actually listening to the answers. It's the difference between description and metaphor.

This contrast between such formal and informal settings for conversation is unfair, but so are most examples used to prove a point. There are many levels to conversation, but the best conversations are acts of collaborative creation. They create a shared understanding where it did not exist before.

"Conversation enables us to rapidly build shared contexts," says Xerox's John Seely Brown. "If the world isn't changing very much, then the shared context you had a year ago can be brought up very easily. But to interpret rapidly changing phenomena or generate radical change, you have to be able to rapidly create new shared contexts."

MORE THAN A FEW WORDS

The role of language in innovation has never been more intriguingly portrayed than by Nobel physicist Werner Heisenberg in his memoir *Physics and Beyond: Encounters and Conversations*. In the preface, Heisenberg asserts that "Science rests on experiments; its results are obtained through talks among those who work in it and who consult one another about their interpretation of these experiments. . . . The author hopes to demonstrate that science is rooted in conversations." For Heisenberg, conversations are as passionate and intense as any journey into theory and experiment.

Indeed, the role of language in science is the central theme in Heisenberg's memoir—both as a means to explore the new frontiers of quantum physics and to explain how the new generation of physicists all related to one another during one of the century's most exciting intellectual adventures. Metaphor is as important to good science as a good theory or a new instrument.

The shift from Newtonian mechanics to quantum physics required not only a new way of looking at physical phenomena, but a new language to describe it. One of the conversations Heisenberg reconstructs occurred with his mentor, the great Danish physicist Niels Bohr. "Bohr was full of the new interpretation of quantum theory and as the boat took us full sail southward in the sunshine, there was plenty of time to tell of this scientific event, and to reflect philosophically on the nature of atomic theory. Bohr began by talking of the difficulties of language."

The Dane points out to the young German that the conceptual problems facing the theoretical physics community are beyond the boundaries of explicable metaphors. "We intend to say something about the structure of the atom but we lack the language in which we can make ourselves understood. We are in much the same position as a sailor marooned on a remote island where conditions differ radically from anything he has ever known and where, to make matters worse, the natives speak a completely alien tongue."

These were not the idle musings of a hyperintellectual. "[Bohr] inspected the language with which an idea was expressed in the way a jeweler inspects an unfamiliar stone," according to one account, "slowly judging each facet by holding it before an intense light."

Heisenberg's memoir (as well as several excellent histories of physics) recalls that the physicists frequently discussed the role of language and metaphor in their work. The physics community struggled to cast their new science into symbolic forms that would be rich with meaning and provide a base upon which to craft further theory and experiment.

Of course, there is far more to physics than words. The new physics of fields and forces demanded and got new forms of mathematical expression. Galileo, a physicist of an earlier era, once said that the language of nature is written in mathematics. The new math of quantum physics was as much a language to Heisenberg and Bohr as German and Danish. Quantum physics was a child of both literary and mathematical metaphors. Without both these languages, the new physics couldn't have evolved.

If we define language as a set of symbols we use to convey meaning, then we all use several languages to express ourselves. Language becomes a high-bandwidth activity. There's body language, the little shifts and movements and expressions that either conceal or betray our feelings; there are spoken and written words, of course; perhaps a few equations, musical notation, a rough sketch, a fine drawing.

Or electronic spreadsheets like Lotus 1-2-3, a computer program that allows managers to create dynamic presentations that represent the financial nooks, crannies, and projections of the business ledger. The spreadsheet can be programmed to reflect various assumptions in the business environment in a way that anyone familiar with finance can quickly and easily grasp. So Lotus isn't just a way to package financial information; it is also represents a lingua franca of finance. The numbers in the rows and columns are the nouns; the formulae that twiddle those numbers are the verbs; and the underlying assumptions that drive them are the adjectives. Knowledge of the business provides the necessary contexts for interpreting all those symbols and processes.

The spreadsheet is both metaphor and language. For many businesses, spreadsheet proficiency is as vital to success as verbal proficiency. If mathematics is the language of nature, perhaps spreadsheets are the Esperanto of business.

VISUAL LANGUAGE

Clearly, there is much more to language than strings of sound or letters forming words, sentences, and paragraphs. Art critic/psychologist Rudolf Arnheim dismisses mere words as the true instruments of thought. In a chapter entitled "Words in Their Place" in his book *Visual Thinking*, he suggests that "language is essentially stabilizing and conservative" and that its real power for thinking is in facilitating "the mass evocation of images." (Marshall McLuhan notes that "We employ visual and spatial metaphors for a great many everyday expressions. . . . We are so visually biased that we call our wisest men visionaries or seers!")

Arnheim goes on to add that "purely verbal thinking is the prototype of thoughtless thinking, the automatic recourse to connections retrieved from storage. It is useful but sterile. What makes language so valuable for thinking then cannot be thinking in words. It must be the help words lend to thinking while it operates in a more appropriate medium, such as visual imagery."

Visual and verbal languages are complements. Who hasn't felt the mental itch during a conversation to snatch up a pen and paper to illustrate a point or sketch a conclusion?

In cognitive science, there is a tremendous rivalry between those who believe people think in images and those who believe that words are the vital ingredients in the crucible of thought. It's impossible to resolve that question here. What matters, though, is the way inner languages of word and image are outwardly expressed.

Consider Albert Einstein's famous remark on his thought processes: "The words or the language, as they are written or spoken, do not seem to play any role in my mechanisms of thought. The physical entities which seem to serve as elements in thought are certain signs and more or less clear images which can be voluntarily reproduced or combined."

It's clear that our conventional perceptions of language are just too narrow. In her delightful book on creativity, *Notebooks of the Mind*, Vera John-Steiner lavishes attention on the role of visual languages in thought. These languages aren't shackled to the intermediary symbolism of letters and numbers; they have the unique properties of images.

"While language is a socially constructed and conventionalized mode of expression, no corresponding single visual language exists," John-Steiner notes. "There is, consequently, a great diversity of graphic and plastic means used by creative individuals in shaping and communicating their inner notions."

"Visual thinking—the manipulation of our visible world to generate meaning—is both a hidden internal process and something that can be extended into material form," adds Australian graphic designer David Sless. "In other words . . . it is the public manifestation of private reflection."

A picture isn't just worth a thousand words—it is the grammar and lexicon of a visual language. The quick sketch to illustrate a point is a visual counterpart to the verbal metaphor. Xerox research chief John Seely Brown, a pioneer in collaborative learning systems, confesses that he's a "functional illiterate when it comes to sketching," which he calls "a primary language." The role of the sketch in collaboration, says Brown, is as fundamental to conveying ideas and images as language. The difference, he notes, is that fewer people are as fluent sketching as they are speaking or writing.

The sketch as language reinforces a fundamental truth about human culture: that image and language can't be divorced. As anthropologist Edward T. Hall notes, "The history of art is almost three times as long as that of writing and the relationship between the two types of expression can be seen in the earliest forms of writing, such as Egyptian hieroglyphics."

A picture may be worth a thousand words, but the right word is worth a thousand pictures. Images, like words, are constrained by the culture and context of their creators. Yet underlying them both is the struggle to take an idea and give it shape. In Albarn and Smith's *Diagram: The Instrument of Thought*, the authors state, "The diagram is evidence of an idea being structured—it is not the idea but a model of it, intended to clarify certain characteristics of features of that idea. . . . Through appropriate structuring, it may generate different notions and states of mind in the viewer."

This craving for visualization extends even to our sense of place. In his intriguing book *The Image of the City*, urban designer Kevin Lynch asked dozens of Boston residents to draw maps of their city. The landmarks they included or ignored revealed a great deal about where they lived and how they felt about the city. Lynch discovered that people carried a "mental map" of the city inside their heads that they used to orient themselves and give directions to others. Research with Parisians by cognitive psychologists revealed that different age groups have different mental maps of their cities and their neighborhoods. These maps are the metaphor for the way the residents view where they live. Mere words, mere addresses don't adequately capture the way they see their city.

One of the great challenges of communication (and collaboration) is to convey these mental maps. How do you get others to see the world as you do? Architects, graphic designers, industrial designers, and scientists can't trust alphanumeric arrays to capture the ideas and images crystallizing in their minds. "Every time there is a dispute," observes French sociologist Bruno Latour, "great pains are taken to find or sometimes to invent a new instrument of visualization, which will enhance the image, accelerate the readings . . . and conspire with the visual characteristics of things that lend themselves to diagrams on paper—coast lines, well-aligned cells, etc."

When words and numbers fail us, we feel we have no choice but to turn to representations that give us another way of grasping reality. Maps and three-dimensional models are frequently the tools of choice. "I would say that models constitute a language too," the late Nobel laureate Linus Pauling once observed. "They hold information and communicate it. Also, the construction of the model may represent the development of a theory—and with a model, it needs to be a precise theory. If you have fuzzy vague ideas, then you find that you can't build a model because a model must be precise."

The popular influence of architects like Frank Lloyd Wright and Michael Graves can be as much attributed to their facility as visual artists as the buildings they've made. While Mao said that "Power grows from the barrel of a gun," in architecture and design, influence grows from the point of a #2 pencil. The ability to model reality in multiple modes—with text, image, conversation, sculpture, and so on—is an indispensable part of creativity and collaboration.

These verbal and visual languages all weave into a continuous flow of communication that shapes understanding. According to psychologist Rom Harré, "We construct our worlds in talk of various kinds. Every exchanging of symbolic objects is a kind of extension of that conversation, I believe. So we have, as philosophers, or psychologists, or sociologists, to look at the properties of talk, the form of conversations, if we really want to get to the heart of what it is to be a human being, engaging with other people in constructing a social world."

The title of this chapter, "Language Matters," is thus flawed. *Languages* matter. Languages of all kinds are our tools to re-create and communicate experiences that are as visual, musical, and tactile as they are verbal. We need all the languages we can muster to create those shared understandings. *Understanding* may be the point at which all these different languages intersect.

We need tools and technologies that will make the process of conversation as swift and effective as possible. Media—the sketch on a piece of paper, the printed word, the video image, the telephone transmission—are the vessels for language. Indeed, one can't divorce language from the media that carry it. As surely as the printing press transformed the written word and television transformed the image, the emerging technologies of collaboration will transform the power and potency of all our languages.

7

Collaborative Tools: A First Look

*The next breakthrough won't be in the individual
interface but in the team interface.*
JOHN SEELY BROWN

*People come out of a Colab session saying, "We've just
done ten hours of work in ninety minutes," and they
can't believe it.*
MARK STEFIK

WHAT IS A COLLABORATIVE TOOL?

OVER LUNCH IN THE CAFETERIA, YOU AND A COLLEAGUE WRANGLE
over how best to structure a particularly troublesome negotiation.
The discussion slowly devolves into an argument. He heatedly insists that the key points should be organized in a sequence that
makes absolutely no sense to you. You assert that presenting the
points his way runs counter to logic and diffuses the impact of the
best argument your side can muster.

Your colleague responds that you've completely misunderstood
the priorities. His sequence of points might take the edge off the
best argument, but it prevents your adversaries from directly attack-
ing the weakest part of the proposal.

"Look," he says, taking out his black felt-tip pen, "I'll show
you."

He snatches up a napkin, unfolds it, and quickly outlines the structure of his arguments—underlining the key points for emphasis. He picks up another napkin and sketches out your presentation. He spreads out the two napkins on the table and points back and forth between them, explaining the error of your ways.

"Just a second," you say, reaching for your pen, "that's not right." (Unfortunately, you have a ballpoint, so you have to borrow his pen.) You modify a word here, cross out one of the points there, and switch the order of two items on his outline. He acknowledges that it isn't a bad idea and adds another argument from your list. You nod approvingly.

He picks up another napkin and outlines the new key points of the presentation, using the other two napkins as references. "Is this what you're saying?" he asks. You say yes, adding one more item to the list.

You genuinely like the modifications. So does he. The disagreement has vanished. Your colleague fixed a weakness in the negotiating stance and you managed to preserve most of the impact of your best argument. The two of you argue briefly over who takes the third napkin back to the office to be transformed into a nice laser-printed memo. The other two napkins get crumpled and tossed into the trash.

The felt-tip pen and the paper napkins are collaborative tools.

WHEN JOHN DYKSTRA, who has directed special effects for such films as *Star Wars*, meets with clients—producers, directors, what have you—to discuss new creative concepts, he greets them with a phalanx of three industrial designers armed with sketchpads. As Dykstra and his visitors chat, the three designers are furiously sketching—tangibly visualizing—the ideas being tossed about. As the sketches become intelligible, Dykstra points to one and says, "Is this what we're talking about?" If the client agrees, the other two industrial designers immediately key into the distinguishing features of that sketch, adopting its tone and style. Dykstra, the clients, and his trio of artists can go through dozens of iterations to come up with the look of a project or a special effect. The conversation interweaves with the sketches as a visual prototype is created. "You have to create a kernel from which you can grow a new concept," says Dykstra, "and you have to stimulate people to go beyond what they normally do in a conversation. . . . By causing people to think on their feet, you get fresher ideas."

This little microcommunity of industrial designers, clients, and sketches is Dykstra's collaborative tool.

You, THE SALES manager, and the convention organizer have until a six P.M. deadline to agree on the design and layout of your company's trade-show booth. This is the key industry show and you're launching a new family of products that the chairman is extremely enthusiastic about. It's already three-thirty and there is still no agreement. You quickly draw a sketch of the L-shaped floor plan, rough in where the new products should be displayed, and fax the diagram to the sales manager. Fifteen minutes later, he calls you back screaming that your layout is stupid and that he's sending his version of the way the exhibit layout should be.

The sales manager's sketch is better drawn than yours, but he's given too much space to the high-commission items and put some of the newer products in the back of the booth. You sketch in some changes on his diagram and fax it back with a note that points out the chairman's interests. A few minutes later, you receive a fax that keeps your modifications but has one more new product added. The layout is fine, but it looks a little cluttered. You call the sales manager. He's adamant: you changed the space allocation, he determines what has to be in the booth.

It's five o'clock and you fax a redone diagram to the trade-show floor coordinator with a scrawl at the bottom asking if there's any more space. Twenty minutes later, he calls you back and says you can have another hundred square feet, but it will cost you. He faxes back your layout with the additional space dotted in. You like it, but it's not in your budget. You fax it off to the sales manager with the dollar figure scribbled in. Ten minutes later, the fax comes back with his OK and initials. You fax the final version to the trade-show office. They acknowledge receipt. Everything's settled.

The collaborative tools here are papers, pens, telephones, and faxes.

THEATER DIRECTOR JONATHAN Miller, who has a keen aesthetic sense but can't draw to save his life, relies on his collection of three thousand postcards to communicate visually with his set designer. "We swap postcards and Xeroxes with each other," says Miller. "I show him how I want something to look, how the light should fall, how a cloth should drape. This is how we communicate when words aren't adequate."

PICTURE TWO ENGINEERS, colored felt-tip pens in hand, chatting away as they sketch out design permutations for a new product on the office whiteboard or college students launching a group assault on the blackboard to solve a particularly annoying problem in linear algebra. This is how work really gets done.

WALK THROUGH VIRTUALLY any research lab or university and you're bound to find the office walls lined with blackboards or whiteboards, all scribbled and sketched upon. (In contrast, the walls of the business offices are either completely bare or feature some tasteful print or poster.) Indeed, the blackboard/whiteboard is the most pervasive of collaborative media. You won't find a world-class researcher at a world-class facility anywhere without a blackboard in the office. (This tradition goes back to medieval universities in Germany.)

With the notable exception of colored chalk, there has been no fundamental advance in blackboard technology in over five hundred years. But, like paper, this hasn't prevented the blackboard from being an astonishingly reliable and resilient collaborative tool, as the following example demonstrates.

"On any given morning at the Laboratory of Molecular Biology in Cambridge," one observer writes, "the blackboard of Francis Crick or Sydney Brenner will commonly be found covered with logical trees. On the top line will be the hot new result just up from the laboratory or just in by letter or rumor.

On the next line will be two or three alternative explanations, or a little list of 'what he did wrong.' Underneath will be a series of suggested experiments or controls that can reduce the number of possibilities. And so on. The tree grows during the day as one man or another comes in and argues about why one of the experiments wouldn't work or how it should be changed."

"I would point out something peculiar," says Francis Crick. "That when two scientists get together, they each get out a pencil and start sketching."

Actually, as Crick well knows, scientists often do much more than that. In Crick and Watson's bid to find the double helix—Crick a brilliant mathematician/crystallographer, the young Watson an expert on bacteriophages (a type of virus)—the scientists found that the key to their success was a collaborative tool of their own invention. Rather than rely exclusively on X-ray crystallography patterns, organic chemistry data, and pencil sketches, the two continually built and rebuilt metal models of their proposed DNA structures. Ironically, such model building was looked upon by their colleagues as a peculiarly grubby form of three-dimensional draftsmanship.

"Helices were in the air, and you would have to be either obtuse or very obstinate not to think along helical lines," says Crick. "What [rival chemist Linus Pauling] did show us was that exact and careful model building could embody constraints that the final answer had in any case to satisfy. Sometimes this could lead to the correct structure, using only a minimum of the direct experimental evidence."

Both Watson and Crick recall in their memoirs that these jury-rigged metal structures were an indispensable part of the way they tested their theories, fitted in new data, and created shared understandings about their individual perspectives.

"Only a little encouragement was needed to get the final soldering accomplished in the next couple of hours," Watson recalled in his *Double Helix*. "The brightly shining metal plates were then immediately used to make a model in which for the first time all the

DNA components were present. In about an hour I had arranged the atoms in positions which satisfied both the X-ray data and the laws of stereochemistry. The resulting helix was right-handed with two chains running in opposite directions."

Now at first glance, there's nothing at all unusual here. This is everyday stuff. These tools, call them collaborative or not, are readily at hand. And no one would argue about their usefulness. They readily embody the visual and verbal languages that people need when they have to do more than just transmit information. They make collaboration faster, better, and more effective. In the real world, collaborative tools, however primitive, are a pervasive and indispensable part of the creative process. That's why you find blackboards lining office walls in universities and R&D labs all over the world. People on the path of innovation and discovery need to sketch and they need to build. They need the insights that only a visual or tactile representation of the problem can evoke.

Imagine being forced to express yourself at work in words of only one syllable. Yes, you would be able to communicate effectively in most situations, but the frustration level would be as high as the precision and richness of your language would be low. The images, maps, and perceptions bouncing around in people's brains must be given a form that other people's images, maps, and perceptions can shape, alter, or otherwise add value to.

"If you have a model, you know what the permissible structures are," says Nobel laureate Linus Pauling, the main rival to Watson and Crick in the race to the double helix. "The models themselves permit you to throw out a larger number of structures than might otherwise be thought possible. But then, I think that the greatest value of models is their contribution to the process of originating new ideas." Model building is now quite a bit more respectable in biochemistry than it was in Watson and Crick's day. That such tools were an integral part of the discovery of the double helix helped make that so.

Collaborative modeling pops up in all sorts of contexts. Cardiac surgeons and plastic surgeons huddle over models, charts, and computer screens to plot out their operations. Architect Kevin Roche, a protégé of the great Eero Saarinen, says that his firm crafts as many as forty models of a proposed structure to give his clients a sense of spatial and aesthetic orientation. Industrial designers increasingly rely on models and prototypes to design *with* users instead of *for* them. Instead of relying simply on what people say, designers of new products and services often encourage customers to build a conceptual model of the innovation and actually diagram how they want to use it. Diagrams are then hardened into prototypes that customers can see, feel, and manipulate.

Rapid prototyping—the ability to quickly build a computer simulation, a mechanical model, or even a cardboard mock-up of the innovation—has become a key to such customer collaboration. The prototype becomes the vocabulary of the innovation, and each successive prototype enlarges that vocabulary and deepens both designer and customer understanding. In effect, says John Rheinfrank, a designer with FitchRichardsonSmith who has worked with both consumer and industrial clients, the conceptual models and prototypes "become the clay" that customers help mold into the final product. "We're still trying to unravel what it means to design a product where the content of the product is constantly negotiable." This holds true whether the product is a computer display, a telephone keypad for an office system, an insurance claims form, or state-of-the-art computer software.

These rapid prototypes aren't one-shot deals: they aren't frozen in final form. They're collaborative learning and design tools. They're visual and conversational stimuli. They're a medium of expression. There's nothing intrinsically sophisticated about them— they represent an attitude as much as they do a technology—but they help get the job done.

In many respects, these collaborative tools—blackboards, whiteboards, metal models—are as essential to the process of creation as new instruments have been to the advance of science and technology. The telescope and radio telescope completely redefined astronomy. The gradual evolution of these collaborative tools are similarly redefining collaboration. People can create and discover things with one another in ways that were previously impossible.

What would it mean if the power and versatility of these simple tools for collaboration could be amplified tenfold? A hundredfold? A thousandfold? What if technology could augment the process of collaboration with the ease that a pocket calculator augments computation? What new kinds of conversation and collaboration would occur? How would conversation and collaboration be different? What new insights into creativity and discovery would these new tools yield?

These questions are at the very core of this new epoch of interpersonal interaction. The blackboard may have served us well for hundreds of years, but maybe it's time for a change. The issue isn't *automating* collaboration; it's using technology to enhance the collaborative relationship. Technology here doesn't substitute for people; it complements them.

In the sixties, Douglas Engelbart (in many respects the conceptual godfather of collaborative technologies) had no tools or prototypes to prove his thesis that technology could augment intellect—the technology simply didn't exist. So he cleverly demonstrated the converse: that technology could "disaugment" intellect.

Engelbart asked a few people to write with a pencil. He analyzed that sample. Then he attached a brick to the pencil and asked them to write some more. After a few minutes, Engelbart coolly observed, the quality and legibility of the writing had markedly deteriorated. The brickified pencil corrupted easy expression.

If one could handicap intellect by attaching obstacles to existing media for expression, Engelbart argued, why couldn't one augment intellect by removing the obstacles inherent within existing media?

In the collaborative context, those obstacles can be as obvious as the fact that napkins rip, people have illegible handwriting, and blackboards run out of space. But there are other, more subtle ways that traditional media constrain the collaborative process as surely as if a brick were attached. Picture a global telephone network that has just one tiny glitch: an automatic two-second delay between speakers. From the moment you say hello to the instant you hear a response, four full seconds elapse. (Check your watch the next time you're on the phone.) What kind of discussion can you have under those circumstances? What does an argument sound like? What would spontaneity mean under these constraints?

What does collaboration mean within these constraints? Even in ordinary conversations, the strictures of taking turns, interrupting, and maintaining conversational flow can make a collaborative effort very difficult. Like the brickified pencil, the time-delayed telephone corrupts fluent expression.

This little experiment in "disaugmentation" underscores another point: even under the best of circumstances, it's difficult to keep track of what's been said in conversation. Conversations—time-delayed or not—are ephemeral; the words vanish the instant they've been uttered. Even when taking notes, one can rarely, if ever, get a perfect transcript because of the inevitable discrepancies between what's said and what's heard. People generally respond to what's just been said, not something said seven or eight minutes earlier. Conversations don't have memories; only their participants do.

The serial and ephemeral nature of conversation, then, subtly √ works against collaboration. In most conversations, people take turns exchanging information, not sharing it. In most conversations, the absence of memory means a useful phrase or expression can be distorted or lost. We frequently rely on the transactional model of communication discussed earlier. For most of us, that looks like this:

Sender/Receiver ············· **Conversation** ············· **Receiver/Sender**

The collaborative model—the model that captures the napkins, faxes, blackboards, whiteboards, musical notations, and the helical intricacies of DNA models—is quite different:

Shared space literally adds a new dimension to conversation, a dimension embracing symbolic representation, manipulation, and memory. Participants must also have near-equal access to the shared space—or else it really isn't shared, is it?

Participants can communicate with one another directly and through the medium of shared space. Changing the conversation can lead to a change in the shared space and vice versa. Symbols, ideas, processes, sketches, music, numbers, and words can be put in the shared space to be expanded, organized, altered, merged, clarified, and otherwise manipulated to build these new meanings. **It takes shared space to create shared understandings.** Conversation is vital, but it isn't enough.

Shared space exists wherever there is effective collaboration. Whether we collaborate to discover something we don't know, to create something new, or to solve a problem that confounds individual solution, shared space is invariably an indispensable tool. You see it in the models that molecular biologists like Watson and Crick build and the annotated scribblings exchanged by Eliot and Pound; you hear its results in the songs created by a lyricist and composer (the piano and the scribbled notes create both acoustic and visual shared space for their work); you see its results in the works actors, directors, and set designers present on the stage; and you find it expressed in the prototypes of virtually every significant invention of this century.

You can play with them, turn them upside down, or spin them on their axis. But these shared spaces aren't just intellectual exercises. They must provoke the senses as well as the mind. Collaborators can literally experience what they're doing while they think about it. Like the keyboard of a piano or a personal computer, the shared spaces are dynamic. And shared spaces can have very selective memories in order to retain the best points and features of a design.

They are also highly malleable and manipulable; it's easy to tinker with, edit, or alter them. Whether the shared space embodies a musical riff or a quick sketch, adding tone or inflection is a simple process.

These collaborative tools frequently work in real time; it doesn't take hours or days to use them. They're highly interactive; just tap them and they respond. Similarly, they readily accept new data and information; they are highly adaptive and adaptable. A new perspective, a new word, or a new chord can easily be mixed in. Collaborators can explore *what-if* scenarios without shattering the shared space. These collaborative environments are also relatively easy to make and discard; there's a low barrier to entry and exit. Yes, there's an emotional and intellectual investment in them, but not an irrevocable commitment.

Shared spaces can be divorced from time or distance or both. A blackboard can easily be worked on asynchronously, with collaborators leaving notes and annotations for one another at all hours of the day and night; it can also be worked on synchronously, with collaborators making a joint assault. Similarly, a fax machine and a telephone can annihilate distance for collaborators. Successful shared spaces create the aura of copresence: they make collaborators feel like they're together, even if they're not. That model is always manipulable; the sheet music is editable; the blackboard accessible.

Most important, perhaps, it's easy to play in the shared space. Formal protocols may exist, but they need not be rigidly enforced. Play allows for curiosity and serendipity, two historically essential ingredients for discovery and innovation. The shared space becomes a frame of reference, a medium, as much as a collaborative tool. Indeed, it becomes a collaborative *environment*.

Shared space heals the rift between spoken language and visual language. In our culture, we've divorced representation from human interaction. People treat speech and writing—or speech and image —as binary, either/or, competitive with each other. Speech is dynamic and interactive; words and pictures are static and designed to be observed. This is as silly and frustrating as watching but not listening to an orchestra play Mozart or hearing a Busby Berkeley musical on the radio.

Visual and verbal languages should work in concert as part of a seamless continuum of expression we can share. The problem is, we are still in the silent movie era of shared spaces and collaborative tools. The tools are too disjointed, our shared spaces too restrictive for us to reap the benefits of multimedia collaboration. Our tools force us to endure collaboration as a more discontinuous and fragmented experience than it could or should be.

To wit, napkins are fairly limited as shared spaces go. Blackboards and whiteboards—the established workhorses of shared-space collaborations—are better, barely. As Xerox Corporation researcher Mark Stefik notes in *Beyond the Chalkboard*, "Space is limited and items disappear when that space is needed for something else, and rearranging items is inconvenient when they must be manually redrawn and erased. Handwriting on a chalkboard can be illegible. Chalkboards are also unreliable for information storage: . . . figures created in one meeting may be erased during the next. If an issue requires several meetings, some other means must be found to save information in the interim." (Of course, napkins are portable.)

To put a collaborative spin on the Sapir-Whorf hypothesis, just as language shapes the process of thought, these shared spaces shape the process of collaboration.

Technology will not only remove the obstacles but it will amplify the power of shared spaces. New collaborative tools and techniques will transform both the perception and the reality of conversation, collaboration, innovation, and creativity. John Dykstra's sketching squad, the fax machine, and Jonathan Miller's photocopied postcards are just the first stutter steps to a next generation of collaborative media.

COMPUTER-AUGMENTED COLLABORATION

The next generation of collaborative tools is being explored by organizations ranging from Apple Computer to MIT to Lotus Development Corporation to Electronic Data Systems to Coopers & Lybrand. These organizations intuitively appreciate the importance of both technology and interdisciplinary innovation.

Perhaps the single most striking aspect of these efforts is that they were all born of necessity and not academic theory. At EDS, researchers in Ann Arbor concluded after an extensive survey that GM work groups needed a better way to meet. At Xerox's Palo Alto Research Center (PARC), a pair of researchers who frequently worked together on new ideas decided to build a set of computer-based tools to augment their collaborations. Stanford University researcher Fred Lakin decided that a computer would be a more versatile graphics display tool than a set of flip charts. Palo Alto's Bernard DeKoven discovered that computer-generated shared space was the best way to get people to participate playfully in meetings. Coopers & Lybrand learned that clients needed to work with visual representations of their strategies, problems, and opportunities.

Indeed, back in 1984, Royal Dutch Shell strategic planner Peter Schwartz whipped up a crude computer model for a Hewlett-Packard calculator and hooked it into a Kodak Ektachrome projector to get the company's managing directors to consider the possibility of an oil price crash. At first, the managers resisted—"We don't play with models in the board room." So Schwartz started playing with the model. Gradually, the managing directors began to participate. After an hour, they were so intrigued that they set up a meeting for the following Monday. "They couldn't leave," Schwartz recalls. "They were totally hooked." This jury-rigged collaborative tool encouraged Shell to better position itself for the coming downturn in the price of oil.

Collaborative technology is being driven by genuine *need*—not by a pie-in-the-sky idealism about how people should work. People are building tools they actually use—not guinea-pig-ware for academic exercises.

Perhaps the most cogent work in the new era of collaborative technologies has been done by the Xerox Palo Alto Research Center. The research—which is, appropriately enough, highly collaborative—blends disciplines from anthropology to software engineering. The initial findings are rich in insight and future applications. They hinge upon a very pragmatic sense of the way work gets done in organizations and a contempt for the techno-macho syndrome where nerds armed with slide rules call the shots.

At Xerox PARC, the notion of personal computing gives way to interpersonal computing. The computer becomes the medium for shared space. "Collaborative computing will be much, much more pervasive than personal computing," claims Mark Stefik, an artificial-intelligence expert who oversaw much of the lab's work on collaborative tools, "because while not everyone needs a personal computer, virtually everyone needs to collaborate."

This shift away from personal computing to interpersonal computing has tremendous implications for both computer technology and the way people interact with it. "When we move from personal to interpersonal," assert Stefik and colleague John Seely Brown, "the requirement for personal intelligibility of the subject matter shifts to a requirement for mutual intelligibility; the meaning of conversational terms shifts from being internalized [inner speech] and fixed to externalized and negotiated; our view of language shifts from a kind of description to a kind of action. But these points are just a beginning. *The new technologies enable conversations with new kinds of properties; we need new concepts to understand their nature.*" (Emphasis mine.)

There are several ways to inject the computer as a medium of collaboration. For the moment, consider a meeting room with a semicircular conference table where each participant has his own personal computer. At the front of the room is a large whiteboard-sized screen that can display high-resolution computer data. During the meeting, the participants can send computer data to one another and they can place it on the large screen for display. This is, crudely, the setup for Xerox's eponymous Colab to support meetings. Colab is a useful model to begin exploring the next generation of collaborative tools.

To promote shared viewing and access, Colab was built around a team interface concept known as WYSIWIS (pronounced "whizzy whiz") for "What you see is what I see." The Colab software lets participants partition the large screen into multiple windows (the equivalent of miniwhiteboards) that can be enlarged, shrunk, thrown away, moved around, linked, clustered, or stored for later retrieval. Participants can also "telepoint" to windows and objects on the screen to identify subjects of interest or topics of concern. All the constraints of the traditional whiteboard—limited space, static representation of symbols, lack of permanence—disappear.

The large screen becomes a community computer screen where everyone can write, draw, scribble, sketch, type, or otherwise toss up

symbols for community viewing. It's the shared space. People can produce on it or pollute it.

This collaborative environment does have a touch of Starship Enterprise/a-personal-computer-in-every-pot overtones to it, but there's more here than an electronic whiteboard. This technology completely changes the contexts of interaction. For one thing, a conventional conversation normally has rules of etiquette that govern turn-taking. These rules evolved around the constraints of an oral meeting, where only one person can speak at a time lest the conversation degenerate into babble. But in the environs of Colab and shared space, there are visual channels that can either augment or conflict with the spoken word. Conversation isn't the only activity going on; it's not the only domain of interaction. In ordinary conversation, a speaker responds in some fashion to the previous speaker's comments; in this new environment, people may feel more compelled than at "ordinary" meetings to respond to something that appears on the screen. Traditional notions of conversational etiquette go out the window (pun intended) if one person writes a controversial message on the community screen while another talks about something else.

In an oral conversation, the words have a soap-bubble quality: they float around, evoke some comment, and then pop and disappear. In a computerized medium, ideas are both external and manipulatable. When one "speaks," one doesn't just utter words—one moves objects. People can create icons—clocks, calendars, machines, spreadsheets—to represent certain ideas and concepts. Others can modify or manipulate these icons until they become both community property and a visual part of the conversation.

For example, a group can meet to design a chart for an important sales presentation. Both in conversation and on-screen, the design criteria can be specified—number of variables to be displayed, size of the chart, special symbols (if any), title, fonts, comments, and so on. People can toss up visual suggestions for group consideration and everyone can decide what looks best. An icon from one window can be moved and merged into a chart layout suggested by another. The collaborative group can tweak, stretch, and compare charts in a multitude of ways. They can produce a prototype of the final chart in a way that just couldn't happen in a room with a whiteboard.

A crude but effective meeting tool developed by Xerox PARC enables a group to create an outline of ideas. Cognoter is designed to help organize ideas for papers, presentations, talks, and reports. The end product is an annotated outline detailing the critical aspects of the project.

Xerox PARC people structure a Cognoter Colab session into four parts:

- brainstorming ideas,
- organizing ideas,
- evaluating ideas,
- generating an outline.

The brainstorming mode represents the antithesis of the standard wait-your-turn meeting session. A participant picks an empty space on the shared screen and simply types in all the ideas he has. Everybody can see what's being typed and this can inspire conversations within the group. People can annotate items, expand them, ask questions, elaborate—and have everything recorded on-screen. (Usually, there's no criticism of what's listed—this is a classic brainstorming session where the purpose is to generate quantity, not quality.)

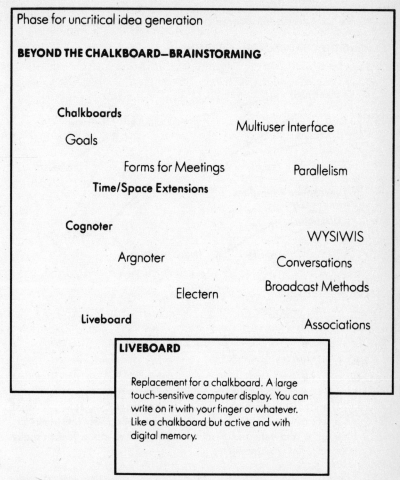

Brainstorming: In the brainstorming phase, Colab participants suggest ideas that are promptly displayed on the large screen. Text explaining the ideas in greater detail is entered into special "windows" that can be called up and displayed if desired.

The next step is organizing all these ideas. The Cognoter software lets people sort through, group, link, categorize, and order all

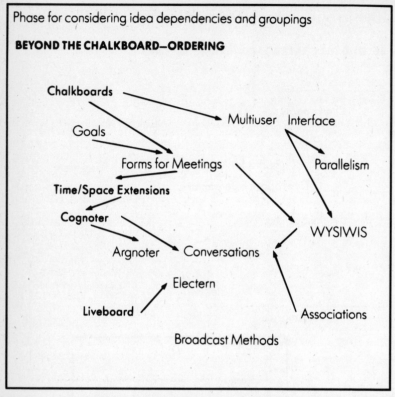

Phase for considering idea dependencies and groupings

BEYOND THE CHALKBOARD—ORDERING

Ordering: The ideas are then put in order on the screen by creating a visual link. This is a very dynamic outlining procedure and, collectively, these links display the hierarchy and networks of all the brainstormed ideas. Ideas usually have one or more links to other items.

these ideas. Themes emerge. Similar expressions are clustered together. Redundancies are eliminated. Arrows are drawn between clusters to delineate relationships. The skeleton and muscles of an outline begin to emerge. The verbal conversations increase as people decide what ideas belong where in the shared space.

Then, people evaluate their ideas. They rank them in order of

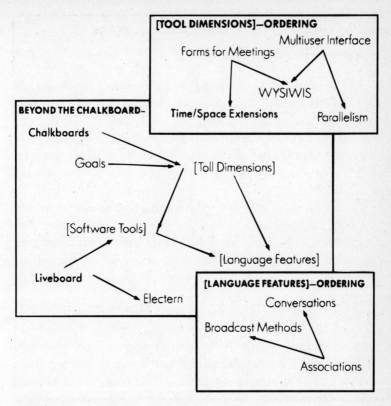

importance, annotate and expand the concepts that need to be explored in greater depth, and prune away the branches of the outline that will probably bear no fruit. The conversations here often degenerate into arguments and disputes as participants come to grips with their personal perspectives and the divergent priorities of other group members. (There may be tension here between participants wanting to revise existing alternatives and those wanting to derive new ideas.)

Finally, each participant gets a printout of the final outline and sees how this outpouring of ideas has been structured by the group.

Xerox PARC has another piece of Colab software called Argnoter, which is described as an "argumentation spreadsheet." In contrast to Cognoter, Argnoter software divides the meeting process into

- proposals,
- arguments,
- evaluation.

The idea behind Argnoter is that most misunderstandings and disputes derive from three main sources: personal positions, unstated assumptions; and unstated criteria. Argnoter is designed to make these all explicit and represented in the shared space. "It's tough to have a hidden agenda in an Argnoter meeting," says John Seely Brown. Shared space is where the real intellectual dueling takes place.

Ostensibly, there may seem to be nothing revolutionary here, but exploring ideas and arguments in the context of shared space can completely transform conversation. The software injects a discipline that encourages people to create, visually and orally, a shared understanding with their colleagues. The technology motivates people to collaborate.

"The coordination of intellectual work around manipulable icons draws on familiar skills for the coordination of physical teamwork," Stefik and Brown observe. "When one participant wants another to work on an item, it is possible to pick up the item and drop it in the work space of the second participant. This is very much like the physical act of picking up a physical object (e.g., a football or a hammer) and handing it off to someone else." When ideas become objects that can be manipulated, meetings become more concrete.

The manipulative power of the medium makes it easy to categorize objects. Groups doing personnel rankings or project evaluations can shuffle through and sort the appropriate icons into whatever categories they agree upon—a major advantage of the WYSIWIS team interface. Everybody can see what's going where all at the same time.

Another profound change for collaborative conversations is the possibility of equal access to the data. Anyone and everyone can "play chairman" and easily send data to the screen. In ordinary meetings, as Stefik and Brown note, one has to get out of the chair, walk to the board, pick up the piece of chalk, etc. Colab makes it logistically easier to participate.

More significant perhaps, is the notion of parallel voices in the conversation. Clearly, in an ordinary conversation, everybody can't talk at once. But in this environment, oral contributions aren't the only way to participate. People can silently enter ideas for community consumption. Instead of having to wait your turn and risk having the glimmer of an idea evaporate into the ether, you can enter it in a special window on-screen without orally interrupting what's going on. Of course, unlike most meetings, even those with transcriptions and minutes, there is a complete record of what data, icons, and processes flowed across the shared space of the community screen.

A few interesting initial observations emerge from this technological stew. For one, oral conversation tends to ebb and flow with the activity on the screen. Sometimes, visual language drives the conversation; other times, oral conversations drive the screen. Colab meetings have a different rhythm than ordinary meetings.

As might be expected, there are tensions between the needs of the group to govern the shared space and the needs of the individual to express himself, creating occasional contention for screen space. Indeed, one Colab participant noted ruefully that "we felt we were spending an inappropriate amount of time managing display space rather than attending to the business of the meetings. Management of screen real estate is a key issue."

Indeed, space itself becomes a measure of meaning. Big windows assume greater importance than smaller windows. Something in the center of the screen dominates a window tucked into the lower left-hand corner. Stefik recalls some meetings degenerating into what he describes as "scroll wars" and "window wars" where various individuals and factions struggled to capture screen space like generals trying to crush data insurgents in an information war.

The medium also engenders its own idiom and humor. When people dwell for too long on a point, some prankster might thrust the clock icon right into the middle of the screen, enlarging it to humongous size, and letting it tick away. People get the message.

When confronted with a meeting in an office bereft of Colab-like support, a regular user may ask plaintively, "How do I point?" Similarly, when faced with a diminishing space on the office whiteboard while scribbling away, a Colab user may ask, "How do I shrink this?" or "How do I move this over there?"

Like the frustration someone used to an electronic spreadsheet feels when confined to a paper ledger, a "frustration with the ordinary whiteboard develops when one has experienced superior media," says Stefik.

No one yet claims that collaborative tools will boost interpersonal productivity ten- or a hundredfold—although Stefik likes to say that most Colab meetings "see new ideas exploding across the screen like popcorn." The point here is that by using this technology, a meeting turns into both a tool and a collaborative environment.

Colab is not the future; it was a rough-hewn prototype lashed together by some good ideas and intriguing software. Colab, says Stefik, "is shaped too much by today's technology—it's an accident of current technology," but it does offer a provocative peek into the potential of collaborative tools.

"We now make Colab jokes at non-Colab meetings," says Stefik. "People bitch 'Why aren't we doing this in Colab?'—the people who don't get workstations (as they do at Colab meetings) are very, very frustrated people. Normally nice people become scowling and unhappy. Some of us have become Colab addicts."

Addiction is too strong a word, perhaps, to describe the way users of General Motors/Electronic Data Systems' Capture Lab feel about their computer-augmented environment—but lust is not. Some GM groups insist they couldn't get their work done outside the lab; they claim that it cuts the necessary time by a factor of ten. That claim may be exaggerated, but it underscores the notion that the computer-augmented collaborative environment can give a group a sense of empowerment. Almost without exception, the Capture Lab reports, every GM group that has used the lab has wanted to continue using it. One GM group insists that a job that normally took four months to accomplish was achieved in two all-day Capture Lab sessions.

The Ann Arbor–based Capture Lab is part of the Center for Machine Intelligence, a research organization run by GM's Electronic Data Systems subsidiary. The lab itself is designed to function as a conference room with a distinctly computational flavor. Several key General Motors working groups and task forces use the Capture Lab for their meetings.

In contrast to Xerox's Colab, the Capture Lab room consists of a large oval conference table with eight Apple Macintosh IIs embedded in it (so that they don't interfere with participant eye contact). There is a large screen at one end of the room; the proprietary software enables any participant to "take control" of this main screen from their personal computer. The room is spacious, if a bit drab, and the computers are designed to blend into the décor rather than call attention to themselves.

As with Colab, the Capture Lab technology and environment—the network of shared space—transforms interpersonal interaction. The most successful meetings tend to be those where people collaborate to create a document; the meeting is used to do work rather than just talk about doing work. Control of the screen is passed about like a baton in a relay race—the participants each take turns as the meeting's scribe. This rotating scribe approach and the nature of the technology assures ready access to the screen. Lots of conversation complements the information being entered on-screen.

To be sure, some people accustomed to more traditional meeting formats have difficulty adjusting to the notion of a personal computer and a central display as collaborative tools. For example, which person sits where at the table is significant. The power seat at the table gives one a view of all the participants and the main screen. Invariably, this is where the senior people end up. A sociologist observing various meetings at the Capture Lab recounts that some high-ranking participants tried to turn their subordinates into their own personal scribes, with varying degrees of success. Eventually, many of these "dictators" decided to grab a keyboard.

The Capture Lab, like Colab, generates its own style of interaction, collaboration, conversation, and presentation. Being in a Capture Lab meeting is not unlike being in a production room editing a movie or being in the control room in the van directing the coverage of a football game. There are multiple perspectives, multiple players, and a sense that everything is moving just a little faster than normal. There's a kinetic quality to the discussion and people feel that their words are tangible things—that they can reach out to the screen and move them around, edit them, blow them up, or file them away.

There's also a tactile and kinesthetic quality. People point. People use speech and physical gestures to draw attention to and away from the screen and themselves. People raise their voices to talk to the screen and lower their voices as they talk to one another. Something is always going on. There's either the clicking of keys, text or images moving on-screen, someone talking, or someone shifting in his chair. The experience isn't breathtaking or overwhelming, but it is disorienting to people who are more comfortable at ordinary meetings. The frames of reference have all shifted. You don't look at people the same way, you don't talk with people quite the same way, and you certainly don't interact with information the same way.

Participants tend to be more sensitive to what's going on around them. They're simultaneously more open and more self-conscious. They're open in the sense that they know that everything they say can be enhanced and modified by themselves and by the group. They're self-conscious because they know that what they say can become part of the record—so they want to measure their words with care.

At first glance, all these different responses to computer-augmented shared spaces might simply reflect the uncertainty that comes from novelty. But a deeper look confirms that these rooms evoke different behaviors because they are designed to evoke different behaviors. Conversations have a different quality and urgency in these collaborative environments because the technology makes it easy to share information in profoundly different ways.

There are both qualitative and quantitative differences between these technology-rich collaborative environments and the ordinary meeting room. If the laws of supply and demand are any indication, the new environments are a great success. The Capture Lab is booked solid, and additional labs have been built. More immediately, some groups are building their own ad hoc Capture Labs with Macintoshes and overhead projectors.

Armed with twenty-four IBM personal computer workstations, two rear-screen projectors and an electronic copyboard, the University of Arizona's College of Business and Public Administration offers its own flavor of meetings environment—a flavor that has been eagerly gobbled up for internal use since 1987 by IBM, the world's largest computer company.

Although the system is text based with nary a hint of graphical capabilities like its CoLab and Capture Lab cousins, it has gotten rave reviews both from IBM's vast internal market and visitors to the Arizona site. Moreover, IBM—which quantifies everything it possibly can—has done studies asserting that these "Decision Support Centers" generate over 50 percent in person-hour savings in meeting time and a 92 percent reduction in time required to complete a project.

"IBM runs on task forces," says one Decision Support Center manager. "Typically, one of those task teams can go on for three weeks. . . . What we found is those kind of sessions which often dragged on and on and on would conclude much more quickly in these rooms. . . . The tools lead you to have more structure. Instead of taking three weeks, the task teams could get their work done in a day and a half. You can get in forty-five minutes of brainstorming what once took half a day—and spend the rest of the time prioritizing what's important."

As in the other systems, participants can simultaneously type and transmit all their ideas onto a central, shared screen. This system supports only text, not graphics. The on-screen ideas are then clustered and analyzed according to the relevant criteria and then prioritized. The thrust of these TeamFocus software tools isn't radically different from a Colab—there's Brainstorming, Issue Analysis, Prioritizing, Policy Formation, and Stakeholder Identification. But there is definitely a different cast to the technology.

For example, anonymity is encouraged. IBM observes that this helps keep people focused on the issues instead of individuals. "Conversations are much more content-oriented as opposed to challenging or getting into personalities. It works extremely well with highly opinionated people who would be prone to dominate a meeting."

Another crucial difference is that these centers all rely on facilitators to coordinate and conduct the meeting. Indeed, it's not clear whether the technology is used to augment the facilitator or the facilitator is used to enhance the technology. However, IBM stresses that the most valuable aspect of the Decision Support environment is the hard copy—the transcript—of the meeting. "The physical output is vital."

One of the cleverest and most provocative shared space designs comes from Hiroshii Ishii and Monoru Kobayashi of NTT Labs in Japan. Their ClearBoard prototypes represent a brilliant new metaphor for collaborative creativity. ClearBoard is designed to create a shared drawing medium for pairs of users—although the idea is extensible to larger groups.

To quote Ishii, "We came up with the new metaphor of 'talking through and drawing on a big transparent glass window.' We named it ClearBoard."

In essence, collaborators literally collaborate *through* the shared space of what looks like a transparent pane of glass that they can sketch, write, and draw upon. This enables them to look directly at each other, recognize body language cues, and converse around their shared space collaboration. Via network technologies, of course, ClearBoard allows collaborators to collaborate remotely: the ClearBoard window can be virtually created to allow a calligrapher in Tokyo to collaborate with a student in Osaka.

Of course there's a problem: the collaborators have no common orientation of "right" or "left" as they work together. However, Ishii and Kobayashi ingeniously solved this problem by mirror-reversing the video-image. That enables both collaborators to have a common left/right orientation. The result is a shared space that creates a fascinating medium for both verbal and visual dialogues. The ClearBoard metaphor has yet to evolve into a commercial product but it is subtley forcing more conventional groupware designers and videoconferencing technologists to reevaluate the way they establish shared space for collaboration.

Whether physical or virtual, face-to-face collaborations are different from side-to-side collaborations, observes Ishii—the interactions are qualitatively distinct. But are they better? In some contexts, they appear to be. But the essential point is that a clever collaborative design metaphor forces both creative individuals and ambitious technologists to think about the role of new media in supporting new kinds of dialogues.

A wackier approach to collaborative environments can be found in the POD, an octagonal meeting room an English computer company uses for brainstorming and other kinds of interactional creativity. Each side of the room has its own medium—butcher paper, video projector, computer projector, whiteboard—to be used depending upon which stage the meeting is in. When the group is looking for multiple ideas, multiple walls are used. When the group seeks harmonic convergence, everyone focuses on a single wall. A round table (this is England, after all) in the middle has a hole in its center for various equipment and wires; it gives the optical illusion of drawing everybody into the center: sort of an organization's collaborative black hole. Clearly, the focus here is collaborative environment over collaborative technology—and the point is clearly made. One is literally surrounded by spaces aching to be shared.

A common design guideline of all these collaborative environments is that real people are in the rooms at the same time—physical presence is important. Obviously, not all collaborations require physical presence. Phone conversations, fax messages, and video-conferences all permit productive collaboration at a distance. Indeed, some collaborations work best that way. But there is still something important about being in the same place at the same time with someone. A study of collaborative interaction in engineering design by John Tang from a joint Stanford University/Xerox PARC project "revealed that gestural actions are a prominent and productive aspect of the group's activity." He argues that collaborative work spaces should convey gestures and "enable the fluent intermixing of listing, drawing, and gesturing." Collaborative tools should empower human expression, not handicap it. That's far easier to accomplish when the collaborators are physically together.

Nevertheless, cross-country collaborative tools are also being explored. "In rooms filled with computers, cameras, microphones, and xylophones," reports the *Wall Street Journal,* "Xerox Corporation scientists in cities 500 miles apart have been collaborating as if they were in the same building." The company has scientists in constant real-time communication between Palo Alto and Portland, Oregon. The workers watch and talk to one another via video and speakerphone connections that are always open. They share documents over a network that links their desktop computers.

"The all-day video and audio connections make a big difference, letting the offices interrelate casually as well as formally. The main links connect the common areas at the center of both labs, each of which has a camera and a big-screen monitor. . . . A few workers have cameras and monitors in their own offices. . . . People in both cities regularly eat lunch on camera, chatting with each other on the screens."

The xylophones? That's how one captures attention. Xerox put a xylophone in each office and gave each researcher a personal melody. Tap the right keys to summon the desired researcher. Of course, the pervasiveness of a video and audio presence means that new rules of etiquette have to evolve. The point is not that this technical kluge represents a breakthrough—it probably doesn't—but that organizations are trying to come to grips with the challenge of making collaborative efforts productive even over great distances. Simply creating communications links isn't enough. One has to craft the communications technology in a way that creates shared spaces for collaboration, not just pipelines to exchange data. MIT's Media Lab has pioneered and packaged an array of technologies designed to digitally transmit presence. The idea is to use technology as a medium to create a sense of *copresence* between individuals and groups.

Similarly, Bell Communications Research—the laboratory of the Regional Bell Operating Companies—has explored a "virtual hallway" called CRUISER. CRUISER provides a blend of video and computer software and hardware that instead of physically moving allows participants to "browse" the hallways by video and chat to see what's up.

Indeed, this effort to add value to traditional communications devices also extends to the fax machine, a collaborative tool that works superbly with paper. But suppose you could "fax" three-dimensional models? America's Defense Advanced Research Projects Agency has funded work in "selective laser sintering." This technique starts with a picture of an object on a computer screen. The computer then slices the image into horizontal layers. Just as a two-dimensional image is computer-constructed from pixels, for "picture elements," the solid is broken into voxels, for "volume elements."

Once the three-dimensional image is completely stored and transmitted over the network, a laser begins redrawing the item—sliver by sliver—on layers of powder that fuse and solidify wherever the laser strikes, one sliver per layer.

A similar idea—stereolithography—allows the virtual transmission of three-dimensional replicas by using liquids that harden when hit by ultraviolet laser light. The laser etches a pattern on the top of a bath of plastic, then a platform lowers the hardened pattern, exposing another liquid layer for the next slice to be hardened.

Both these methods are slow, but electronics companies, aerospace firms, and car companies are all very interested. The idea of being able to telecommunicate three-dimensional shared spaces literally adds a new dimension of possibility. These are the tools that not only make distance irrelevant but invite collaborations where they had previously been impossible. Engineering, architecture, medicine—any field where three-dimensional models offer more insights than two-dimensional representations—will find their collaborative infrastructures reshaped by these technologies.

There is a tacit, if unarticulated, design ethic lurking beneath all these emerging real-world examples. **The real purpose of design here is not to build collaborative tools but to build collaboration.** These rooms, these tools are media and environments that both encourage and enable collaboration. We don't yet have a design tradition for collaborative tools in the way we have design traditions for buildings and furniture or for the graphic arts, but, as our understanding of collaboration deepens, that aesthetic will evolve.

The POD, Capture Lab, Decision Support Center, and Colab rep resent the first glimmers of a design tradition in collaborative environments.

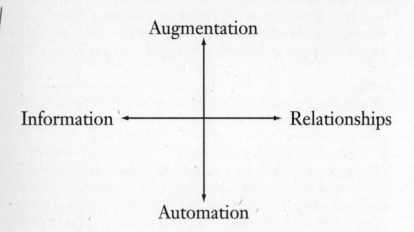

THIS SIMPLE MATRIX offers a useful diagnostic for assessing the design impact of technology on the organization.

It's fair to say that for the last forty years the central role of organizational technology has been to automate the process of information management in the organization. That's the guiding principle of management information systems groups and data processing departments. It's at the core of mainframe and departmental computing. Even a lot of the newer client/server architectures are designed around this requirement. Of course, much of personal computing—including electronic spreadsheets and word processing—finds its origins in automating information. Conversely, technology can also be used to augment information management. The same spreadsheet that automates a bookkeeping chore can be used to explore *"What if?"* scenarios for future budget challenges. The same desktop media software that automates a slide show can be used to create a dynamic, interactive presentation in collaboration with an audience. An organization can develop analytical tools to add value to all the data it has collected.

But perhaps the sharpest distinction between automation/augmentation can be found in the artificial-intelligence domain of "expert systems," which are software designed to replicate the decision-making rules of experts. Many times, expert systems are designed with the idea of using the technology to replace the expert. Sometimes, the expert systems are designed to enhance the ability of experts to make better decisions. Expert Systems designed to automate expertise feel very different from expert systems designed to augment it.

Similarly, there are profound differences in technology designed to support information management and technology designed to mediate relationships. An example of technology designed to automate relationships management is the ubiquitous phone mail. The machine is a substitute for presence. Electronic mail frequently qualifies as a relationships automation technology as it substitutes for the memo management tasks that occupy so many organizations. The rise of work flow technologies and reengineering also serve as examples of technologies designed more to coordinate relationships than transmit information.

The upper-right quadrant—the place where relationships are augmented—is the domain of collaborative tools, technologies, and media. Electronic whiteboards, distributed shared spaces on networks, and prototypes (both real and virtual) belong in this quadrant.

It's important, however, to stress that no quadrant is more valuable than another in the context of organizational management. Each sensibility serves a valuable function.

The matrix has proven to be an exceptionally helpful diagnostic tool. I have handed out transparencies with this matrix on them and asked each member of a group of project managers to put in the appropriate quadrant where their particular project belongs. Then I've stacked the transparencies on an overhead projector. More often than not, what we see is a total scatter pattern. In other words, people are trying to work together to implement systems and technologies about which they have fundamentally different perceptions. That guarantees trouble.

The value of the matrix diagnostic is that it encourages people to be more explicit about the kind of network technologies they're trying to implement. Do we want the emphasis to be on automation or augmentation? Relationships management or information management? What design emphasis makes the most sense for us? What makes the most sense for our users? Mapping the options can be essential to picking the right ones.

8

The Ecology of Meetings

*We meet because people holding different jobs have to
cooperate to get a specific job done. We meet because the
knowledge and experience needed in a specific situation
are not available in one head.*
PETER DRUCKER

I don't know why the hell we're meeting.
ANONYMOUS FORTUNE 500 MANAGER

We're meeting managers to death.
ROBERT LEFTON, CONSULTANT

HAROLD GENEEN RAN HIS MEETINGS THE WAY HE RAN ITT—WITH
an unslakable thirst for detail, a ruthless focus on the numbers, and
a brutal insistence not just for facts, but for what he called "unshak-
able facts."

These semimonthly meetings in Brussels and New York would
frequently run past midnight, and executives who could not answer
Geneen's persistent queries were often humiliated before their
peers. Geneen's ledgers, exquisite memory, and ironclad backside
enabled him to dominate. The meetings served a dual purpose: they
confirmed Geneen's primacy and let every one of the company's top
managers know where the others stood in the numbers game. These
rituals of power and coordination served Geneen and ITT's share-

holders quite well for a time. For better and worse, these meetings defined ITT's culture.

Former Reagan administration Office of Management and Budget director David Stockman, on the other hand, recalled with disgust a budget meeting with the president and Defense Secretary Caspar Weinberger in the early years of Reagan's first term. Armed with a sheaf of spreadsheets and charts, the technocratic Stockman argued for moderate growth in defense spending. The savvy defense secretary, who had known Reagan since his days in the California governor's mansion, riposted with charts that called for a far larger increase. The chart showing the OMB-proposed defense budget was illustrated with a wimpy-looking soldier with a teeny-tiny gun. The Defense Department budget chart featured a Rambo-like commando bristling with lethal weaponry. The president looked impressed. Stockman lost his budget battle.

Symbolism is often where you find it, but it's clear that these meetings were as much theater as they were business. The participants were playing their designated roles. These meetings weren't just managed; they were stage-managed. Weinberger's charts and Geneen's ledgers weren't just tools, they were props, bits of stagecraft designed to conjure up an impression. There's nothing wrong, evil, or improper about that. But it reveals some fundamental truths about relationships.

Erving Goffman, the late sociologist, wrote frequently about the notion that all the world's a stage. His books—notably *The Presentation of Self in Everyday Life*—are classics. They reveal just how ritualized, formalized, and sterilized many of our relationships have become. He shows people as preening peacocks; putting on a good act is enough. "Excellent performance" is a double-edged phrase in America today.

One can argue about the scope of Goffman's thesis, but his descriptions are a little too painful to dismiss. Accuracy has its own eloquence. The reality is that most people *do* hate meetings. Most people *are* sickened by the mixture of boredom, frustration, and waste that comes with the daily/weekly/monthly meeting. Much ado about nothing. Repetitious posturing and display. Yes, their colleagues and peers may be bright enough, but when everyone gets in the same room, the whole is less than the sum of its parts.

At a manager's conference in Boston, a Procter & Gamble executive polled the audience with a series of simple questions.

First he asked, "How many of you spend over half your day working directly with other people?"

Roughly two thirds of the managers raised their hands.

He then asked, "How many of you feel most productive when you're working on your own?"

Fully three quarters of the people raised their hands.

The P&G executive paused for effect and asked, "Is it possible that where we spend the most of our time is the least productive part of the day?"

I've seen people literally flinch when they hear they'll have to be in a meeting for over an hour. In too many organizations, meetings have become nothing more than unfunny jokes that breed contempt at each retelling. It's difficult to describe the pain and despair that these people feel. Gifted professionals and just plain folks content to deliver a day's work for a day's pay physically gnarl and tense when they describe the meetings they've been in. They're furious at the memory. These emotions cut across age, ethnicity, and education. People know they have to interact; survey after survey confirms that American managers typically spend fully half their working days in meetings. Most people crave the opportunity to be and work with others. And yet there are these awful feelings of impotence and frustration.

These people are not happy actors. They're all performing live in skits and sketches that are usually neither enlightening nor entertaining. The occasional agenda sometimes serves as a script, but even with the script, the performances are perfunctory. There seems to be something intrinsic to most meetings—to most group interactions—that renders them so wasteful.

Most people don't have a contempt for their own time or for the time of others. Most people want to be productive; they want to work well with others; they want to be more effective. If nothing else, they want to feel less frustrated.

For all intents and purposes, meetings have become the formal structures of collaboration in organizations today. Meetings are supposed to be the times when people get together to solve problems, plan for the future, and/or get their work done. Not all meetings are supposed to be collaborations—some are, quite properly, reviews or presentations designed to disseminate information. On the other hand, there are meetings that are expressly called to create shared understandings within a department or throughout an organization. Effective collaboration is the goal. Unfortunately, these meetings tend to be bizarre hybrids of inefficiency and ineffectiveness.

It's easy to say that meetings should be better run, that there should be an agenda, that the meeting leader should encourage participation and deflect efforts by the more loquacious to dominate. There's a lot of blather about the importance of "being sensitive" and "being a good listener" and "being prepared." It's all so easy to say, but it's also meaningless. What's more, it misses the point.

The structure of meetings in everyday life practically dictates that they will be wasteful, repetitious, and frustrating. They're antithetical to meaningful collaboration. These structures mean that meetings can't help but oscillate between the stage-managed and the improvisational. But it's not purely a matter of office politics and personality. Just as people behave differently on the street than they do at home than they do onstage in front of an audience of a thousand, most meetings take place in environments that encourage counterproductive behavior.

Look at a typical meeting. It doesn't matter if it's a brainstorming session or a program review. Maybe half a dozen to a dozen people in a well-lit room, seated around a table—rectangular or round. The leader is either at the head of the table or is the focal point of attention. Maybe there's a flip chart with an agenda and vital statistics of the day; perhaps an overhead projector with transparencies and the requisite number of wax pencils. People talk. More precisely, individuals take turns talking.

The group shifts their attention to each new speaker. They look at the speaker, seeking visual cues on everything ranging from the speaker's sincerity to his intellectual competence. His tone is analyzed realtime for nuance. *Is there a hidden agenda? What does he really mean?* Somebody responds directly. The speaker responds in turn. Perhaps a third person chimes in with comments or criticism. There are dialogues, exchanges, little games of verbal volleyball. Others in the group may make side comments or mutter among themselves. People may lean back in chairs, clear their throats, or perform other acts to attract attention. Occasionally, someone may refer to the flip chart or write a point on the transparency. If there's a whiteboard in the room, someone may walk over to it to illustrate a point. The group leader may go around the table soliciting comments.

Maybe there's an argument; perhaps an intellectual prima donna or an ego-driven bully tries to dominate the meeting. Maybe one or two people don't comment at all or limit their contributions to one or two questions or complaints. Platitudes, clichés, and buzzwords dominate the conversation. People occasionally glance at the boss to see how he's reacting. In a traditional meeting, people adopt the roles they're most comfortable with in this situation. There may be a healthy exchange of views or a mess of conflicting perspectives. It doesn't really matter. Occasionally, the single most important element of the meeting is the clock. Meetings run out of time. People have to go on to the next meeting or back to their own work. Eventually, somebody reads back their notes and the leader says, "So, we're all agreed then? This is what we'll do next."

The meeting's particular purpose seems almost irrelevant—negotiation, arbitration, planning, brainstorming, or just touching base. These patterns seem eerily transcendent. No matter what the industry or location, these frustration formats are disconcertingly consistent. They seem to be pathological malignancies of social behavior—and they are. This is why cynics define a camel as a horse designed by a committee. Given that numerous surveys reveal that most managers spend at least half of their time in meetings, this whole interpersonal ritual comes off as a cruel existential joke.

What's going on is a very primitive, almost tribal, power game based upon a perfectly reasonable misunderstanding of what communication means. What we have here is a linear montage of speeches, soliloquies, conversations, arguments, interjections, visual displays, gestures, and grunts all presented within a certain time frame within the same room. It's called a meeting. Many people believe that this is where communication takes place, that this is how things get done. To some extent, that's true. People can also sleep in the bathtub, even though that's not what it's designed for.

A typical meeting is an exercise in futility akin to remodeling a bathroom into a bedroom suite. It can be done, but the result is extremely cramped, hard, and uncomfortable. Nor is it conducive to intimacy or relaxation. In practically every way, most meeting environments can't help but subvert genuine efforts to create understanding. They're cramped, hard, and uncomfortable. The typical meeting environment subsidizes the excesses of individual communication at the expense of collaborative community.

How can this be so? Meeting mechanics and dynamics focus on the individual. The ecology of meetings breaks people and their environment into incompatible niches. The group is nothing more than a collection of individuals who happen to be sharing physical proximity and a common problem at a point in time. When someone talks, *he* is the focus of discussion. People look at *him*. People react to what *he* says and how *he* looks. Gestures are often as eloquent as words. What a speaker says and who he/she is are inextricably linked in the minds of listeners. The meeting is a carousel of egos, each grasping for the brass ring of attention. The group does nothing. These conversations and exchanges are all between individuals and overheard by the rest of the participants. Words vanish even as they are uttered. Speakers contribute *their* comments. People exchange *their* ideas. Participants yearn for approval and acknowledgement of *their* contribution. They're trying to present themselves in the best possible light. They're trying to make *their* point.

"If a meeting is a game," asks Bernard DeKoven, a meetings facilitator, "how do you win? You win if 'my point is the one that everybody likes most.' "

Like actors desperate for applause, people make their points and use whatever props—flip charts, 35-mm slides—they can scrounge up to reinforce them. Sometimes, they like their points so much that they repeat them over and over again. People are enamored of their presentations and many meetings are nothing but a sequence of them. Geneen's ITT meetings and the Stockman-Weinberger encounter spring to mind. But why not? Everything about the design of the meeting encourages *individuals* to make their points, not the group to create a shared understanding. Too frequently, people measure group productivity as the sum of individual participation. There's nothing in the ecology of meetings that encourages collaborative creativity, problem solving, or decision making.

True, a gifted leader is capable of creating a meeting environment that fosters collaborative conversations and brings the group to greater understanding and focus. But it's unrealistic to expect that the majority of people who run meetings are gifted enough to create such environments spontaneously—just as it would be unrealistic to expect a gifted leader to run a proper meeting if the lights failed or if a busted thermostat roasted the room at ninety degrees.

The ecology of a meeting is the interplay of ideas, personalities, and environment. There's a wealth of material on the social psychology of meetings. Books on successful meetingsmanship and "how to win at meetings" crop up on bookshelves everywhere. The advice is solid and well intentioned. But the focus is almost exclusively on strategy and tactics. Insights into the influence of the meeting environments are scarce. (A well-known consultant suggests that the quickest way to speed up meetings is to eliminate the chairs!) But by reshaping the meeting environment, by redefining its ecology, one can dissolve many of the barriers to fruitful collaboration. In many respects, it's easier to get results by changing the environment than by trying to persuade people to behave differently.

One insight, offered by Michael Doyle and David Straus in their miniclassic *How to Make Meetings Work*, is that all meeting ecologies can be split into two parts: content and process. Content addresses what is said; process is the way it gets said. Doyle and Straus argue that there's a kind of Heisenberg principle trade-off involved between the two. If the person running the meeting is concerned about the process, he may do so at the expense of active participation by others at the meeting. If the focus is on process, the meeting leader may be too concerned about who should speak next or who hasn't spoken at all. Of course, the leader may—consciously or subconsciously—skew the discussion in ways that reinforce his own views at the cost of contributions by others.

That's a major reason why Doyle and Straus champion the concept of *facilitators*—outside consultants or disinterested third parties who express no opinions on the content side but keep the meeting focused on the task at hand. The idea is that a skilled facilitator removes much of the mechanical burden of the meeting from the group and enables everyone to participate more effectively. Of course, to say that the content of a meeting is irrelevant to the process is foolish. But many organizations—from Ford Motor to Apple Computer to Stanford University—have discovered that facilitators can redefine meeting ecology by redefining the meeting environment.

The key is to create an environment that shifts attention away from the individual participant and toward community expression, changing the ecological rules to require greater interdependence between the participants and their environment. One place to start is by eliminating presentation props that are static, unchanging, and unresponsive. You do this by creating an environment that is dynamic and interactive, an environment that links individual expression to group accomplishment. You do this by providing collaborative tools that are simultaneously accessible to everyone and belong to everyone. You create an environment where shared space—not freeze-dried presentation—becomes the primary medium of communication and collaboration.

A NEW ECOLOGY OF MEETINGS

Some people believe that large sheets of paper taped to a wall (readily accessible to colorful Magic Markers) make the best shared space for meetings. No doubt they can be. Yet the constraints of pen and paper limit, even cripple, much of the versatility of collaborative expression that shared space can provide. Even the size of the paper can affect what's written—Is there enough space? Is there too much?—and it's tough to shift a thought around once it's written down.

Ideally, you'd want magic paper endowed with properties that make it easy to store, retrieve, and manipulate all sorts of information, whether text or numbers, charts or diagrams. You'd want paper that simplified the task of outlining ideas or linking concepts. Of course, that magic paper already exists in the form of the computer screen. Playing with information on a computer screen is as simple as punching a few keys on a keyboard or pointing and clicking with a mouse. The versatility of the computer makes it a logical medium for shared space.

The idea is to shift the focus of attention from the individual ego to a computer screen. The computer screen becomes the new focal point of the meeting ecology. It redefines all the relationships within the group because it becomes a new medium of communication. It's a source of light as well as information. Instead of just looking at the speaker, people also look at the screen.

This basic technological approach is often called *computer-enhanced* meeting or *computer-augmented* meeting. These are misnomers of sorts. People don't say they're in the middle of a blackboard-enhanced meeting or an overhead-projector-augmented meeting. Nevertheless, the technology's presence is so forceful and pervasive that the meeting almost has to be defined in that context.

For the moment, let's assume that a stenographer (or a facilitator) is typing up the discussions at a meeting even as people speak, taking "living minutes." As people talk, their comments appear on the screen, the main source of light in the room. People can see themselves being heard. What appears on-screen changes constantly as people talk. These changes command attention. Everybody sees this at the same time. Because everyone has access to the screen, the screen becomes the community medium. It becomes the shared space. Shared space transforms the ecology of a meeting as surely as a change in season transforms the ecology of the rain forest. This ecology of shared space completely transforms the perceptions of conversation, information, communication, and collaboration. The perceptual bias of the medium is toward a melding of oral and visual communication.

The shared space becomes a representation of the discussion. In some respects, it *is* the discussion, because it captures the conversation and makes it visible and accessible to all. The screen becomes an intelligent mirror of the meeting, reflecting the comments and contributions of the entire group instead of only individual points.

Shared space endows the group with what only the participants had previously possessed: memory. Group memory creates a new context for group discussion. As shown by Xerox PARC's Colab experiment, this distinction is crucial. In a purely oral conversation, the words are ephemeral, floating around the room, evoking a comment or two only to pop and disappear into individual minds. But this mirror converts speech into text. On a computer screen, those words are everyone's. In this shared space environment, one doesn't just utter words—one creates objects that become community property and tools for conversation.

In addition to redirecting focus and creating a visual group memory, this new factor further transforms the ecology of the meeting. These visual objects are manipulable. They can be moved from here to there. They can be shrunk down or blown up. They can be molded, twisted, and shaped in all sorts of ways. They can be made more aesthetically pleasing or left in a simple Bauhaus form-follows-function state. You just can't do that with ordinary conversation.

But what's more, all these visual objects can be shuffled about and linked together as the group sees fit. The visual objects don't stand alone but become parts of hierarchies, priorities, and networks of meaning. Comments can be ranked and grouped together in appropriate categories or linked into a discussion map that can be edited instantaneously.

Most significant, perhaps, is that what's displayed can be physically printed out, copied, and distributed to all the group members and any other relevant parties. I can't overemphasize how significant this is. It transforms the traditional meeting ecology—to discuss a topic, come to a conclusion, or make a decision—into an *act of shared creation*. The ability to create a tangible product completely revolutionizes what a meeting is. The meeting becomes a group process to create a group product. It's the difference between talking about what you'll have for dinner and actually cooking the meal. The focus shifts from planning and reviewing work to actually *doing* work. That people can end a meeting and then literally grasp a document that captures what the meeting was about and what the group's priorities are transforms the entire experience. Note that the hard copy can appear literally moments after the meeting concludes. There's no need for delay or dissonance. The immediacy reinforces the idea that the meeting is a genuine act of creation.

BEHAVIOR

The combination of these elements dramatically alters the way the group interacts. The environment is far more responsive than that of a traditionally structured meeting. Many of the behaviors associated with typical meetings either disappear or are transformed. Long-winded soliloquies become short gusts. The quantity of speech is different; the quality of speech is different. The individual ego evolves into a collective ego. The focus is no longer on who said what but on what's on the screen. It's not that comments are anonymous, it's that presenting them on the screen physically decouples them from the speaker. The comment literally becomes a contribution to the meeting. Others are free to add to or build on the comment as they see fit.

Contributions are worded more succinctly, and those words tend to be less abstract. Participants become very selfish about making sure that they are heard correctly and that their comments are transcribed accurately. Participants aren't just speaking to be heard; they're speaking to be seen. They're sensitive to that. People try to make comments that will generate other comments. The immediate feedback—the visual reinforcement of spoken comments—encourages contributions.

And yet, there seem to be fewer digressions than in typical meetings. Perhaps that is because one can literally see the digression before one's eyes; it disrupts the flow. Conversely, there is a psychic communal reward for memorable phrases that appear on-screen. Similarly, the disincentive for longish monologues is obvious.

Participants talk as much through the medium of the screen as they do directly to one another. The number of dialogues and three-way discussions drops dramatically. It seems as if some people are comfortable talking directly to the screen while others prefer to have one eye on the screen and another on whoever's talking. (Interestingly, groups meeting in well-lit rooms tend to treat the screen as a complement to the discussion, while groups meeting in darkened rooms eschew eye contact in favor of focusing on the screen.)

Participants watching the flow of comments on the screen begin to say things like "Hey, this point relates to something earlier," or "Wait a second, doesn't that contradict what you said ten minutes ago? Let's see." With just the tap of a key, the screen scrolls back to the desired place on the list of comments. Another tap and the entire string of comments—or graphics or numbers or charts—is on display.

Bernard DeKoven, who has facilitated hundreds of computer-augmented brainstorming sessions, has structured the meetings in three phases that he calls "the C-Cycle." The first phase is *collecting* comments; the next is *connecting* them; the third is *correcting* them.

In the collection phase, people just talk. They list ideas and concerns. They raise questions. The flow isn't linear or continuous; it seems more thematic. Comments serve as springboards for other comments. There is a tacit relatedness. People are literally performing a memory dump on-screen. They don't seem to worry about saying the same thing in a slightly different way. There's no concern about a particular contribution being remembered by everyone, because it's being recorded. Participants don't feel an urgent need to blurt out their comments in hopes of hopping on a train of thought. There's little disagreement during this phase, which can last over an hour. The group then creates links and connections between the comments. Patterns of expression emerge. This is where disagreements spring up. People push to word comments more sharply and explicitly. They argue over what comments should be grouped together or linked. Sometimes comments have to be copied and then linked to several comments. These tend to become categories. Basically, what's happening is that structure is being imposed on what had been a free flow of comments. The digressions become more obvious—they're not linked to anything. The subtler but significant points gradually rise to assume their rightful position in the newly oriented discussion map that's being instantaneously edited on-screen. Of course, some of the links evoke further comments, which are appended to the screen. The conversational tone tends to be analytical and helpful. People sound genuinely curious and concerned about making the appropriate links. Participants do a lot of verbal and physical pointing. People verbally grab what's on-screen and move it around. There's an animated, almost playful quality to the discussion—as if the group is assembling a Tinkertoy structure of ideas on-screen.

The most difficult phase for brainstorming groups is the correcting phase. Actually ranking categories and links brings out the sharpest disagreements between group members. This is where ego clashes resurface. What's important to note, however, is that clashes tend to be about real differences of opinion, not over misunderstandings. One of the real virtues of group memory is that facts and assertions can be easily tracked for context and accuracy. At this point, the group talks as much to itself as it does to the screen. People begin to negotiate the text and appearance of the document. It's usually at this point that the group leader reasserts primacy.

When a consensus is reached or imposed, the technographer (as DeKoven calls the meeting recorder) prints out what's on-screen. The participants come away with a structured ranking of suggested ideas along with the discussion associated with them. Again, it's difficult to adequately convey the feeling of accomplishment when people actually carry away a tangible product at the end of the meeting. These aren't "someone's notes"—they're the group's notes. The document becomes part of the group memory and a frame of reference for future discussions—either one-on-one or in another meeting. As Xerox's John Seely Brown emphasizes, it's often more important to preserve the process of the meeting than its outcome. Marilyn Mantei, a researcher who has observed the General Motors electronic meeting room, notes that there are fewer surprises after the meeting because most of the ambiguities have been ironed out both on-screen and on paper.

Of course, meetings do not always flow. People get stuck in ruts. But even here, the technical prowess of the computer-enhanced meeting can help jiggle a conversation back on track. DeKoven, for example, likes to change the visual emphasis of the meeting: literally have people peer into a different screen. So he scrolls the screen or shifts the perspective on the outline. One "cheap manipulative trick" he describes is to "shuffle the minutes"—that is, use the computer to rapidly riffle through and re-sort all the comments that have appeared thus far. That usually evokes a laugh and a comment or two.

David Braunschvig, who ran computer-augmented strategic planning sessions for Coopers & Lybrand, and is now an investment banker at Lazard Frères, frequently splits the screen into the two sides of an argument to "deemotionalize" the discussion. By creating a visual schism of the participants' disagreement, their intensity is focused on the screen—not on one another. The technology lets people deal with potentially volatile conflicts in a way that transfers the volatility to the computer. Sometimes he opens up a third screen—literally new territory—where he offers the participants a place for consensus and agreement.

Another facilitator takes one on-screen comment and proceeds to change its size, its type font, and then make it flicker like a stroboscope. These efforts to change the conversational pace are the counterpart to telling a joke to break the tension. The fact is, it works. This is another reason why the computer screen can be a powerful collaborative tool that shapes the way groups interact.

The technology can be so powerful in shaping the flow and tempo of a meeting, says Braunschvig, that sometimes the best tactic is simply to turn it off. "We've discovered that, at certain points in a meeting, the screen can be a distraction. We just flick it off and have the facilitator quietly take notes while the participants just talk. Then we turn the screen back on with a structured summary of that discussion. It completely changes the rhythm of the meeting and people refocus their energy on the screen more productively."

These techniques also work across cultures. As organizations increasingly become more global and more multidisciplinary in their efforts to manage problems and generate opportunities, they are confronted by enormous cultural gaps. Americans, Europeans, and Asians do not all communicate or collaborate with one another by fiat. Multinational meetings are frequently fiascoes. The only participants who profit from them are the translators. The idea that an ad hoc group of sharp marketing, sales, and R&D people can be tossed into a room and come out with perfect solutions is a delusion. The reality is that bridging cultural differences—national or disciplinary—is fast becoming one of top management's greatest headaches. These problems are independent of an organization's size or mission. The difficulties inherent in getting people with different vocabularies to speak the same language are extraordinary. Clearly, traditional meetings aren't up to the task. A different environment is necessary.

"Americans and Europeans are different from the Japanese—we're heterogeneous," says Braunschvig, who has facilitated cross-cultural collaborative meetings. "People come with mixed perspectives that might otherwise build barriers. We have to compensate, and this technology helps us share a common platform."

In other words, *the collaborative tool becomes a lens to focus cultural diversity*. In Xerox PARC parlance, shared screens offer WYSIWIS—"what you see is what I see." A flexible collaborative tool—one that facilitates the easy display of both words and images—improves the chances for creating a shared understanding. More explicitly, it gives participants from different cultures a medium to search for and create shared meaning: *Is this what you mean? Suppose we changed this word? Is that what you mean? Suppose it looked more like this? Is this what you're talking about?*

Shared screens don't mean that Frenchmen will understand Americans or that Japanese will speak German. They do, however, create a forum where nuances and subtleties can be tamed in real time—and recorded. The shared space has a memory; Confucius once remarked that "Pale ink is better than best memory." In this new era, a flickering video-display screen is even better than pale ink.

In this new environment, participants literally have the opportunity to define their terms. The same holds true for interdisciplinary interactions. Marketing people still won't speak fluent R&D, yet both sides will be able to use the shared space to illustrate and explain their concerns. The group's diversity doesn't have to work against it. Used effectively, the shared space really does become a lens that can take the broad spectrum of expertise in the room and focus it explicitly on the task at hand.

PROBLEMS

But altering the meeting ecology also has its downside. Fuzzy thinkers and people who have difficulty articulating their thoughts are penalized. Participants who shotgun comments and digress look like muddled thinkers. Perhaps people defer too willingly to the glib participant who's always ready with a facile phrase (although flashes of humor can also be lost in the transcription). One definite problem is the raving egomaniac who views the screen as his private fiefdom instead of community property. These egomaniacal twerps are so thick and insensitive that even the mutters and protests of others don't get through. They are polluters of the shared space. In practice, people are usually sensitive to the screen as community property and don't want to be seen as monopolists. Indeed, most people are very concerned about not littering on the screen or becoming verbal graffiti artists.

In contrast, a few participants are genuinely selfish in another way. They literally can't let go of their ideas. The notion of making a contribution to shared space without their name being actually attached to their ideas is too much for them to take. They're quiet and explore back-channel ways to make themselves heard. These are the people who have to be stroked and coaxed into understanding that being a part of a group doesn't make them any less of an individual. These people must have their anxieties and expectations managed before and after these meetings.

Similarly, political participants and group members with hidden agendas find the new environment distasteful. By decoupling contributions from personalities, charismatic and political power is diffused. Politics and gamesmanship never vanish, of course, but unless the player wants to pull a coup d'état and capture the screen, it's very difficult to schmooze, flatter, or intimidate someone into going along with a point of view. A player with a hidden agenda also quickly discovers that since the purpose of the process is to flush out what people think, his agenda isn't likely to stay hidden for long. Worse yet, it becomes transparently obvious what that player is trying to do as that hidden agenda gradually leaks out on-screen.

In another context, Harvard Business School professor Shoshana Zuboff has noted that "The electronic text displays the organization's work in a new way. Much of the information and know-how that was private becomes public. Personal sources of advantage depend less on . . . private knowledge than upon developing mastery in the interpretation and utilization of the public . . . electronic text. This kind of mastery benefits from real collaboration." In other words, it may be politically beneficial to be generous with information in this sort of meeting environment.

Another problem is that it's difficult to capture nuance or the subtler elements of a sophisticated discussion. The appropriate words don't always reflect the appropriate tone. It can be done, but it requires a particularly gifted technographer. What's more, some people become self-conscious when speaking on-screen and worry as much about what will appear as what they say. Quite simply, some people don't like being recorded on-screen just as some people don't like being recorded on tape. The reality of a record can be intimidating. In fact, DeKoven recalls several instances when he was explicitly asked *not* to record a particular line of discussion, much as a court stenographer is asked not to make something part of the record.

But unquestionably, the greatest problem facing the meeting environment is abuse by the group leader. Lowell Steele, a former General Electric executive, remarks that "if you want to control a team meeting, get to the blackboard first. . . . The person who determines what is written down and the words that are chosen controls the meeting." That holds in spades for shared space. When the leader takes over the technology and plays gatekeeper, the shared space no longer lives up to that description. Some leaders are more ham-handed about exercising their power than others, but the results are essentially the same: the meeting decays into a session where the leader simply dictates (pun intended) his thoughts onto what was supposed to be a community screen. The technology becomes an amplifier for an individual rather than a common tool for the group. The domineering personality runs roughshod over the collaborative qualities of the environment much in the way a single factory can pollute the river that provides water for the entire community.

DeKoven ruefully recalls one chief executive of a small company who half-jokingly suggested that the shared space be reapportioned on the basis of rank. Because he was the CEO, this CEO argued, his vote should have a greater weight than the votes of his colleagues. That way, the ideas the CEO wanted could "win" the approval of the group.

The point is clear: This technology is not a panacea. No technology—not the rack, the iron maiden, not even a gun pointed at someone's head—is more powerful than an individual's pride, ego, and personality. If the wrong people are at the meeting, the most supportive technology in the world won't make a difference. The best a technology can do is change the environment—change the ecology—of ideas, people, and interaction.

Not all meetings are collaborative or need to be. But when there are problems to be solved, innovations to be created, decisions to be made, the ecology of shared space offers tremendous potential to those willing to exploit it. Using a computer screen as a shared space can be a powerful collaborative tool and environment.

Do the benefits outweigh the potential for abuse? That's a decision that can only be made from experience. But is there any real question that most current meeting environments are toxic-waste dumps of time and talent? Is there any doubt that more people leave meetings feeling frustrated than invigorated? Is there any question that people want to feel and be more productive when they meet with others?

Insisting that people dramatically change who they are seems too much to ask. Asking people to drop out of professional roles they've spent years rehearsing and perfecting seems unrealistic. Personality transplants just don't exist. But is it unrealistic or unfair to ask people to make an effort to participate in an environment that is designed to encourage collaboration? One that tilts the focus away from ego and toward the group?

"We are talking about using technology to fundamentally change the way groups interact," says Rob Fulop, who has conducted scores of these computer-augmented collaborations. "People are used to having hidden agendas or waiting for a moment alone with the boss. They're not used to sharing their ideas in this way."

But once they get immersed in this new environment, their perceptions change. "They become hypersensitive to the process," he notes. "There's almost a meta-meeting—people spend a lot of time discussing the criteria of the meeting and how it's being conducted. The big change is that people are now getting together to make stuff instead of just talk about making stuff."

The fundamental question is the fundamental challenge: In what ways can organizational meetings generate productive and profitable collaborations? The challenge is to meld the best of the individual with the best of the group in ways that are efficient, effective, and empowering.

That challenge never goes away.

9

Collaborative Organizations and Technological Mythmanagement

FRANK GILBRETH, ARTICULATE DISCIPLE OF "SCIENTIFIC MANAGE-ment," may be best known as the obsessive protagonist in *Cheaper by the Dozen,* a book and later a movie about an efficiency expert's attempt to run his household like a factory. Children were workers and the clock commanded nearly as much obedience as Mother and Father. Gilbreth viewed technology and technique as keys to running the business of domestic bliss.

Even more than his guru Frederick Taylor, Gilbreth was fascinated by the way technology could be used to redefine the workplace. This was a man who never met a stopwatch he didn't like.

Gilbreth was as captivated by the dimensions of space as he was of time. A motion study of bricklaying in 1909 enabled him to devise an adjustable scaffold for piling up bricks that tripled worker output. He pioneered time/motion research by means of cyclegraphs. These pictures were produced by attaching small electric lights to a worker's body and making photographic time exposures of motions, which appeared as continuous white lines. This made it possible to see the path of a motion and reconstruct it in three dimensions with a stereoscopic light. But that was just the beginning. For still further precision, Gilbreth adapted a motion picture camera to take chronocyclegraphs, which, he wrote, would show "the paths of each of several motions made by various parts of the body and their exact distances, exact times, relative times, exact speeds, relative speeds, and directions." In an article on scientific management of households, Gilbreth boasted that with chronocyclegraphy "we can now for the first time record the time and path of individual motions to the thousandths of a minute." His wife, Lillian, who worked with him, conceived of a new managerial position—the speed boss—whose job it would be to demonstrate to a worker how a task was to be done in the specified time.

Gilbreth's innovative use of new technology—movie cameras were then in their infancy—revolutionized perspectives of the factory floor. On-the-job motion was transformed from a continuous process to a set of discrete, measurable, and identifiable parts. Those parts became the building blocks of a redesigned, and presumably more efficient, workplace.

Suddenly, technology wasn't just a means of production any more. In the hands of a Gilbreth, technology becomes a triple threat: a tool, a medium, and an environment. The chronocyclegraph let the observer analyze reality in a way it had never been analyzed before. This tool is also a medium, a frame of reference, a means of expression. The chronocyclegraph, like a lens or a prism, offered a new way of conveying the information that underlies the reality. As a result, it also redefined the environment. As surely as turning off all the lights changes what people see, injecting a new perspective of the everyday changes how people perceive. Imagine the shock of recognition and disbelief flickering across the face of a turn-of-the-century foreman as he watched a chronocyclegraph of the men on his assembly line. The stop-action, slow-motion flow of visual information would forever change his perceptions. Everything the foreman took for granted would be shattered into neatly analyzable fragments by the reductionalist reality of the chronocyclegraph.

This is the real power of technology: not just to serve as a tool or medium but to redefine the way people perceive their environments. Technology *is* the environment and it inevitably shapes the way people relate to one another.

That begs a few questions. How do you design workplace technologies that effectively support the collaborations that are vital to an organization's growth? What does collaborative design mean in the context of our traditional workplace environments? The Gilbreth example highlights the role that technology can play in forcing people to reevaluate every fundamental assumption that they have about the places where they work. Our existing information infrastructures make it too difficult for people to think out loud. Our workplace designs don't adequately reflect the role of collaboration in adding value.

Go into any office building—or any office—and you'll see that the physical design of the workplace is filled with both brash and subtle cues about expectations and realities. Paintings may or may not adorn the walls; the chairs may be plush or streamlined Bauhaus; offices may be private or just another waystation in a maze of cubicles; people may have networked computers or IBM Selectrics atop their desks; conference tables may be intimate and round or long and rectangular; clocks may or may not be easily visible. The design of a workplace is often more eloquent than any manager, worker, or entrepreneur in articulating the real values of the organization.

Robert Becker points out in *Workspace* that "The physical setting is simultaneously a symbol of efficiency and an instrument of power. The physical setting functions non-verbally to promote power relationships we choose to ignore or suppress in our discussion of organizational decisions. . . . Changes in the physical environment were taken as very tangible evidence by employees that management was concerned about their work environment and welfare. The environmental changes operated as part of a nonverbal communication system."

Physically altering the workplace is one of the most powerful and influential things an organization can do. Harvard Researcher Shoshana Zuboff quotes a benefits analyst at an unnamed insurance company describing how management redesigned the workspace to kill off chatting: "We used to be able to see each other and talk. Sure, sometimes we talked about what we were going to make for dinner. . . . Then, with the new system, they put in two filing cabinets between us, because we weren't supposed to see each other anymore. But there was still this small space. . . . One day, a manager walked by and I was asked who left this space there. I said that was how they left it when they put the cabinets in. The manager had them move the cabinets together because they don't want us talking." This furniture was designed to increase productivity because it put everyone in their own little cubicle.

The converse of such petty tyrannies occurs in organizations that pack people together in order to encourage interaction. Because numerous studies indicate that physical proximity leads to greater frequency of interpersonal contact, many newsrooms and research and development organizations are laid out in an open office design to encourage serendipitous encounters. Privacy and quiet are sacrificed to the belief that too much interaction is ultimately more effective than too little. Of course, such a layout is economically efficient use of space for an organization, too.

Another reason workspace designers frequently give to justify an open office format is that workers will have the chance to see where they fit into the organizational scheme of things. Alas, in at least one organization, the switch to the open office layout had a dubious impact on employee morale. "In this instance, [employee] observations clearly indicated that their work had less impact than they had perceived before the move," Becker reports. This new awareness created a sense of impotence.

These design efforts are nothing less than an attempt to shape the pattern and flow of information within the workspace. The famous Procter & Gamble one-page memo, the office voice/mail network, the desktop-publishing system, the weekly staff meeting are all technologies and techniques to manage attention as well as information. Managing *attention* is the gateway to managing priorities.

Consequently, a new brand of techno-emphasis has gradually been seeping into the mainstream of management thought. In a *Harvard Business Review* article, "The Coming of the New Organization," Peter Drucker, the grand old man of managerial thought, argues that "The typical large business twenty years hence will have fewer than half the levels of management of its counterparts today and no more than a third of the managers. . . . The typical business will be knowledge-based, an organization composed largely of specialists who direct and discipline their own performance through organized feedback from colleagues, customers, and headquarters. For this reason, it will be what I call an information-based organization."

Information technology, Drucker says, makes this organizational transformation inevitable. "The information-based organization requires far more specialists overall than the command-and-control companies we are accustomed to," Drucker writes. "Moreover, the specialists are found in operations, not in corporate headquarters."

Evolving networks of specialists—with access to data at their fingertips—will get the job done differently. "In pharmaceuticals, in telecommunications, in papermaking," Drucker says, "the traditional sequence of research, development, manufacturing, and marketing is being replaced by synchrony: specialists from all these functions work together as a team, from the inception of research to a product's establishment in the marketplace."

Drucker believes that the university, symphony orchestra, and hospital offer models for the information-based organization of the future. Specialists will want to remain specialists: a talented bassoonist does not yearn to play first violin; a surgeon doesn't want to do a stint as an anesthesiologist.

The challenge of these new organizations will be to create new visions and incentive systems for their talented teams of specialists. As Drucker puts it, top management must now learn to cope with "the shift from the command-and-control organization, the organization of departments and divisions, to the information-based organization, the organization of knowledge specialists."

This theme of the specialist-driven organization coincides with the concept of "collective entrepreneurship" proposed by former Harvard lecturer Robert Reich:

> Under the old paradigm, companies are organized into a series of hierarchical tiers so that supervisors at each level can make sure that subordinates act according to a plan. It is a structure designed to control. But enterprises designed for continuous innovation and incremental improvement use a structure designed to spur innovation at all levels. Gaining insight into improvement of products and processes is more important than rigidly following rules. *Coordination and communication replace command and control. . . .*
>
> Because production is a continuous process of reinvention,

entrepreneurial efforts are focused on many thousands of small ideas rather than on just a few big ones. And because valuable information and expertise are dispersed throughout the organization, top management does not solve problems; it creates an environment in which people can identify and solve problems themselves.

Alas, neither Drucker nor Reich explicitly discusses the role of collaboration, tools, or language in these new organizations. Theirs are grand visions that loom tantalizingly above the grimy details of implementation. They grasp the significance of technology even as they fail to offer a technology design ethic to cope with this fundamental shift in organizational dynamics. In sum, they treat technology as something that an organization manages rather than as a medium to create organizational environments.

Paul Strassman, formerly the vice president of corporate planning for Xerox, is more explicit:

Technology allows an organization to deal with the problem of how knowledge is shared. The verbal process of disseminating information is terribly inefficient. Hardly anybody writes because you can't really write down all you know. And even if you write, nobody will read it. So there are meetings, and meetings to plan reports, and meetings to review the status of reports. And what these meetings are about is people just trying to figure out what they are doing. . . . All that talking, finessing, and gaming around the table comes from people who, in the absence of a clear sense of direction and strategy and culture, constantly invent and reinvent the rules. . . . The technology makes it possible for meetings and memos to become unnecessary. Coordination becomes simpler.

Or more complex: It depends on your metaphors for media in organizational design. People talk about lateral networking versus hierarchical command-and-control, but what does that mean, really? Do these distinctions matter, or are these simply phrases that sound impressive but are practically meaningless?

Picture a strapping six-foot-plus giant, muscles taut and bulging, perfectly proportioned—a flesh-and-blood incarnation of a Michelangelo sculpture. But give this demigodly creature the nervous system of an earthworm. Clumps of basal ganglia are not enough to let this creature survive. This misbegotten nervous system couldn't even handle the autonomic functions of controlling the heartbeat and respiration, let alone the sensations of touch, sight, sound, and smell. The nervous system of any organism shapes the way it interacts with its environment. To a large extent, the adaptability of the organism depends upon the adaptability of its nervous system.

The same holds true for organizational organisms. The way external data are gathered, processed, analyzed, and distributed within the organization and acted upon determines the organization's fitness for survival. An organization without an adequate nervous system is a cripple. Media technologies—the memos, telephone calls, fax transmissions, and personal communications—are the neurons, synapses, nerve pathways and spinal cords of the organization. These are the networks that matter. Some of these nervous systems evolve via Darwinian selection in the marketplace; others are rigorously planned, designed, and implemented.

As surely as nervous systems shape the patterns of perception for organisms, technology shapes the patterns of information flow through the organization. The design and implementation of media technology invariably molds the structures and processes of the organization. If you put eyes on an animal's feet, it has a dusty view of the world. If you put ears on its tail, why should anyone be surprised that the animal only hears danger after it goes where it isn't supposed to be? If the animal lacks a larynx, how can it call for a mate or cry out to warn its young? Biological evolution would never yield such crippled animals, so why should the organizational evolution of nervous systems be so troublesome?

Organizations are plagued by design emphases that encourage toxic inefficiencies. That's why we have to examine the way new media redefine what it means to share and coordinate information. An organization may have an excellent customer service arm that can't send messages to the marketing arm. An organization may be brilliant at talking to itself but have few receptors for external stimuli. Simply disconnecting a few phone lines can bring the most sophisticated organizations to a befuddled halt. Like a nervous system, the organization's media infrastructure determines reactions and response. In an old-fashioned organization, eliminate the flow of paper memos and the regular staff meeting and then sit back and watch people try to compensate for the absence of these vital organs of perception and transmission. The response is even more frantic at a high-tech workplace like an equities trading room: let the computers go down and people become blind, deaf, and dumb. Their information windows to the world are shattered. Excising media from an organization is like pithing a frog or performing a lobotomy: the organism still lives, but it's not good for very much.

What happens to the nervous system when the environment changes? How does a nervous system cope with rising complexity? Lower organisms, with their preprogrammed ganglia and limited degrees of freedom, struggle to adapt or they die. Higher-order animals with brains, like man, think about what to do.

Organizations try to meet complexity with complexity. The organization hires or develops specialists to help it cope. Whether in research and development, finance, engineering, marketing, or distribution, the organization manages complexity by acquiring expertise. As the joke goes, a specialist is someone who knows more and more about less and less until he knows everything about nothing. In contrast, the general manager—who runs the specialists—knows less and less about more and more until he knows nothing about everything.

So how do organizations navigate between the Scylla of general ignorance and the Charybdis of trivial omniscience? Some of them simply redraw their organizational charts. The faces at the staff meetings change, and a different list of phone numbers is issued to managers. In other words, the organizational network is rewired, but the underlying media structures remain unchanged. The perceptual biases of the organization don't shift.

Other organizations invest in technology as the solution. They automate; they reengineer; they buy the latest networking equipment; they buy the whole concept of the information-driven organization. They're betting that they can plug technology into the organization as easily as a computer can be plugged into a wall socket. But the notion that connecting people up and managing information yields more effective and more productive people is flawed.

We need to shift away from the notion of technology managing information and toward the idea of technology as a *medium of relationships*. Organizations need to get a better understanding of the complex ecologies of media that shape, deflect, and define one another. To use technology as a medium to create collaborative environments requires us to remember that each technology dictates its own strengths and limitations.

For example, before the telephone enjoyed widespread use, organizations were run purely on paper and by word of mouth. Memos and meetings were the media of communication, command, and control. There was nothing else.

Telecommunications redefined everything. Distance became less relevant. "Call me!" replaced "Send me a memo!" The casual phone call supplemented or replaced the casual meeting. The meeting that once spawned a flurry of memos now spawned a flurry of phone calls. The casual memo became a little less casual and more of a cover-your-ass or corporate memory device. Now, the very medium one chooses to communicate through communicates something. Calling a meeting means something different from making a phone call. Sending a memo implies something else. Technology has reached the point where a handwritten memo is perceived differently from one that's typed.

Just as the telephone defined the role of the existing organizational media of memo and meeting, electronic mail is reredefining them all. MIT professor Tom Malone, a pioneer in the design of electronic mail systems and software agents, talks about how the new communications technology has changed the way people in organizations communicate. Where they would once make a quick call, they now flash a quick electronic mail message. Where they would send a paper memo, an electronic mail memo now suffices. In fact, says Malone, the ability to send electronic mail messages cuts down on the number of meetings that people hold. And when people do meet, he says, they don't spend their time talking about the sorts of things that they could better handle over the electronic mail network.

This reaffirms just how fundamental technology is to the way that people relate to one another in organizations. Clearly, electronic mail systems change both the quantity and quality of communication. But scratch a little deeper, and you'll agree that, in essence, electronic mail is just another way to send a message.

INFORMATION
DISTRIBUTION/TRANSMISSION/PROCESSING

The fundamental problem is that organizations and their philosophers remain trapped in the distribution/transmission/processing information paradigms. Whether that's because of inertia or conceptual impotence is irrelevant. The value of the information doesn't lie in the media that process it, but in the people who interact with it. The issue isn't rewiring the organization or adding new technology—it's deciding what *kind* of medium the information technology should be. What should the perceptual bias of the organization be? What kind of nervous system does it want? What kind of nervous system should it have? What values are embodied in the design of the network?

Today's organizational media are designed to facilitate individual decision making and communication. A manager using a networked personal computer to manipulate and massage his data might as well be masturbating with it. Traditional information technologies reinforce a pattern of exchanging information rather than sharing it.

Lotus Development Corporation's Irene Greif points out that there are actually two dominant models for computers in organizations: the first is personal computing "with an emphasis on fostering individual creativity and innovation"; the second is the systems approach "with its emphasis on controlling the flow of corporate data." "Neither choice supports work groups," she notes.

Why should this be true? For the most obvious reason: it's the easy way out. Organizations rarely design for collaboration because it's alien to the way the organization thinks of itself. Most organizations have never used technology to augment their collaborative efforts. Why should computer and telecommunications technology be any different?

In practice, most organizations are content to shoehorn their traditional styles of interaction into the newer media. Consequently, the results are frequently more confusing than productive. Take electronic mail in a Fortune 500 company, for example. The ability to send messages electronically probably means that the volume of paper memos declines. That may or may not be good: there's no inherent guarantee that electronic mail memos are any more informative or incisive than paper-based memos. Certainly, many managers complain that they are inundated with junk electronic mail, but most are quick to praise the virtue of quick turnaround and short response times. And yet electronic mail is widely perceived as just another way to transmit information. There is nothing inherent in the design of most electronic mail systems that encourages the creation of shared space and collaboration.

 In fact, *the design of these systems usually reinforces the ability to communicate at the expense of collaboration.* Carnegie-Mellon University professor Sara Kiesler, who has extensively studied the way electronic mail is used in large organizations, has commented that "When social definitions are weak or nonexistent, communication becomes unregulated. People are less bound by convention, less influenced by status, and unconcerned with making a good appearance. Their behavior becomes more extreme, impulsive, self-centered. They become, in a sense, freer people."

In other words, the system often isn't designed to encourage any other behavior but self-indulgent communication.

The most compelling example of this can be seen in the explosive rise of desktop-publishing technology. For decades, people wrote up reports, had them typed up by the secretarial pool, and, if these reports were really important, had them typeset and bound before distribution to top management.

The emergence of personal computers and—as importantly—high-quality printers offering an array of type fonts, design formats, and other tricks of the print shop made publishing superb-quality documents relatively easy and affordable. All of a sudden, departments turned themselves into desktop publishers, printing manuals, reports, and brochures in a variety of eye-pleasing designs. Crisp typing and clean layouts weren't enough anymore. Now the reports had to have the latest in typefaces and be filled with charts, diagrams, and graphics. The organization's lowest common denominator for acceptable printed material rose. The metaphor shifted from producing reports to producing documents.

As desktop publishing goes, so go desktop presentations. Organizations, pleased by the new aesthetics of print, are counting on computer technology to elevate media standards and move beyond 35-mm slides and overhead transparencies. Industry analysts project that desktop presentations, like desktop publishing, will blossom into a multibillion-dollar market.

Similarly, huge organizations like General Motors and General Electric get excited about creating local area networks for their personal computers and linking these networks to one another and to larger corporate computers. Indeed, the rise of computer networking is a fundamental dynamic in information processing today. Even smaller companies are plunging into networking, confident that this technology is a key to unlocking greater productivity. These computer networks are to data what the telephone networks are to voice. It's the triumph of connectivity over content.

However useful and relevant these technologies are to the way an organization manages its information flow, the fact remains that they fall squarely within the traditional paradigm of distribution and transmission. There is nothing inherent in these technologies that encourages collaborative relationships. In truth, these technologies add value to the traditional modes of packaging information, but that's basically all they do.

The social conventions and protocols surrounding these media similarly reflect this distribution/transmission paradigm at the expense of collaborative support. Back when office architecture was new "media," the classic example was who gets invited to a formal (or informal) gathering and who got to sit where. When paper became the medium of choice, the questions changed to "Who sent the memo?" and "Who was on the route list?" and "Who could respond to it?" With the tremendous explosion of desktop publishing, one sees a subtle redefinition of paper protocol. People don't just send memos or reports—they send documents.

The telephone, of course, spawned its own conventions. "Many managers imagined they would use the telephone to enhance their control," says Kiesler. "They thought they could use the telephone as a broadcast device for transmitting orders and information to their employees. But the telephone performed even better as a conversation medium than a broadcast medium. Thus it gave employees a chance to talk to their supervisors, to exchange information, and to send it up the hierarchy as well as receive it. The telephone did not militarize the workplace; it democratized it." (Of course, be very careful about how frequently you try to call the boss.)

Nevertheless, the urge—and the need—to collaborate is so strong that people will grasp for whatever media they can to do it. The media style of the organization is almost irrelevant. People can —and do—use these media as a means to collaborate.

For some people, the desire to create shared space is simply a natural impulse that always manifests itself in a technology. These are the people who whip out a yellow pad at a conference table, jot a few notes, and then push it across for others' comments. These are the people who use yellow Post-it notes to create a shared space for comments on an interoffice memo. These are the people who always hold meetings in conference rooms with whiteboards instead of overhead projectors.

But these collaborative efforts occur incidentally to the organizational nervous system rather than because of it. That collaboration is such a pervasive, prevalent, and persistent organizational phenomenon despite these technical barriers simply underscores just how basic and necessary it is.

The classic perception that professional work begins with the individual decision-making unit and proceeds when management adds these units together to make larger and more complex decision-making units is tempting but ultimately wrong. Nobody in their right mind sees organizational reality as the sum of individual decisions. There's too much politicking, irrationality, and lobbying, too many informal meetings and formal presentations for that.

The real basic structure of the workplace is the *relationship*. Each relationship is itself part of a larger network of relationships. These relationships can be measured along all kinds of dimensions—from political to professional expertise. The fact is that work gets done through these relationships. As Bell and Flores put it, "The ingredients of the work are not the bodies and tools and spaces, but the questions and commitments and possibilities that bring forth things. This is a very different basis for thinking about an enterprise than as a collection of decision units that process and communicate information."

The tools that support such relationships simply don't necessarily look or feel like the tools that support individual decision making and communication. Designing for collaboration means that the emphasis shifts from networks of information distribution and transmission to networks of shared spaces. The question no longer is "What do I do with this?" but "Who else should see this so I can understand and use this better?" The issue isn't just *processing* information—it's *creating* information with others.

In a case study of Honda, the superbly innovative Japanese automobile company, Ikujiro Nonaka, a professor at Japan's Hitotsubashi University, discovered that the new-product development system is geared around collaboration. The company holds *tamadashi kai*, meetings to create and share information, between the development, manufacturing, and sales departments and structures the work flow in a way that literally forces collaboration. One Honda manager asserts, "I am always telling the team members that our work is not a relay race—that's my work and yours starts here. Every one of us should run all the way from the start to the finish. Like in a rugby game, all of us should run together, passing the ball left and right and reaching the goal as one united body."

Honda is already famous within corporate Japan for its huge meeting rooms—and all of them are glassed-in so that people can peer inside to see what's going on. The media environment is structured to encourage constant interaction between team members. Media traditionally associated with Western organizations—memos, phone calls, computer printouts—are relegated to secondary status. "I think it's pretty difficult to articulate really meaningful know-how in text, figures, or other measurable forms," said one Honda engineer. "The knowledge is alive . . . because it changes continually. . . . The best way to transfer it is through human interaction."

The rise of network computing offers similarly intriguing ways to animate knowledge. In her book *In the Age of the Smart Machine,* Shoshana Zuboff quotes a manager at an international bank describing the impact of a new computer and telecommunications network that links the far-flung departments: "The new technology really brings people together. You need people who can understand electronics, programming, and the complexity of information. It requires teamwork because you need to have different specialties and understanding to work together. This type of computer system will always bring people together because you *have* to discuss what you see, what you understand, what you know and, what should be done." (Emphasis mine.) Zuboff conjures up the compelling metaphor of an "electronic text" to describe this emerging web of digital readouts.

The irony here is that this enormously large, enormously complex, and enormously expensive computer system wasn't, in fact, built with collaboration in mind. The bank managers wanted to use technology to reassert control over their people and their data. Collaboration occurs here by default rather than by design. It's a necessary byproduct of this system's complexity. Indeed, it is these upward spirals of organizational and environmental complexity that are the spur to so much collaboration.

The problem is that most organizations neither appreciate nor recognize that collaboration is the best way to cope with that complexity. They mistakenly believe that increasing the number of communication channels is enough to coordinate and direct the enterprise. This delusion is based on the belief that more is better and that multiple channels of communication will build in the redundancies, safeguards, and variety necessary to manage complexity. In truth, people are already overwhelmed by the existing information flow. The issue is the quality of collaboration, not the quantity and frequency of communication.

People who build information tools are increasingly sensitive to their design bias and limitations. The personal computer software industry, which rose to multibillion-dollar status on the strength of enhancing personal computations and communication, is now aggressively exploring the potential of using software to support groups. This so-called groupware takes the view that personal computer software can be extended to groups; that software can be grafted onto the way people work together. That may be true, but the reality is that most software designers know far more about collaborating with computers than with human beings. And, of course, they design around that core of knowledge. The result is that most of what's called "groupware" is designed more like a prosthetic than an augmentation of how people naturally collaborate. Technology is always more likely to succeed when it extends what people tend to do naturally rather than require a new repertoire of behaviors. Groupware is one of those names that succeeds more on the basis of a familiar suffix than on the power of a compelling idea.

Nevertheless, both as a market opportunity and as a design challenge, a growing community of people who design tools for individuals have concluded that they should begin to design tools to support relationships. Lotus Development Corporation chairman James Manzi jokes that, sometime in the future, software boxes may be labeled *Now . . . with Group!* as an added inducement to get people to buy. Lotus Notes, of course, has become the world's most successful groupware product. Indeed, Lotus itself now acknowledges that much of the success of Notes comes not just from its ability to manage group databases but its ability to support collaborative interaction. Notes is now seen as a medium of relationships management as well as information management.

Similarly, such rising groupware products as Novell's Group-Wise, Collabra's Share, and Group Technology's Aspects all reflect the emerging awareness that designing software to support human interaction requires different functions and options than building software that merely enables groups of people to manipulate data. Indeed, the explosion of the Internet phenomenon—with people communicating and collaborating via usegroups and the World

Wide Web—is the most stunning indicator that technology is more compelling as a medium of community than as a tool for information.

This shift in design emphasis scales from global technologies like the Internet to enterprise-wide networks defined by Lotus Notes to the unit of collaboration: the pair. John Doerr, a venture capitalist with the enormously successful Kleiner, Perkins, Caulfield & Byers, has coined the term "pairware" to describe what he believes will be one of the fastest growing segments of this market: technology that supports those intense two-person efforts that require rigorous coordination and collaboration to succeed. "I can think of several relationships that I'm in right now where I need this," says Doerr. Pairware could be the conceptual nucleus for a host of approaches to collaborative tool design.

The rise of collaborative tools will puncture the myths of the information organization as the technovision of the future. The clichés aren't wrong—they're just not right. The clichés used to be "It's not what you know—it's who you know." Or "It's not what you know or who you know but when you know it." The collaborative cliché will be "It's not just what you know, who you know or when you know it, it's how you create value with other people." Collaborative media will make value-generating relationships possible in ways that traditional media architectures now preclude. These new media of collaboration will completely transform the organizational nervous system. In the same way that the evolution of living things led to human culture, the evolution of organizations will lead to richly profitable collaborative relationships.

10
Collaboration Design Themes

PICASSO AND BRAQUE COLLABORATED ON THEIR ART QUITE DIFFER-ently from the way Apple Computer cofounders Jobs and Wozniak collaborated on their computer. The Wright brothers approached heavier-than-air machine flight in ways quite alien to Gilbert and Sullivan's approach to comic opera. The way a community of nine-teenth-century painters launched a shocking new art form called impressionism isn't the same as the way an equally inspired group of twentieth-century scientists like Bohr and Heisenberg crafted a shocking new discipline called quantum physics.

And yet, though the characters, personalities, eras, and fields are all different, certain aspects and themes of collaboration constantly recur. They seem to transcend business, the arts, and the sciences as well as language, culture, and time. The overwhelming majority of successful collaborations have these themes and characteristics woven through them. That doesn't mean that replicating these be-haviors guarantees successful collaboration. What these behaviors reveal, however, are patterns of interaction that have consistently led to successful collaborative outcomes.

Like friendship, romance, and other basic human relationships, these patterns of collaboration have withstood the test of time. There is an overarching continuity that is really quite impressive. There is no recipe for a successful collaboration any more than there is a recipe for a successful friendship. Nevertheless, there are definitely ingredients to a collaboration that can largely determine how successful it may be.

1. COMPETENCE

The obvious is frequently overlooked. A collaboration of incompetents, no matter how diligent or well meaning, cannot be successful. Whether in business or biochemistry, a certain minimal threshold of competence for the task at hand is required of each member of the collaborative team, or else the whole is less than the sum of its parts. History confirms this. James Watson of *Double Helix* fame may have been christened Lucky Jim by a fellow Nobel laureate, but no one questioned his basic competence. The Wright brothers may have run a bicycle shop, but they were superb model builders burning with ambition and had the intelligence to understand aerodynamic phenomena. Individual collaborators don't have to be brilliant, but, at the very least, they must be competent to deal with the problem they face. A collaboration can compensate for an individual technical or conceptual gap, but it can't paper over a fundamental deficiency.

2. A SHARED, UNDERSTOOD GOAL

Picasso and Braque were struggling to express their ideas in new painterly and nonpainterly forms. The impressionists were all intrigued by the ways light could be represented. The quantum physicists pushed to explain the paradoxes of subatomic symmetries. Wozniak and Jobs wanted to build a personal computer that could be sold cheaply. Pound and Eliot wanted to create great poetry.

These are not open-ended relationships. Indeed, the relationships are inherently subordinate to the goal. Many of the quantum physicists were friends, but that was a byproduct of their intellectual quest. A collaboration is not described in terms of the relationship but in terms of the objective to be achieved. In this respect, collaborations are classic examples of management by objective—except that the focus is almost exclusively on the objective rather than the task of managing. Collaborative scientists tend to answer questions about their work in the context of how far along they are in understanding a particular set of phenomena. Theater ensembles and collaborative movie directors talk about how close they are to achieving what they consider the best performance. Engineering and development teams are concerned about when their creations will finally work.

The collaboration is treated as a means to an end—not an end in itself. When the collaboration is going exceptionally well, people talk about it. When it's going particularly poorly, people talk about it. Otherwise, they treat the collaborations as a medium to accomplish their goals.

3. MUTUAL RESPECT, TOLERANCE, AND TRUST

Wilbur and Orville Wright got along famously; Lennon and McCartney did not; Watson and Crick took their time deciding how they really felt about each other. (The first line of Watson's *Double Helix* is "I have never seen Francis Crick in a modest mood.") It turns out that successful collaborations don't require friendship or even that the collaborators like one another very much. Collaborative emotions tend to be utilitarian.

Like competence, however, there must be a minimum threshold of mutual respect, tolerance, and trust for a collaboration to succeed. Successful collaborators tend to ignore the more irritating quirks and idiosyncracies of their colleagues. Whether these peccadilloes range from excessive garrulousness to moody abruptness (and collaborations fall across the entire spectrum of interpersonal relationships), successful collaborators tend to focus on managing one another's strengths rather than one another's lesser qualities. It is implicitly understood that the task at hand transcends personal annoyance.

Trust is almost always assumed; there is precious little gamesmanship about proving oneself trustworthy or responsible. Nor is this a fragile trust. A collaborator has to break a commitment or betray a confidence or consistently underperform before the collaboration comes apart. The collaboration exists precisely because the collaborators believe they need the other to get the job done.

4. CREATION AND MANIPULATION OF SHARED SPACES

All collaborations rely on a shared space. It may be a blackboard, a napkin, a piano keyboard, a rehearsal room, a prototype, or a model.

Independent of whether the collaborators are artists, scientists, professionals, managers, or mechanics, collaborators are inevitably drawn to a shared space to share the ideas and insights that will solve the problem or achieve the task. The shared space becomes a partner in collaboration.

These shared spaces usually permit real-time access by all the collaborators. They serve as both a model and a map for what the collaborators are trying to accomplish. A blackboard with equations; a rehearsal room where actors, director, and crew gather; and a rough prototype of an invention all serve as shared spaces for collaborative interaction. As much as the collaborators themselves, these media serve as references and touchstones for the act of collaboration. Shared space is essential as a technique to manage conversational ambiguity. In effect, these shared spaces are the collaborative tools that people wield to make sure that the whole of the relationship is greater than the sum of the individuals' expertise.

5. MULTIPLE FORMS OF REPRESENTATION

The quantum physicists spent an extraordinary amount of time devising both a verbal and visual language to describe quantum phenomena to go along with the mathematical language. Medical experts rely on techniques that range from diagnostic imaging (X ray, CAT scan, MRI, and so on) to blood tests and biopsies in order to build multiple representations of a patient's condition. Molecular biologists are quick to build computer or Tinkertoy three-dimensional models of organic structures to complement their experimental data and discussions. Theater directors rely heavily on critical interpretations of text, actors' impressions, set designers' suggestions, and audience reactions to fine-tune performances.

These multiple forms of representations frequently occur in shared space. Correspondingly, the shared space can be the reference point for other representations—a model can be a reference point for a conversation or an equation can generate an image. Because there frequently is confusion over language, collaborators look to other representations to triangulate their perceptions and impressions.

But the fundamental point is that since collaboration inherently fuses multiple perspectives to address a task, it must use multiple representations to manage those perspectives. For all intents and purposes, collaborators require a repertoire of different languages to hone in on the problem to be solved or the innovation to be created. These multiple representations create a web of information that makes it significantly easier for the collaborators to construct meaning. To put it another way, each level of representation—mathematical, linguistic, structural, conversational, visual—represents a different lens through which to view the collaborative task. Some views put others in context; some are deceptive and create illusions; still others reveal precisely what needs to be seen. However, it is the availability of these multiple representations that enables the multiple collaborators to collectively grasp the key elements of the task.

6. PLAYING WITH THE REPRESENTATIONS

The impressionists enjoyed playing with light; the cubists enjoyed playing with geometry and multiple media. Watson and Crick enjoyed tinkering with their metal models of the DNA molecule. Distinguished theater directors like Peter Brook and Jonathan Miller let their actors and set designers play with various interpretations of the performance. Great jazz musicians view improvisation as a form of play.

Instead of treating uncertainty as a problem to be solved, successful collaborators treat uncertainty as opportunities to be explored. The uncertainties fuel the sense of play and experimentation. Even the scientists aren't initially searching for solutions—they're trying to get a sense of the degrees of freedom the problem allows. They're playing with the parameters and underlying dynamics to see what constraints they have to obey. In contrast, the artists play with the parameters and dynamics to see what constraints they can shatter.

Successful collaborators take play seriously. They tend to view their shared spaces and multiple representations as Silly Putty that can be stretched and molded to test their ideas. Exaggeration, oddball perspectives, and understatements all fall under the anything-goes category that collaborators freely indulge in as they try to sort out their options. Even doctors struggling to diagnose a troublesome set of symptoms "play" with the diagnostic possibilities by picturing what the ailment might be if a certain fluid level was higher or how a patient might respond if a new drug was introduced into the treatment program.

The multiple representations and the shared spaces serve, in effect, as a conceptual and technical playground for the collaborators. Their thoughts and behavior there commit them to nothing. At the same time, the playground puts them in a position to make a commitment when they feel ready.

7. CONTINUOUS BUT NOT CONTINUAL COMMUNICATION

Francis Crick describes his own pattern of collaborative communication as "continuous but not continual," and it turns out that this pattern holds for the majority of collaborations examined.

Unless it is mandated by circumstance—an emergency in an airline cockpit or a hospital operating theater—collaborators do not maintain constant communication. Instead, they focus on trying to create a rhythm, a tempo, and a flow of communication that prevents them from interfering with one another while assuring that events are proceeding apace.

In effect, successful collaborators create patterns of communication appropriate to their relationship and their task. Particularly in the arts and sciences, there are no formal reporting schedules in a collaboration. In an organization or a project with a deadline, meetings are usually held less for the purpose of collaborating than to disseminate relevant information about where the collaborators stand vis-à-vis their deadline. In other words, the initiative for the communication comes from the collaborators themselves, not from any externally imposed arbiter. This maximizes both flexibility and spontaneity—two qualities of communication that successful collaborators stress are essential. Successful collaborators try to create an appropriate flow of communication rather than a structure for communication.

8. FORMAL AND INFORMAL ENVIRONMENTS

As a general rule, collaborators collaborate along a spectrum of different environments—both formal and informal. That distinction is somewhat arbitrary.

For example, in a hospital, the classic formal structure for a collaboration is grand rounds, where the top medical staff supervise a survey of patients with both residents and interns in tow. Interns, residents, and attending physicians formally review patient charts.

However, there are dozens of other less formal and even casual collaborative episodes in the hospital. Interns and residents collaborate with the nurses. The nurses collaborate among themselves to decide whether or not to call a doctor or administer a medication themselves. Doctors collaborate with lab technicians to get more information on clinical tests or collaborate with other doctors in casual hallway discussions about a particularly difficult diagnosis. Doctors and nurses collaborate with patients to clarify their understanding of certain symptoms; even cafeteria conversation can review the disease du jour or a troublesome diagnosis.

It's difficult to tell when a formal collaboration blurs into an informal discussion and vice versa in this environment. Yet it's clear that medical personnel depend on the entire range of collaboration to treat their patients effectively.

Similarly, biomedical researchers in major labs seemingly depend on both formal and informal settings to accomplish their work. The staff of Nobel laureate Walter Gilbert's molecular biology lab at Harvard was famous for repairing to the local pub to continue research debates that began back at the lab benches. (Indeed, some members of the lab even put out an underground newspaper documenting and generating the latest lab gossip.) Watson and Crick didn't limit their discussions of DNA to their offices in Cambridge's Cavendish Lab. The quantum physicists traveled all over Europe together and were particularly fond of boat rides, mountain climbing, and long walks in the country.

Of course, the French Impressionists and the Cubists achieved notoriety in Paris for their willingness to turn sidewalk cafés into salons for debating the merits of their respective aesthetics. At the same time, however, these painters worked conscientiously in the more formal environs of their studios as they experimented with their art. They also exchanged letters and sketches.

On a more technological level, one of the fastest-growing young computer companies in America, Compaq Computer Corp., was launched after a few of its founders sketched a prototype of their proposed portable computer on a paper napkin over a meal.

As one surveys the sociology of science and art, it's striking—but ultimately not surprising—that creative communities and collaborators meet in a variety of formal and informal environments. One could make the case that because these people are all working intently on the same problems that it's inevitable they work together in different settings. However, a more powerful argument could be made that it is precisely because people collaborate in both formal and informal environments that they expand their ability to solve problems.

In both the biographies and the comments of great scientists and artists like Niels Bohr, Georges Braque, Francis Crick, and Vincent van Gogh, it's consistently the informal meetings, the café arguments, and the wilderness trips that are cited as pivotal events in the creative cycle. Of course, the "Eureka!" also strikes at the laboratory bench or in front of the easel or at the more "appropriate" settings. But one can't ignore the possibility that informal collaboration fathered the inspiration that hatched in the more formal setting.

The fact that great collaborations occur in so many formal and informal settings dictates that tools for collaboration should also be robust enough to cope with a change in scenery.

9. CLEAR LINES OF RESPONSIBILITY BUT NO RESTRICTIVE BOUNDARIES

Collaborative relationships are not managed in the classic meaning of the term. There is no division of labor in successful collaborations comparable to the way most organizations define the phrase. Typically, most organizations assign specific responsibilities to individuals and expect them to deliver the goods on schedule and at the appropriate level of quality.

In a collaboration—particularly in the sciences and engineering

—individuals are explicitly responsible for certain tasks but are also free to consult, assist, and solicit ideas from their collaborators. In other words, the individual has both a defined functional role and a charter to go where the task takes him. Collaborators are expected to ask one another the tough questions.

There is little turf warfare in the successful collaboration precisely because the collaborators are supposed to create collective solutions to problems. Richard Feynman, the brilliant physicist who worked on the Manhattan Project in Los Alamos and who later won a Nobel Prize, recalls being astonished by how freely scientists of all stripes could participate in the informal colloquia that Robert Oppenheimer organized about how best to build the atomic bomb. At the best hospitals, the specialists willingly collaborate with attending physicians, nurses, and residents to diagnose and treat the patients. Everyone remains responsible for their own functional duties, but everyone is encouraged to create shared understandings about the entire task.

10. DECISIONS DO NOT HAVE TO BE MADE BY CONSENSUS

One of the most persistent myths about collaboration is that it requires consensus. This is emphatically not so. Collaborators constantly bicker and argue. For the most part, these arguments are depersonalized and focus on genuine areas of disagreement. Then again, collaborators argue precisely because they come to the task with different perspectives and backgrounds—which is exactly why they're collaborating.

For obvious reasons, collaborators usually agree about the directions they are taking. Braque and Picasso had their serious disagreements, as did Watson and Crick. That didn't preclude them from pushing ahead. If collaborators consistently diverge, the collaboration ultimately dissolves. To that extent, collaborators enjoy a tacit consensus about where they're going or they're not collaborators.

However, in collaborative efforts, from making *Gone With the Wind* to building the atomic bomb, it's clear that chance, circumstance, and necessity dictate that, ultimately, key individuals will make decisions about where the collaboration should go. Consensus is often irrelevant to the act of creation or discovery. The real challenge is for the collaboration to generate the collective ideas and insights that accomplish the desired task.

In effect, collaboration is the medium that creates value, but the imperatives of the organization (or marketplace) determine how the fruits of that collaboration will be realized. Collaboration doesn't mean consensus—nor should it.

11. PHYSICAL PRESENCE IS NOT NECESSARY

Even before telecommunications redefined presence, there have been successful long-distance collaborations. Thomas Wolfe and his editor, Maxwell Perkins, enjoyed a tremendously productive correspondence of both letter and manuscript. So did T. S. Eliot and Ezra Pound. Francis Crick points to Cambridge University mathematicians Hardy and Littlewood, who collaborated by letter for years even though they worked only a few hundred yards apart. The relative purity and elegance of mathematical proofs helped make distance irrelevant.

That mathematics, physics, and chemistry each has its own lingua franca makes scientific collaboration by correspondence so pervasive. Albert Einstein frequently collaborated by letter. The quantum physicists enjoyed energetic correspondences throughout Europe. Letters and monographs served effectively as shared spaces.

The continuing rise of fax machines and computer networks has dramatically transformed collaboration in the sciences; long-distance collaboration can now be nearly instantaneous. Scientists of all disciplines increasingly rely on the Internet to exchange information. The fax machine has become a particularly ubiquitous mode of information distribution. While many computer networks are only good at exchanging text, fax machines can easily transmit graphs and sketches. One molecular biologist at MIT's prestigious Whitehead Institute says that researchers all over the world fax one another sketches of protein and enzyme structures all the time—and the recipients turn around and fax them right back with comments, criticisms, and alternate perspectives. Today, they use the Internet instead of faxes. "We do things in an afternoon that used to take a week of Federal Express and phone calls," he says.

While video conferencing and other high-bandwidth communication technologies are available but not pervasive, it's clear that the existing telecommunications infrastructure is acquiring a collaborative overtone. While there is no substitute for face-to-face contact, these technologies render physical presence a useful but not necessary part of a successful collaborative experience.

12. SELECTIVE USE OF OUTSIDERS FOR COMPLEMENTARY INSIGHTS AND INFORMATION

Successful collaborations are not solipsistic. As intense and demanding as most professional collaborations are, successful collaborations have historically relied upon a network of outside advisers who are familiar with either the technical area, the personality of the collaborators, or both.

In the case of the quantum physicists, the molecular biologists, and the impressionists, the collaborative communities attained a critical mass at which the lines between formal and informal collaborators frequently blurred. In many respects, these communities were self-sustaining and were constantly invigorated by new entrants to the field who brought new perspectives.

In specific collaborative instances, however, it's clear that outsiders play a crucial catalytic role in achieving successful outcomes. For example, Octave Chanute, a past president of the American Society of Civil Engineers and author of *Progress in Flying Machines*, entered into what would become a decade-long correspondence with the Wright brothers in 1900. Chanute's worldliness, experience, and patronage were fundamental to the brothers' pioneering flight at Kitty Hawk in 1903.

Similarly, Stanford University's Frederick Terman served as a mentor to the young William Hewlett and David Packard, the parents of Silicon Valley's first and, in many respects, most successful electronics company. Terman lent both business and technical expertise to his charges. The same holds true for marketing guru Regis McKenna's role in positioning Apple Computer, the offspring of Steve Jobs and Steve Wozniak.

On a more explicitly technical basis, Watson and Crick depended on information gleaned by Rosalind Franklin and Maurice Wilkins, among others, to turn the mosaic of information into the model of the double helix.

What's intriguing to note, however, is that all these collaborators *solicited* this outside assistance. It was not imposed upon them. Successful collaborators are constantly on the lookout for people and information that will help them achieve their mission, but they do so on their own terms. Apparently, one cannot impose assistance upon a collaboration, even if that assistance would be precisely what the collaboration needed to meet success.

The crucial point, however, is that the most successful collaborations are not inwardly focused to the exclusion of outside data. Historically, successful collaborators have had their antennae exquisitely tuned to who's doing what in relevant fields. Successful collaborators rarely hesitate to establish links—if not ties—to other people who can provide either specific doses of necessary information or useful insights to guide the collaborative effort. These outsiders rarely become an ongoing part of the collaborative process, but they do serve specific functional roles at critical junctures in that process.

13. COLLABORATIONS END

One should always enter a collaborative relationship with the idea that it will end. Collaborations are purposeful; once the purpose is achieved, the need for the collaboration usually evaporates. In that sense, successful collaborations are more like trysts than great romances. Once the operation is a success or the crippled plane lands or the new product attains commanding market share with great margins, the collaboration usually ends. Most collaborations are task specific.

That's one of the reasons why Watson and Crick ended their splendid collaboration. After discovering the double helix, what do you do for an encore? In contrast, Crick enjoyed a fruitful twenty-year collaboration with molecular biologist Sydney Brenner because the two worked so well together as a team. Instead of the relationship being subordinate to the task, the task was subordinate to the relationship.

In practice, a consistently productive long-term collaboration is as rare as a great friendship or a great marriage. Because collaborators are also individuals, it's completely understandable that they grow apart over time. They are captured by new interests and perspectives—and new collaborators. The collaborative conflicts that once sparked creative epiphanies eventually spark noisy disagreements.

To a large extent, these changes are both inevitable and predictable. Collaboration sometimes changes people in ways that make continued collaboration impossible. People and their collaborations are not static, inflexible machines—they are dynamic relationships that respond to changes in both environment and expectation. Rodgers and Hart didn't write the same musicals as Rodgers and Hammerstein. Braque and Picasso, while intense collaborators, ultimately had different perspectives on art. Watson and Crick have different aspirations in science.

The idea that even the most successful collaborations come to an end is simultaneously sad and liberating. On one hand, it's a pity that such a productive and beneficial relationship ultimately dies. On the other hand, it reaffirms that people are individuals who are free to go their own ways and pursue other interests, either on their own or with a new set of collaborators. The reality that collaborations end may indeed be one of the best reasons why bright, talented people are willing to be a part of them. The long-term benefits can greatly exceed the short-term costs.

PEOPLE WHO WANT to design or use collaborative tools, people who plan to build or work in collaborative environments, need to be aware of both the opportunities and the constraints these themes suggest. Damon Runyon once noted that "The race isn't always to the swift or the battle to the strong—but that's the way to bet." No doubt, many collaborations have succeeded outside the themes mentioned here—but the odds favor the collaborators and technologies that respect them.

11

Building Collaborative Architectures

*As larger groups begin working together in design, we
need not only looser roles but more public ways of
thinking aloud.*

JOHN CHRIS JONES • SOFTECNICA

DESIGNING FOR COLLABORATION REQUIRES AN ARCHITECT WITH A
sense of humor. After all, collaborative relationships have to cope
with the misunderstandings as well as the epiphanies, and the tools
should be able to support them all with grace. Creating an environment that stimulates the relaxed intensity that marks effective collaboration is a craft, not a science. It requires both an aesthetic sense
and a grasp of functionality. The architect must be able to design
formal tools for informal collaborations and informal tools for formal collaborations.

Ideally, these architectures should be able to support collaboration at any time, at any place, at any level. They should support the
cascade of serendipitous personal interactions that turn into informal collaborations that turn into formal meetings that turn into
ongoing relationships that turn into results. They should be able to
handle a variety of interactions, from the casual chat in the cafeteria
to a huge meeting with hundreds of participants.

The difficulty lies in trying to create tools and environments to
support something we don't quite yet fully understand. The difficult
questions surrounding collaboration are startlingly similar to those

surrounding intelligence or creativity. How do you nurture it? How do you inspire it? How do you manage it? Designing structures that encourage effective collaboration is no less challenging than designing a house that people enjoy living in as much as they enjoy looking at.

Collaborative design has yet to find its Frank Lloyd Wright, Raymond Loewy, or Le Corbusier. Most likely, it will take a collaborative community to build the appropriate tools and environments. But to really take collaborative design seriously, one has to be willing to play with the concept. This requires an appreciation of two basic design themes:

- Collaborative tools and environments aren't just designed to support individuals or groups or meetings—they're designed to support relationships. Those relationships can be one on one or group interactions, but the key here isn't to optimize the efforts of individuals but to optimize productive relationships between individuals.
- Collaborative architectures support a process, not an output. One is not building a slaughterhouse where the architectural design directly contributes to a specific outcome. A collaborative environment should be designed to support the various processes of interaction—conversations, sketches, arguments, agreements—and not to predestine or predetermine any specific set of results. The trade-off here is balancing the demand for flexibility and adaptability with the need for some sort of structure that can hold the contexts and contents that these collaborations generate.

In the same way that the well-designed office encourages accessibility, the best of these structures makes collaboration easy to the point of being inevitable. One of the most heavily used whiteboards at the Xerox Palo Alto Research Center is the one in the lounge area by the coffeepot. Multicolored scribbles, scrawls, and sketches are tattooed all over it. There's no question that there's a lot of thinking going on here. In their brilliant monograph *Toward Portable Ideas*, Mark Stefik and John Seely Brown wonder how much better and more powerful a collaborative tool that whiteboard could be if it went computer.

"After productive conversation one wouldn't need to just re-

Colab-like environments might lead to a fundamental redesign of all the areas where formal and informal meetings take place. One could take a conversation that began at a coffeepot, move it into a wall-mounted computer display and retrieve items on a display from a previous conversation, or forward the contents of the board so that the conversation could continue in someone's office.

member the ideas or copy the content to paper!" they write. "Explaining an idea to a colleague is simplified greatly when the context-setting sketches on a whiteboard are available. To this end, means for moving the contents of [an electronic whiteboard] should be direct and simple. One could forward the data to an office [electronic whiteboard] ('Send this to my office') or file it in a database. Similarly, one could retrieve an idea to show a colleague at the coffeepot ('Get the big-idea window from yesterday's conversation')."

Their basic architectural design scheme is to offer a "seamless environment of tools for conversation that extends from offices to the coffeepot to the formal meeting room." They want to extend the notion of seamlessness right to the office cafeteria. Instead of having to scribble the latest greatest idea on a mustard-stained napkin, the cafeteria tables should have embedded interactive flat panel displays that induce you to engage in shared scribbling between bites.

In this context, ideas wouldn't just be externally represented and manipulable (as previously discussed) but portable as well. They could easily be carried (or flow) from location to location, whiteboard to computer to printout and back again. There need be no discontinuity between the intimacy of personal creativity and the added value of collaborative creation. Structures should be designed to embrace collaborations wherever they occur.

The thing that's so compelling about seamlessness and portability is that it automatically changes the way information and interactions are treated within the organization. This fundamental design assumption is every bit as profound as the physical layout of the workplace. Are there private offices or is there an open office layout? Are there hallways that encourage people to meet one another? Are there community rooms, a cafeteria where people can sit down and break bread? Are there windows offering generous views, or is the workspace disconnected from the outside world? Just as the external and interior design of a workplace help determine professional interactions, seamless and portable tools in that workplace will encourage collaboration.

To underscore the point, a telephone on every desk is considered an indispensable part of the communication infrastructure of the organization. Technologically speaking, a telephone in every office and conference room creates a seamlessness and portability of conversation. The telephone helps make physical distance irrelevant. You wouldn't think of designing a workplace without effective telephone communications. Why not design workplaces that pay attention to the needs of effective collaborations?

Just as the telephone on every desk spawned a new generation of instantaneous organizational communications—confirming information, spreading gossip, tapping an expert's brain, setting up an impromptu meeting—an environment fostering seamlessness and portability will generate new forms of collaboration that we can't yet fully appreciate. If nothing else, the barrier of entry to collaboration will be reduced and the context of individual work redefined.

In the collaborative environment, a fundamental change in the properties of the medium occurs. The focus shifts from a display of results to a shared awareness of process. People can see, and if necessary participate, in crafting these outputs. Yes, it is possible to design an environment where the imperative for collaboration overwhelms the perfectly understandable desire for privacy and personal space. This holds true for physical environments as well—you don't want to jam people together or place each of them in splendid isolation. The collaborative architect has to recognize and appreciate the inherent tension between shared space and personal space. The two are not, however, mutually exclusive, and different people have different perceptions of these spaces. The smart organization respects both the individual and the collaboration.

Indeed, collaboration isn't a function of people peering uninvited over one another's personal computers or blackboards. Personal interaction is required. The idea is to empower a relationship, not indulge workplace voyeurism. Effective communication often requires taking risks. To say something new, important, or not obvious is to risk being misunderstood. In conversation, we depend on feedback to signal understanding or misunderstanding, and we use that feedback to establish mutual intelligibility. If the bandwidth of the conversation is too low, correcting the misunderstandings is too difficult. If the organizational setup precludes discussion, or if the mean time between encounters is too low (i.e., there's little chance of bumping into people in the hallways or the cafeteria), then participants will have few opportunities to fix the misunderstandings that occur during more formal meetings. One has to design collaborative environments that can quickly heal misunderstandings even as they help spawn new ideas.

But how does an organization encourage its people and itself to make the transition from one environment to the other? How does one begin to build a bridge to more powerful collaborative tools? As Stefik and Brown observe, "The gulf between an informal whiteboard and a formal computer tool is so broad that many people never cross it."

The trick, they argue, is to reduce that gap through a sequence of smaller, more manageable steps: whiteboards whose contents are easily saved and retrieved; whiteboards with windows; whiteboards that are networked to other whiteboards.

"There must be a seductive gradient," they write. "Simple ends need simple means. The gradients should be such that a small investment in learning has a large payoff in increased capabilities, quickly drawing one further into the tools. For example, the use of a [computer-augmented whiteboard] could start out as being identical to the familiar whiteboard. Learning how to quickly erase, save, and retrieve should be very simple. Learning how to use windows and multiplex the use of space is the next step. Through simple explorations [users] should encounter new possibilities."

Of course, new social phenomena emerge from these environments and around these tools. Just as the strategically located water cooler becomes a critical node on the office grapevine or the photocopier becomes the printing press for the memo fanatic, collaborative environments and their technologies will yield their own meetings facilitators, collaboration gurus, and snipers, as well as collaboration voyeurs—people who just want to watch. New technologies create new communities. The challenge is to make sure that the seductive gradient doesn't turn into a slippery slope that sends people plunging into free-fall. If the technology isn't useful, it shouldn't be used.

Tools for collaboration should allow a seamless transition between individual work and collaborative efforts. "If collaboration tools fail to do that and require that people use one kind of tool for individual work and a different kind for group work," says Stefik, "then collaboration technology will fail." Le Corbusier once commented that one should always design for the next level: when you design a chair, keep the table in mind; a table and chair should be designed for the context of the room, and so on. This must also be the design dictum for collaborative tools. One should design them with the next level in mind; collaborative tools must gracefully extend into collaborative environments.

DOCUMEDIA

Meeting that design challenge requires a radically different perception of media and a new respect for the way competent individuals relate to one another in a group. Documedia is the name I assign to these computer-based collaborative media and environments, partly because *docere* is the Latin verb meaning "to teach" and collaborative media help collaborators learn what they really want to do and how best to do it; and partly because while most collaborations produce documents as products, documedia is more than just a document—it's producing a media hybrid of information, communication, and results. (I also prefer the term to "multimedia," which refers simply to a multitude of media, or "hypermedia," which usually features more hype than media.)

The functional specifications and versatility necessary for these tools will require a tremendous integration of visual, textual, and audio media. But instead of these multi/hypermedia being a way for an author or an artist to package information, they will more likely be a communal medium. It takes multiple people to use multimedia.

The documedia that have been described so far are pretty much a tabula rasa, blank pages to be filled by the comments, questions, and discussions of the collaborators. The words and symbols fill up the empty spaces. To put it another way, these documedia—whether facilitated by an expert or handled by the collaborators themselves —are like mirrors that reflect what the group is talking about. Even better, they're mirrors with memory so that people can recall what the conversation looked like just a few moments ago.

Such mirrors can be extraordinarily useful, of course, because they give people a chance to see something they couldn't see before. Just as a room lined with windows can be distracting, a room lined only with mirrors can also be a bit much, letting people slip into narcissistic self-analysis. Collaborative tools and documedia should add value to a collaboration, not merely reflect people's jottings or oral comments on-screen.

As the sophistication surrounding collaboration and collaborative tools grows, there will be a fundamental shift in the nature of documedia. Instead of being just mirrors that reflect a collaboration, documedia will become lenses, tools, and templates that evoke— even provoke—collaboration. That's not to say that future documedia will display Rorschach ink blots for group analysis and discussion (although some groups do merit intensive psychoanalysis). Rather, the idea is to present visual and textual patterns—templates and molds—that can induce appropriate conversations. This is completely consistent with the architectural metaphor. Just as the rooms of a house are designed and furnished to satisfy a particular dimension of home life, these templates are furnished with structures that frame collaborations.

Consider, for example, a group of people from different departments in an organization trying to figure out how to devise a three-year budget. It would make sense, of course, to list the criteria for spending and investment and come to a consensus on what the organization's priorities should be.

Nevertheless, probably the best vehicle to display the trade-offs and projections inherent in any budgetary discussion is a spreadsheet.

The spreadsheet offers a template that can effectively frame the relevant conversation about how one divvies up the money and what the assumptions for financial projections are. The spreadsheet becomes a dynamic model for the different departments to calibrate and revise their assumptions, aspirations, and expenditures. The spreadsheet becomes less a mirror of the discussion than a lens to focus it.

The same holds true when people get together to chart out a project-management schedule, arguably one of the most difficult collaborative exercises an organization performs. Scheduling a project requires a grasp of time constraints, reality, and the hidden interdependencies between key individuals and groups within the organization. For all intents and purposes, a project-management schedule is a map where everyone agrees on direction but not necessarily on the times of arrival.

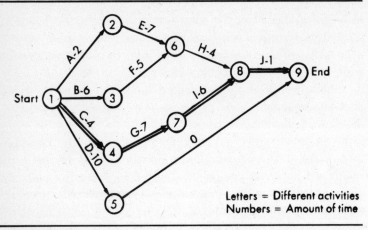

Letters = Different activities
Numbers = Amount of time

CPM/PERT Network

American defense contractors are fond of using PERT (Performance Evaluation and Review Technique) charts to map out their production schedules; publishing companies often use Gantt charts; other firms rely on Critical Path Method charts as their schedule

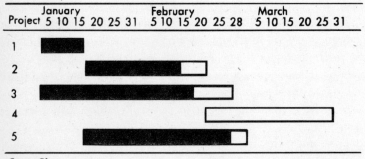

Gantt Chart

display of choice. There are computer-based versions of all these project-scheduling approaches.

Offering a group a scheduling template completely shifts the focus of discussion away from individual statements of obligation to an appreciation of interdependencies. People can literally see a schedule disintegrate before their eyes if one or two of the key hit dates are missed. The ability to display and modify a scheduling map evokes conversation that centers on the process of meeting a schedule, not just a heightened awareness of crucial dates.

"Our basic tool is the unfinished model," says David Braunschvig, who facilitated computer-augmented meetings for Coopers & Lybrand's strategic management consulting group. "We build a lot of unfinished models for meetings that range from writing a document to planning budgets."

Braunschvig found that at least half of his clients eventually wanted to build an in-house capability for collaborative support and that they wanted to be in meetings where they weren't just there to address a task but to actually accomplish something. The template may be unfinished, but the process of collaboration completes it. There is a sense of closure and accomplishment. It's not unlike the satisfaction one feels in solving a puzzle—the crucial difference here being that solving the puzzle is synonymous with dealing with the task at hand.

Braunschvig may display a matrix that represents the group's current perspective of its marketplace. How might that view change if demographics shifted? Prices changed? Competition intensified? The shape and substance of the matrix shifts with the flow of responses. The group reconfigures the matrix to reflect its evolving perceptions of the marketplace. To a large extent, then, designing for collaboration means designing for this feeling of closure and completion. Collaborators want to see themselves completing tasks.

Whether creating a budget, managing a schedule, writing a report, or conducting a negotiation, the documedium deals with and displays symbolic representations of a process. People are simultaneously seeing and playing with a model of reality. The computer enables these processes to be modeled dynamically and interactively. The trend is clear: the nature of both collaboration and documedia technology will push for high-resolution visualizations of the collaborative task.

Think of the way that Walt Disney Studios approached the challenge of creating *Fantasia* in the thirties. Just talking about the characters, the music, and the ideas wasn't enough: they had to be visualized in storyboards and synchronized with little snippets of animation. As documented in *The Illusion of Life*, Disney animation succeeded in part because its animators and technicians were geniuses at collaborating to create images to accompany the music.

Instead of editing a text, working with documedia will feel more like editing a movie. Words will be used to complement and explicate the simulations. Groups will become as concerned about the images they use to represent a process as they are about the words they use to describe it. Most importantly, the discipline of collaborating to define the task at hand visually automatically challenges them to deal with that task. By working with meaningful representations and visualizations, collaborators immediately focus on the challenge of solving the problem—not just talking about it.

There are other visualizations of collaborative processes that are far more intricate and demanding than text:

- Doctors have traditionally used medical charts and such diagnostic imaging tools as X rays, CAT scans, and MRI imagers to create shared spaces to collaborate about patient treatment. Increasingly, doctors are now using on-screen computer simulations of their patients to prepare their operations.

  This is particularly true in cosmetic surgery, where the patient wants to have some understanding of how the operation works and how he or she will look after it takes place. These cosmetic surgeons draw the planned incisions on the computer simulation of the body part involved to illustrate the procedure. Similarly, several cardiac surgeons now rely on computer models of their patients' hearts to determine which procedures would be most timely and effective for treatment. The ability to capture a graphic rendition of the heart, rotate it on-screen, and examine it from several angles before even lifting a scalpel is, perhaps, one of the most rewarding applications of computer-generated shared space. Of course, other specialists can also examine the documedium. Treating the patient becomes a much more explicitly collaborative task. This represents a significant qualitative advance in patient care.

- At Digital Equipment Corporation, a small team of in-house consultants uses computer visualization techniques to literally map the relationships between parts of the organization—particularly those groups having problems. At these meetings, participants create islands, swamps, bridges, and other cartographic representations to symbolize the way their group relates to others in the scheme of things.

  Initially, the groups work in isolation to devise their own version of the big picture. When the different groups get together, they usually find that their maps portray the other groups as the problem-infested swamps and barriers to effective work flow. These mirror-image maps underscore the interdependence of the groups.

  At this point, DEC's consultants create new groups with members drawn from each of the conflicting subgroups, and the maps are redrawn. After several iterations, there is a new set of maps that details the current situation and the goal for the future—along with suggestions for what steps might best be taken next. The DEC employees leave the workshops taking these maps (suitable for framing) with them, along with a much more explicit picture of their relationships and responsibilities.

- Currently, most industrial designers rely on computer-generated graphics for their personal use. The potential for collaborative design is nothing short of immense. If you are designing a product—an automobile dashboard, say—documedia offer the most radically effective real-time approach to bringing multiple talents and perspectives to bear on the design task. Instead of being forced to focus on individual components, the shared-space approach allows teams to explore and understand the trade-offs involved in piecing together a working system.

  A suitably sophisticated simulation may be able to emulate much of the product's real functionality. If nothing else, the designers are in a position to produce working prototypes much more quickly and cost-effectively. Just as important, the documentation and the design methodologies are automatically recorded in an easy-to-retrieve, easy-to-update form—in sharp contrast to the messy paper trails that most traditional design procedures impose.

We've already seen the first halting steps in collaborative design in the realm of computer-based desktop publishing and multimedia presentations. Desktop-publishing systems encourage people to play both editor and designer of documents, reports, and publications. Software to ease the challenge of designing an appealing layout is widely publicized, and every department has at least one amateur art director willing to lend an eye and a hand to produce good visuals. Groupware products like Lotus Notes are excellent examples of software that enables this.

The ad hoc collaborative clusters that form around desktop-publishing efforts are a forerunner to the sort of revolution that documedia will bring to the multibillion-dollar packaging industry. Marketers, engineers, market researchers, and customers will no doubt collaborate on the design of product packages. Market research focus groups will literally be able to select the sizes, weights, colors, and designs of packages for both consumer and industrial goods.

No doubt, many companies will invest in ultra-high-quality computer graphics screens to be able to present full-color facsimiles of proposed packages. These images can all be customized, edited, altered, expanded, contracted, changed, modified, or played with—all within key parameters—until the optimal package is created. This documedia application will likely embrace products ranging from candy bars to book covers to annual reports. With increased technological sophistication, these visualizations will serve as worthy surrogates for the test products.

The next step is to elevate these visualizations into simulations—turning the visual storyboard into a dynamic and interactive representation of the desired process. Increasingly, the ability to mimic reality—with a twist—will become a crucial aspect of collaborative architecture. Collaborators will work in a shared space of a virtual reality that gives them the power to probe a variety of design options. The shared space will become a test-tube medium for new processes and products designed by collaborative teams.

As computer graphics consultant Richard Mark Friedhoff observes, "Visualization need no longer be a solitary inner experience. The computer makes it possible for groups of individuals, even if they are separated by great distances, to collaborate in visual exploration whether in artistic, design, or scientific spheres. The computer *democratizes* visual thinking."

As computer-armed collaborative teams succeed, their work spaces will generate a vocabulary all their own. Just as *interfaces* and *factor analysis* and *chi squares* are the idioms of computers and market research, there will no doubt be a new lexicon and idiom that collaborators will use to describe both their interactions and the idiosyncrasies of their documedium. Perhaps certain windows will get certain pet names or people will grab for the telepointer to poke at a questionable assumption or an undesirable feature in a product rendering. Eventually, people will craft their own signs and symbols to represent processes. People will learn a lot about themselves as they create the new semiotics of collaboration.

It's probably misleading to focus exclusively on the role of unfinished models and realistic simulations as key pieces of conceptual documedia software. In all likelihood, documedia will develop their own unique brands of collaborative software. Just as new media generate their own vocabularies, they also tend to generate new contents that are unique to their strengths. Marshall McLuhan was fond of noting that new media cannibalize the content of their precursors. After relying on literature for their content, the movies developed their own style. After depending on movies and radio for its material, television nurtured its own formats. The same evolution will no doubt apply to documedia.

Evocative templates that make people think about collaboration differently are also a real possibility. Picture a template designed by a collaborative architect who is a cross between Walt Disney and Peter Drucker. This template would simultaneously appeal to the fantastical and the practical and provide images that would stretch the imagination even as they reinforce common sense. It would offer a new way of creating closure, but at a higher level. It would get people to create shared understandings they never knew they could possess.

Perhaps some documedia will be imbued with some degree of artificial intelligence and so-called expert systems that would be capable of interjecting comments and questions into a collaboration, prodding people to explore an assumption a little more rigorously or pursue another line of inquiry. No doubt, some of these expert systems for collaboration will be designed to augment brainstorming collaborations, while others might offer advice on project-management schedules. As business and marketplaces grow more global, there will be documedia templates that augment cross-cultural collaborations.

These documedia must be capable of stretching across time and space, as well as culture, if they are to be truly versatile. The constant design imperative is to assure the feeling of copresence, the feeling that one is always adding value to and building on the contributions of others. Time and distance are dimensions that shouldn't define the limitations of documedia. On the contrary, they are dimensions that offer unique opportunities for collaborators. Shifts in time and distance guarantee different perspectives. The ability to audit the trail of a collaborative medium over time or view its evolution from afar can be valuable in itself. No one wants to read a blackboard through a telescope; on the other hand, the ability to zoom in and out of the collaborative process has its virtues. It's possible to be too close to the shared space. The point is simple: successful collaborative architectures recognize that copresence can exist in several dimensions. The trick is to design documedia that respect this.

But the real challenge of collaborative architectures is to design structures that not only endure and are useful but that *inspire*. Curiosity, excitement, intensity, surprise—collaborative designers must try to evoke all these sensations. No doubt some collaborative architects will prove gifted at creating environments, tools, and documedia for every kind of professional workplace. Perhaps some will prove brilliant at coming up with gimmicky collaborative artifacts that will provoke unusual collaborative patterns. Maybe documedia will develop the equivalents of Cubists, Futurists, and Surrealists who will redefine the way people view collaborative environments. No doubt many collaborative tools will follow the dictum of the Bauhaus: form follows function, with little or no ornamentation.

Ultimately, collaborators will be able to choose from different sets of templates—different documedia and collaborative environments—to find the one that best suits their particular needs of the moment. Reaching for the appropriate collaborative tool or documedium shouldn't be like reaching for a Phillips screwdriver or a socket wrench, requiring you to hunt down a tool kit, sort through a mess, and retrieve what you need. Documedia should be more like a Swiss army knife—something inherently multifunctional, seamless, and portable that you reach for automatically to get the job done. You don't need it all the time, but it can sure come in handy.

12

Collaborative Futures

Ted Nelson, self-styled techno-visionary and author of the cult classic *Computer Lib/Dream Machines*, has designed some of the most fantastical scenarios imaginable about collaborative systems. Like something out of a full-blown sixties acid trip, he envisions clouds of text and imagery materializing over people's heads even as they speak. These clouds are conceptual appendages to the conversation, ever shifting, changing, evolving as the speaker's words shift, change, and evolve: a nonverbal mirror of thoughts. The listener doesn't just listen to what's being said—he sees it swirl and coalesce before his eyes.

Of course, each speaker has his own cloud floating overhead, so arguments look like semiotic thunderstorms giving off flashes of insight. As they talk, people point at one another's clouds and ask questions ("Just what do you mean by that?"). Naturally, these clouds can be melded to create shared understandings or split apart to create multiple conversational climates. The whole idea is that people carry entire environments of expression with them wherever they go. Even casual conversation becomes a multimedia experience; these media are as much a part of an individual's style and personality as his clothes. Just as people would feel naked without their clothes, people participating in Nelson's vision of interpersonal communication would feel collaboratively mute without their media clouds. Those clouds are a natural extension of themselves and their thoughts.

This scenario is right out of the cyberpunk genre of science fiction that treats technology as a template for refashioning pop culture. Cyberpunk is science fiction with street smarts. It portrays worlds where computers are as much prosthetics and partners as utilitarian tools. Cyberpunk's inhabitants get "juiced" on the webs of network technologies that are continually humming with data and information. Technology isn't just a medium of communication —it's *the* medium of communication. The reality of the technology is more compelling than the reality of reality. Reality and virtual reality become indistinguishable. The line between humans and the media they use to project themselves blurs into irrelevance. This is what the future may look like.

The cyberpunk scenario is one of the *ad absurdum* extensions of collaborative tools. But its underlying theme is compelling. Increasingly, new technologies determine the quality of human relationships; they set the boundaries, they define the parameters. This has been true in architecture and transportation as well as telecommunications and medicine. A favorite question of philosophers through the ages has been "Does technology shape culture or merely reflect it?" In truth, it is impossible to imagine what popular culture means in the absence of technology. Technology—as much as personality —becomes the lens through which we view the nature of human relationships.

The emerging generation of collaborative tools will inevitably have as big an impact on the style and nature of personal and professional relationships as, for example, the telephone and television have had. These technologies fundamentally change the things people take for granted in a relationship.

People will go to their collaborative tools as readily as they scribble on a legal pad or switch on the radio to catch the latest news. Just as a lawyer or an investment banker thinks nothing of reaching for a car cellular phone to make a call, professionals will increasingly come to take their collaborative tools for granted. In a realistic scenario of the professional future, people will come to reserve a shared space in fine restaurants as comfortably as they've come to use a phone. The very idea of collaboration will be redefined along technological dimensions.

Personal computers will become interpersonal computers; instead of a keyboard for one, there will be keyboards for two—or more. The computer screen is now a shared space. That restaurant of the future will supply the finest flat-panel display screen with high resolution graphics—comparable to the finest 70-mm film quality. This collaborative tablet will come with the desired number of keyboards and interfaces so that the two or three or four people at the table can collaborate comfortably over their coffee. The mice will be appropriately calibrated so that they won't snag on the table-cloth.

A few years later, these collaborative tablets will evolve into a full-blown multimedia experience that also incorporates the latest in artificial-intelligence techniques. This tablet will project three-dimensional displays of text, graphics, and image. You can write on it, sketch on it, and scan data into it. The tablet will respond to verbal commands—*"Move that paragraph there below the picture of the chairman and make the typeface Palatino Bold," "Why don't we accelerate this part of the schedule and then redesign this gear so that we can be on the shelves in six weeks instead of twelve?"*—and perform automatic voice recording and transcription. You can see the conversation as you speak or choose not to display it on the screen. Similarly, you can play back the parts of the conversation that are particularly important, have the tablet transcribe them, edit them appropriately, and design them into the documedium.

Graphics software will enable you to animate the text and images in ways that turn your collaborative effort into a process akin to shooting and editing a movie. The walls aren't just walls—they're readily accessible displays. The tables aren't tables—they're structures that invite collaborative interaction with models and maps as surely as a window invites you to look outside and see what's going on. Xerox's John Seely Brown, for example, can imagine "architects tightly grouped around a computational desk designed to help them share a common work space."

But those are just the passive elements of the technology. The rise of artificial-intelligence techniques will enable the appropriately programmed table to ask questions and provoke scenarios. For example, a collaborative effort to draft a financial budget might evoke

questions from the tablet: "Have you considered the internal rate of return?" "What if the key project is four weeks late?" "Why don't you format the four-dimensional spreadsheet in *this* way?"

Eventually, programs will be able to learn about the cognitive strengths and weaknesses of the people who use them and adjust themselves accordingly—sort of collaborative thermostats that heat up or cool down the analytical rhetoric when necessary. Admittedly, like Nelson's conversational cloud formations, this is a futuristic assessment of collaborative tools. Yet there is a solid technical core to these techno-visions.

Future conference rooms will bear only the faintest resemblance to today's. This super-conference room isn't just a conference room in the same way that a microwave oven isn't just a bunch of dried sticks and a match. Slide projectors, overhead projectors, and VCRs are wonderful tools for *presentation*—not *collaboration*. Conference rooms will evolve a technical infrastructure designed to support collaborative interaction—the active *sharing* of ideas, images, and thoughts rather than just their display. The room will be designed to augment the way teams interact with ideas—not just with individuals.

Picture a holographic projection of a new product—an automobile, a cereal package, a point-of-purchase display—in the center of a conference table that the participants can rotate, shrink, expand, detail, manipulate, modify, alter, stretch, and multiply according to whatever design criteria they desire. A tap on the keyboard, a spoken command, a conversation lead to side-by-side displays of various alternatives. Tap another key, and the group is literally inside the laser-generated product, viewing it from angles and perspectives that were previously inaccessible. This conference room turns an idea into a virtual reality. Indeed, the whole idea of virtual (or artificial) reality has spawned a movement in the computer hard/software domain dedicated to using technology as a simulacrum for possible worlds. Computer journalist Steve Ditlea compares the development of virtual reality to the evolution of the movies in turn-of-the-century Paris. "Two apparently opposite trends emerged then," he writes. "A realistic documentary bent, characterized by the Lumière brothers, who filmed scenes of everyday life; and an imaginative, fictional inclination, exemplified by Georges Méliès and his fancifully staged *Voyage to the Moon.*"

Fantastical imagery can expand our insights into reality. Virtual reality can help shape real reality. Some of the most advanced work in real-world virtual reality is going on in architecture at the University of North Carolina. As Ditlea describes it, "a deluxe system shows high-resolution depictions of floor plans and 3-D full-color interiors complete with real-time adjustment of the position of the sun and the ratio of direct/ambient light. To navigate through a virtual structure, you can use velocity-modulating joysticks (in what is called a helicopter metaphor), move a headmounted display (the eyeball metaphor), or, in the closest thing to being there, walk on a treadmill you steer by using handlebars (the shopping cart metaphor)."

Clearly, this virtual reality can be a powerful and empowering tool for architectural collaboration between architect, client, and contractor. Virtual realities shouldn't be—and won't be—solipsistic.

Collaborations and their environs will feel more like flying in a jet fighter cockpit simulator than sitting in a movie theater munching popcorn and making clever comments to your neighbor. Futuristic environments will change passive absorption into interactive creation.

At this sophisticated level of high-bandwidth interactivity, the term *collaborative tools* no longer adequately captures their real value: *collaborative environments* is more accurate. Use high-bandwidth satellite and fiber-optic telecommunications capacity to put those three-dimensional images in New York, London, and Tokyo simultaneously, and it's clear that this technology is designed to foster collaborative communities—not just networks. Distance becomes irrelevant. The ability to structure bandwidth becomes paramount. People can choose to collaborate in real time or to make their collaborative contributions off-line by annotating the texts or editing the screen and asking the others to comment on these changes at their convenience.

This is where the real value of collaborative interaction can reside. The shared creation of possibilities and perspectives empowers this global group to look at an opportunity in ways that were once impossible. What's more, these technologies are *designed* to encourage the cross-cultural shared creation of ideas and insights. The telephone is designed to be talked into; the radio is designed to be listened to; the personal computer is designed to be interacted with; these tools are designed to be shared collaboratively. These are the tools of collective creativity.

Consider: A movie consists of twenty-four frames of images that appear every second. These images are synchronized with a sound track to render a dynamic visual and acoustic experience for the viewer. But suppose you could only see one of those frames per second? What kind of experience would watching a movie be? The value of the movie doesn't live in the discrete collection of images, phonemes, and musical notes but in their seamless flow on the screen. What matters is the way these disparate media blend together to create an experience. That will prove equally true for collaborative tools and environments. This kind of flow isn't here yet, but it's coming.

As these technologies converge to create new collaborative environments, people will discover new modes of interaction, new styles of creativity and conversation, and a new desire to work with people to solve problems and craft innovations.

SOCIAL IMPLICATIONS

So what are the social implications of a technology designed to foster new levels of collaboration? What new metaphors will it generate? How will people—consciously and subconsciously—change the ways they communicate with others?

Will collaborative technologies bring about a new degree of socialization? Will new notions of collective creativity redefine the role of an individual in the group? Will they arouse dormant emotions or thought processes, create new standards of conversational literacy and professional intimacy? Might people even behave in ways alien to their own individuality? Will the new technologies become a glue that bonds people more tightly together than conventional media? Can they make people *feel* better and more productive about themselves and their work?

When Henry David Thoreau was told that the invention of the telephone would enable a gentleman in Maine to talk to a gentleman in Texas, he replied, "That's nice—but what will they have to talk about?" Thoreau's query was relevant for that moment, but it has been more than adequately answered in the fullness of time.

The past is the best prologue for exploring the future implications of collaborative technologies. The historian/philosophers such as Innis, McLuhan, and Mumford have exquisitely detailed the way new technologies have transformed the routines and expectations of everyday life.

The technical invention of the printing press, for instance, made the social invention of literacy inevitable. The rise of the printing press—making possible the mass production and distribution of the written word—transformed every aspect of culture (high and low), from the availability of the Bible to the creation of the novel to the transformation of scientific research. Samuel Morse's invention of the telegraph dramatically changed the role of print in conveying the news, which in turn linked people from different parts of the world in ways they had never anticipated. Of course, the telephone redefined conversation and radio sparked the emergence of a mass pop culture that, along some dimensions, rivaled print in influence. The airplane and automobile have completely redefined our perceptions of personal travel. The ultimate impact of television and computer technology has yet to be fully felt. Clearly, these technologies have all fundamentally changed the meanings and metaphors of popular culture.

It's clear then that a **successful technology reframes human experience.** Over time, collaborative technologies will reframe personal experiences and perspectives as dramatically as the clock changed society's perception of time and television reshaped the experience of entertainment. Collaborative technologies will dramatically enlarge our vocabularies of interaction and, most importantly, will evolve into something we all take for granted. Many of our most important relationships will be viewed through the prism of these evolving tools.

The ubiquity of the clock means that people define key aspects of their relationships as a function of time.

- What time is the appointment?
- Is this person on time?
- Why is he always ten minutes late?
- Sorry, our time is up.
- It's time to go.
- If we don't call her in ten minutes, it will be too late.

The technology of time has embedded a unique dimension in our culture. It's almost impossible to divorce the way people feel about and behave toward time from their feelings and behavior toward other people. In other words, the technology of time makes appointments—and the virtue of punctuality and the sin of lateness—possible.

Similarly, the telephone has reframed our perspectives and expectations about conversation. It's easy to forget that the telephone was once a novelty; in its earliest days, the Bell System thought of the telephone as strictly a business tool. In addition to being the keystone technology of a multibillion-dollar industry, the telephone is now the indispensable instrument of telecommunication. Intimate relationships are born and broken over the phone. The telephone has become one of the most vital and expressive media of interaction. Even the manner and mannerisms of its use send a signal.

- Why doesn't he call?
- Why is the line always busy?
- Should we call her and tell her?
- He should have called and canceled.
- What's the matter? He can't pick up a phone and call?
- Why doesn't she take my call?
- Why don't they return my call?
- Don't call us—we'll call you . . .
- Can I put you on hold?
- Mr. Smith is in a meeting—can I take a message?

The telephone's very existence and pervasiveness create a separate context that shapes the way people interact with one another. We're annoyed if we can't get somebody on the phone. We're grateful (or relieved) if somebody immediately returns our call. The tacit protocols of telephone use play an enormous role in determining how effective we are during the day.

Even the technology that surrounds the telephone has transformed our expectations of the medium. A few years ago, people were uncomfortable leaving messages on telephone answering machines. Nowadays, most people are annoyed if there's no machine on which to leave a message. There's no escaping the reality that the telephone frames a significant part of how we choose to relate to others and how they choose to relate to us.

Indeed, some people complain (rightly) that they aren't "good" over the phone. They can't articulate well; they need to look into someone's eyes; they need the added dimension of vision and touch. While this is all true, it's equally true that we often use an individual's ability to communicate on the phone as a yardstick against which to measure him. The artifact becomes a hoop that people are expected to jump through in order to meet our expectations. Whether we consciously think this or are only dimly aware of it, telecommunications technology has unquestionably become a factor in how we feel about people—including ourselves.

Collaborative technologies will raise new sorts of questions and feelings:

- Why doesn't he collaborate?
- Do I really want this relationship to be collaborative?
- Don't you think we should work this out in a shared space?
- I don't think they'd be good collaborators.
- Do you think we should collaborate with her?
- He has a lousy collaborative style.
- Do you think our tools can support this collaboration?
- Why is he hogging the tools?
- Collaborating with her is as easy as talking.
- This group sure knows how to collaborate around these tools.

- This is a lousy collaborative environment. Let's try another display.
- Are our styles of collaboration compatible?

Collaborative tools and environments will spark the same kinds of questions and concerns as other fundamental technologies, which will in turn determine the effectiveness of both individuals and enterprises. "Why won't he get out the good collaborative tools with me?" is a question not unlike "Why won't he talk with me on the phone?" or "Why doesn't he give me more time?" These are the questions that matter. The technology becomes a frame of reference and a new infrastructure for the way people relate to one another.

On the macro level—a societal level—collaborative tools must inevitably spawn a new etiquette and manners. Just as there are polite telephone rituals—"Hello. How are you?"—various forms of collaborative small talk will emerge. It's considered rude to put someone on hold for too long, and many people hate being put on the speakerphone; no doubt, new forms of collaborative rudeness will also evolve. Perhaps someone will use the technology out of turn or hog the shared space. What will be the collaborative counterpart of hanging up on someone or putting them on hold? Perhaps the taboo of collaborative interaction will be smashing a group model or injecting a computer virus into a shared screen. The point is that social technologies evoke new kinds of manners and emotions from their users. Collaborative technologies will be no exception.

New collaborative skills will evolve side by side with collaborative sensibilities. Just as there are gifted telephone conversationalists, talented blackboard sketchers, and superb memo writers, there will be people unusually adept at wielding collaborative tools. Their ability to lead others will be as much a function of their competence with these tools as any particular personal charms. Collaborative leaders will have a repertoire of techniques that can guide a group to a successful solution to a problem, draw out the latent talents of team members, and project an otherwise inaccessible vision onto the shared space.

Some of these talents may reflect an unusual charisma that only collaborative tools can amplify (like the individual who is lousy in person but magnificent over the phone) or just a grab bag of useful techniques that a sharp individual has strung together (the way a skilled hacker can get more out of a personal computer than a novice). As collaborative tools and environments assume greater prominence in an organization, the people who can use them effectively will also enjoy a higher profile. Those who are unable to work with the new technology will gradually pay a price in the same way people with lousy phone styles or the inability to write or speak do. Collaborative fluency will become as important an interpersonal skill as verbal fluency and literacy.

Like other artifacts of a technological age, collaborative tools will serve as yet another way to categorize and evaluate people. How well—and how poorly—people adapt to these tools will matter. For better and worse, collaborative technologies will give individuals and their organizations a new measure of one another.

People working with collaborative technology will become increasingly conscious of what collaboration really means. We will increasingly think of collaboration in the context of its technologies much as we now think of political campaigns in the context of their media coverage and travel in the context of airplanes and automobiles.

COLLABORATING ABOUT COLLABORATING

The design and implementation of collaborative tools changes at least three dimensions of personal interaction:

- the role of language,
- the task of modeling processes and ideas, and
- the perception of how others add value.

For the moment, consider these dimensional changes in the professional sphere. Whether designing a new product, discussing a new advertising campaign, or planning a budget, people will use their collaborative tools to build models of their thoughts. Because collaborative tools make conversation more visual and diagrammatic, they require a new level of conversational literacy. If the telephone renders mute someone who depends on body language to convey his real emotions, then collaborative tools might render the articulate egocentric mute as well.

Spoken language in everyday life will change. It will not become less important, but the new tools will redefine its role—just as clothes are important but the way you're dressed is irrelevant to the person at the other end of the phone. Collaborative tools shift the role of spoken language away from transmitting ideas toward the construction of meaningful models. Thus spoken language will increasingly be used to complement visual imagery and displayed text. The listeners' focus of attention shifts from the spoken word to the shared space. The brilliant conversationalist, the smoothly persuasive salesperson, the glib verbal tap dancer can no longer rely solely on the sound of his voice. That voice is now being processed in parallel to the shared space.

Likewise, the slick presentation that has all the facts and has touched all the bases and is bulletproof has become unsatisfying. Why? Because it doesn't invite collaboration. It doesn't encourage others to make a contribution, to add value. Collaborative tools, on the other hand, will encourage people to design presentations that invite further input and ideas, that beg improvement and closure from other parties. A major drawback to collaborative environments is that they create too much of a bias toward participation, even when it is unnecessary and inefficient. Another concern is that collaborative tools will have the same sort of dehumanizing effect on knowledge workers that automation has frequently had on factory workers.

But what if people aren't active collaborators? To what extent does the group then view them as parasites? Indeed, to what extent does this new technology make people view their colleagues as entities to be mined solely for their knowledge and ideas? In this sense, people simply become vehicles for exploitation: *If you're in a collaborative environment, how come you're not collaborating?*

In the same way that people involved in a collective effort would be resentful of those who don't contribute—or who don't return phone calls or respond to memos—the inability or unwillingness to use collaborative tools may evoke serious tensions between workers.

Conversely, the efficiency minded may choose to use collaborative tools as an excuse not to treat people as individuals but merely as a potential source of added value. On one level, that may be flattering to some individuals. On another level, it represents the classic problem that technology can be corrupted by people who would rather be more efficient than human.

The quantitative rise of collaboration will be the single most obvious impact of these new tools. It's no great leap of logic to believe that, when there are more cars, more people will drive. And when there are more media for collaboration, there will be more collaborating. What's more, many traditional interactions—like shooting the breeze—will eventually take on a collaborative flavor.

Brainstorming will likely be the organizational pastime most quickly transformed by collaborative tools. Most people regard brainstorming—the process of cramming disparate people into a room and forcing them to come up with new ideas—as a waste of time. The process is too random, too unstructured, and usually too unfocused to generate the sort of insights that matter. Computer-augmented meetings, on the other hand, are structured to improve brainstorming sessions. The new technology makes capturing, editing, and playing with fresh ideas relatively easy. There's almost no barrier of entry to a computer-augmented environment: whatever pops out of someone's mouth pops up on the screen. It's a simple task to print out the results of the brainstorming session as a community document and as group memory. Brainstorming experiments have shown that people enjoy—indeed, prefer—the process in the technologically supported collaborative environment.

No less important, however, will be the way ordinary individuals, not just professional groups, will get together to brainstorm. Instead of a phone call to shoot the breeze or just chat, people will drift into collaborative environments just to see what happens.

Collaborative tools will also change the way organizations draft documents, historically, the lifeblood of formal communications. Organizations, particularly corporations, are fueled by paper. Traditionally, one or two individuals have been given the task of drafting a report and then passing it around for revisions and comments. In addition to being extraordinarily time consuming (it is not unusual for significant reports in large organizations to take over six months from assignment to sign-off), the process is fraught with ambiguities and uncertainties. Over time, people's perceptions and memories change. Some factions pay more attention to the drafting of the report than others. Unwarranted politicization can creep in. What's more, people get sick of constantly seeing what was once a pressing matter drag on and on in a bureaucratic shuffle.

The Capture Lab experience at General Motors indicates that group documents can be put together in days, rather than months. Indeed, some facilitators say that group writing offers "the biggest bang for the buck" in the value of collaborative tools. This isn't propaganda; it's the empirical knowledge that the makers of collaborative tools have gained the hard way.

The implication is clear: both executives and middle managers will spend a greater portion of their time collaborating on documents deemed important to their organizations. Budgets, training procedures, strategic plans, quarterly reports, and other documents will increasingly be produced collaboratively in real time, not processed in long cycles of draft and revision.

The focus of collaborative technology shifts from *assigning* work to *doing* work. Shared understandings become more possible more quickly. Collaborative environments will give people in group meetings the incentive to produce something—anything—that can be displayed. The rise of collaborative environments should speed the cycle of document creation and the spread of new ideas. If the collaborative tools are handled well, the quality of ideas and information will improve.

Collaborative tools will not only transform collaboration within the organization but will offer new ways for organizations to relate to their outside constituencies. These technologies can effectively bring outside suppliers and customers in during the design cycle of new products and services. Indeed, collaborative tools will provoke the convergence of an organization's sales, marketing, and design divisions. Collaborative tools are equally certain to transform the sales cycle for everything from retail clothing to high technology equipment; the coordination and flow of vital information accelerates. Collaboration enables coordination.

As customers increasingly insist on products and services tailored to their special needs, how can organizations respond effectively? And how can a company best educate its customers about the novel products and services it offers? The answer rests in collaboratively created prototypes and products.

Shared space offers custom-tailored collaborations. In the past, a widget salesman would bring a widget, or a picture of a widget, to a potential client. Like Willie Loman with a shoeshine and a smile, the salesman would make his pitch with his prop. Maybe the client would ask a few questions, and then they'd haggle over price.

Collaborative sales tools completely transform the sales pitch. Instead of slapping a brochure on the client's desk, the widget salesperson slaps down a computer. A questionnaire flashes on the screen. The salesman skillfully asks questions and weaves the information into the questionnaire as the client responds. A profile of the client's needs is being built before his eyes. If the client wants to add a few comments or explain a few things in a bit more detail, the documedia questionnaire can expand accordingly.

Instead of getting a pitch, the client has worked with the salesman to paint a portrait of his needs. At this point, the salesman taps a few keys and there, on the screen, appears a beautifully crafted sketch of a custom widget designed exactly according to the specifications embodied in the completed questionnaire. The customer and salesman, by using a collaborative tool, have taken an important first step in selecting the best widget to meet the customer's needs.

The customer can now *see* the desired widget. It looks almost exactly like what he needs, except for one or two details. Part of it needs to be made a little larger. *How much? This much . . . no, that's too much . . . that's it exactly.* And it has to be a different color— gray. Another key is tapped. *Yes!*

The salesman uplinks from the computer to the home office to see if there are any widgets in inventory to match these new specs. There aren't, but the home-office computer indicates that these special widgets could be engineered, manufactured, and sent out within forty-eight hours if the customer orders a minimum of two hundred. No extra charge. The customer asks for a guarantee and a penalty clause for failure to deliver on time. The salesman keys the request in and it's approved. An invoice is drawn up then and there, and the order is uplinked immediately.

Clearly, turning a sales pitch into a computer-augmented collaborative exercise completely redefines the sales cycle. The potential for this technology exists in virtually every sales environment. What happens to the traditional roles of salesman and buyer in this new environment? Will customers come to insist upon collaboration? Will salesmen be able to tailor their pitches to take advantage of the technology? More explicitly, will salesmen trained to *sell* be able to *work* collaboratively with their clients? Would they really be selling anymore? Or would they really be performing another kind of service?

Similar questions emerge with regard to the design side of the industrial cycle. As mentioned earlier, many of the best industrial designers increasingly rely on customer input to help fashion the prototypes of their new products. Instead of designing *for* their clients, designers are now designing *with* their clients. Office furniture companies, like Steelcase for instance, bring in their largest customers to work with their ergonomists, chair designers, and interior-design people. Telecommunications companies work with their corporate clients to design office phone systems that make voice mail, call forwarding, and other local area network options easy to use. Even investment bankers are working closely with their clients to design new financial instruments that are custom tailored to meet the issuer's needs. Instead of going back to the drawing board alone, designers are bringing their clients back with them. Collaborative technologies offer a refined and inspiring infrastructure for the designer-client dialogue.

But collaborative tools shouldn't be confined solely to organizational domains. In a time when people are concerned about gaining better insights into themselves, it is likely that collaborative tools will become a foundation technology for therapists. Psychologists already use such vehicles as the Rorschach ink blot test and Minnesota Multiphasic Personality Inventory test to gain a better understanding of their subjects. Why not use computer-augmented shared spaces to create collaborative understandings between patient and therapist? What does such a session look like? Is it filled with words? Pictures? Does the shared space complement a session or does it become the focus of the session?

The emergence of collaborative environments may have a profound effect on traditional modes of psychological counseling. Therapists and their patients will have the chance to sharpen the focus of their discussions using collaborative technologies.

Similarly, marriage counselors often draw up lists of problems and opportunities for their clients. It would not be illogical for counselors to map these problems and opportunities for their couples in a computer-augmented shared space. Because the shared space can be neutral and cool, it can serve as a medium through which the couple can talk instead of shouting or arguing directly with each other.

With the appropriate software and user sensitivity, a shared space can be a vital environment in which people can come to shared understandings about their problems and challenges. These problems won't necessarily be solved more easily, but the media will help individuals to identify their problems more quickly and clearly.

Ultimately, predicting the future impact of collaborative environments is too much like predicting the impact of the telephone after "Watson! Come quickly! I need you!" or of the airplane after Kitty Hawk in 1903 or of the first ENIAC computer in 1946. The changes will be significant, but it's difficult to know either their direction or intensity.

It's fair to argue that more collaborative tools don't necessarily lead to better collaborations, much as the proliferation of word processors hasn't demonstrably improved the quality of writing. However, it's equally fair to point out that technologies like word processing are designed to reduce the physical labor associated with writing, not the cognitive labor. In contrast, collaborative media are designed explicitly to augment the quality of the interaction itself. Word processors don't change your vocabulary; effective collaborative media will.

From the history of collaboration, it's clear that any technology that reshapes collaboration will reshape the fields where collaboration is important. That means that business, science, and the arts will all undergo significant changes as these new media take hold.

Computer network and facsimile machines are already transforming collaboration in international science and business—and those technologies aren't even designed to augment collaboration. The best of all possible collaborative futures offers a world where people can enjoy and indulge their individuality even as they enhance and augment their communities.

The One-Minute Collaborator

You get to see yourself being heard.
BERNARD DeKOVEN

IN THE SPIRIT OF POP-MANAGEMENT BOOKS, THIS CHAPTER OFFERS a quick and dirty summary of how to create a computer-augmented collaborative tool that will make

- brainstorming sessions,
- new client meetings,
- project-management meetings,
- interdepartmental product-design efforts,
- marketing and advertising campaign discussions,
- technical reviews,
- strategic-planning sessions,
- sales presentations,
- contract negotiations,
- arbitration hearings,
- budget reviews,
- quality-circle meetings,
- cross-cultural discussions, and
- documentation-production sessions

more efficient, effective, and productive. Like paper, the technology can be extraordinarily flexible. It can be typed on, sketched on, drawn on, and calculated on. You can do practically everything with it you can do with paper—except fold it.

The best and easiest way to use the technology is for two or three people to go into a room and try to thrash things out informally. The technology makes a wonderful complement to ad hoc groups throwing themselves at a problem. The technology can work for larger and more formal groups as well if people take the right attitude.

QUESTIONS OF ATTITUDE

While blackboards, whiteboards, and overhead transparencies can be useful collaborative tools in their own right, even a crudely designed computer-based collaborative tool can instantly transform a meeting in impressive and useful ways. But to be successfully deployed, the technology can't be treated as just a gimmick or a quick fix. If it's treated like a gimmick, it will become one. The technology is so flexible and versatile that it can just as readily amplify the worst expectations as it can enhance the best.

So accept and respect the fact that this is *supposed* to be a different kind of meeting. Stress that the technology is designed to support collaborative efforts. If the purpose of the meeting is to *present* a lot of information or *persuade* people, then collaborative technology doesn't offer the best approach. But if the purpose of the meeting is to solve problems, explore new ideas, and create new information, then this technology does offer a useful platform for discussion.

The trick is having the willingness to go with the technology when it's helping the meeting flow and the ability to ignore it when it gets in the way. The technology should be treated as both a tool and an environment—something that can be both used and inhabited—but also as something to be kept in its place. Encourage participants to treat it as a medium with which to express themselves. Remember that you're not just using a collaborative tool—you're using tools to create a collaborative environment. You're trying to get people to share their best thoughts and insights with the group in a way that encourages everyone in the group to contribute their best thoughts and insights.

The key is to understand that you're not just having a meeting—you're creating a document. One cannot underestimate the importance of that distinction. It is the fundamental difference between ordinary meetings and computer-augmented collaborations and should be stated outright. Comments, questions, criticisms, insights, and the other discussion particulars should enhance the quality of that document. That should be the group's mission. Participants aren't just exchanging information—they're creating it.

PEOPLE

Numerous studies indicate that both efficiency and quality of decisions degrade when there are more than twelve people present at a meeting. While this is not a hard and fast rule, a meeting that has significantly more than a dozen people rarely enjoys a lively exchange that includes participation by all its members. Computer-augmented meetings suffer a decline in quality when too many people are stuffed into a room—not unlike the way a speakerphone conversation decays when there are more than three people on any end of the line. The technology can be overwhelmed by the weight of numbers.

ENVIRONMENT

Three important dimensions help shape the environment of the computer-augmented meeting: time, light, and layout. All three can have a tremendous impact on the quality of the collaboration.

TIME

While traditional meetings are supposed to run on a schedule, computer-augmented meetings invariably prove less linear and more time independent. The need to compartmentalize a meeting according to time and topic disappears when the technology enables easy access to the entire discussion. One of the main virtues of computer-augmented meetings is that nonlinear skipping from topic to topic is so easy—simply a matter of tapping the right keys. Linking disparate but relevant comments becomes a simple matter of routine, which is why one has to be careful about creating artificial boundaries of "We'll discuss this for fifteen minutes and that for twenty minutes."

In a computer-augmented meeting, time shouldn't be allocated on the *topic* but on the *process:* "We'll spend fifteen minutes establishing criteria; twenty-five minutes listing ideas; twenty minutes connecting them; and thirty minutes arguing about it." Time has a fundamentally different role in a computer-augmented meeting than in one with a more traditional structure. This emphasis on process forces people to pay as much attention to what they're doing as to what they're saying. Managing a computer-augmented meeting means managing the *process* of collaboration as well as the content.

Because of this, computer-augmented meetings consistently tend to run longer than traditional meetings. It takes more time for the process and the technology to fall into a mutually supportable rhythm. Where an ordinary brainstorming session might run for a little over an hour, a computer-augmented brainstorming session would probably run closer to two hours.

Similarly, because it is so easy to explore options and create links between people's comments, groups tend to spend more time exploring and discussing things. This adds to the length of the meeting. The good news is that these discussions tend not to be repetitive or redundant. The bad news is that the meetings do become longer—often significantly so. This is one of the significant trade-offs to be considered when using these collaborative tools. Placing a strict time limit on the meetings will likely frustrate the participants. Listing and linking ideas and comments takes more time. The computer-augmented environment encourages people to discuss things a little more thoroughly than they might otherwise.

Consequently, people planning computer-augmented meetings need to be very wary about the time allocated for the meeting, both the total length of the meeting and the amount of time budgeted for each process. Participants should be aware of these allocations at the beginning.

LIGHT

The amount of light plays a subtle but important role in shaping the texture of collaborative interactions. No one would think of conducting an ordinary business meeting in the dark. Conversely, too much light can vitiate a movie, a slide show, or many other technology-driven presentations. Each medium has its appropriate level of illumination.

With computer-augmented collaborative tools, modulating the light can modulate the interaction. If the room is very dark, the group's attention turns to the sole source of light—the computer screen. People tend to speak directly to (or through) the screen. There are fewer interpersonal dialogues as people focus on what the screen is doing. The darker the room, the more power the screen has over the conversation.

Conversely, in a comparatively bright room, the shared space screen becomes more of a backdrop, a complement to the meeting rather than its focus. These meetings tend to be more like traditional meetings with people talking directly to one another and the screen being relegated to a useful reference device.

In the chiaroscuro ranges—dimly to barely lit meeting rooms—one sees an intriguing mixture of screen focus and interpersonal interaction. As people speak, some of the group look to the screen and the rest look to the speaker. There is a tacit competition between the screen and the individual. The group's attention constantly swings back and forth between the screen and the speakers. In the light, the conversation is more people focused. In the dark, the conversation is more task focused.

Meeting planners should be willing to experiment with the lighting and learn how different groups respond to different levels. No doubt some collaborations work best in bright light while others will do their best work in the dark. In the computer-augmented collaborative environment, light can be a productivity tool and should be treated as such.

LAYOUT

The layout of a collaborative environment should let the technology easily complement the collaboration. The design should be unobtrusive; the computer screens should be an integrated part of the environment, not an intrusion. Ideally, the computer screen becomes a window/mirror that people like to look into as they work together.

The best physical layout for a computer-augmented meeting consists of a shared screen/display at the focal point of a semicircular table. The seats around the table should afford easy line-of-sight access to all the participants as well as the screen. The second best configuration is a round or oval table with the screen perched in clear and easy view of all the participants.

Avoid having people seated at a table shoulder to shoulder and facing a screen as if in an interrogation. It's awkward, inhibits any chance of natural conversation, and physically subordinates the people to the technology, which is always a mistake.

PROCESSES

RUNNING THE MEETING

As a general rule, the group leader should only be the technographer if he or she is prepared to be seen as completely controlling the meeting. When the leader directly controls access to the shared space, it tends to inhibit contributions. The leader essentially becomes judge, jury, and court stenographer all in one. That's intimidating. What's more, the task of technographer is demanding enough. The concentration necessary to put the conversation into shared space inherently conflicts with the focus necessary to lead the meeting. The technographic task should be delegated. If the group leader has a clear understanding with the technographer, this should in no way dilute the leader's ability to run the meeting as he or she sees fit.

There are two real options for technography:

1. Assign someone who is fluent with the computer and the discussion area to be the technographer. This individual is responsible for tracking the flow of the conversations and mapping it onscreen. The key question here is whether

this individual should also be a meeting participant. Is it a good idea for the conversational gatekeeper to put in their two cents worth? Obviously, there is an inherent conflict of interest here. Some individuals will be frustrated if they can't participate in the conversation, but the rest of the group might resent the technographer taking advantage of his role to shape the material that appears on the screen. There is no simple resolution to this problem.

2. Use rotating scribes. The idea is that people take turns at the keyboard depending upon what they have to say or contribute. This works particularly well in small groups where all the participants are fairly adept at using the computer. (This "my turn to drive!" approach is ideal for two-party collaborations.) This method works less well when part of the group is uncomfortable at the keyboard or doesn't know how to use the software.

What frequently happens in these cases is that the technographer role falls into the hands of a couple of people who swap the keyboard between themselves. Occasionally, people who aren't rapid typists and software jockeys take the controls. This can be a bit frustrating but no more so than when slow speakers or stutterers participate in a meeting or when people with illegible handwriting start marking up the blackboard.

Whether one goes with a dedicated scribe or rotating scribes, it should be made crystal clear from the beginning that the technographer must always make a best-faith effort to record accurately what people say when they are saying it. The technographer may seek guidance, advice, and clarification from the group, he may not put his own spin on what's been said. That undermines the whole process.

BRAINSTORMING

Computer-augmented collaborative environments are ideal for brainstorming. They are flexible, forgiving, inviting, and they create opportunities to link ideas in unusual ways and to let people see what they've said.

The approach suggested here blends brainstorming techniques that have worked for David Braunschvig, Robert Fulop, and Bernard DeKoven, who have collectively facilitated hundreds of idea-generating sessions.

First and foremost, people who come to the computer-augmented collaborative brainstorming session should know that the purpose of the session is to generate ideas. Don't dilute the session by dragging in extraneous topics such as personnel or organizational management concerns.

There are several stages in a successful brainstorming session:

Criteria. Before brainstorming, the group should list the criteria it deems important to measure the merit of the ideas.

For a new product, these criteria might include

- cost,
- manufacturability,
- aesthetics, and
- schedule.

For a new advertising campaign, these criteria might include

- budget,
- media,
- humor, and
- client concerns.

This part of the session serves two functions. It makes people aware that there are real-world constraints and disciplines for their ideas, and it creates a checklist that can be useful in testing the validity of the ideas the brainstorming session spews up.

After listing and recording these criteria, blank the screen.

Collect. In this next phase of the session, which might last for thirty minutes, the group should list all the ideas they can think of.

Invite people to spit out their ideas. Anything goes. People can say whatever they want and whatever they think is relevant. The technographer duly records what's being said.

People can talk a bit about the ideas, but the leader shouldn't permit any formal discussions about them. The purpose of this process is simply to gather ideas and get people into a rhythm of contribution. The leader should be doing everything he can to encourage people to participate. The fact that a lot of these contributions are non sequiturs is irrelevant. They'll all be recorded.

Obviously, if people are still going strong after thirty minutes, extend the time for collection. But if things have begun to wind down or if the ideas are sounding increasingly redundant, draw this part of the process to a close.

At the end of this part, scroll up and down through the list a few times and encourage people to make sure that everything has been recorded accurately. This gives people visual reinforcement that their ideas are all there waiting to be explored.

Connect. At this point, the leader encourages the group to establish links and connections between all the ideas. Clearly, many will overlap. The roles of the leader, technographer, and the group will be to rearrange and cluster these ideas appropriately.

People should be talking about why these ideas have things in common and look for the themes and patterns that make a category. The actual merits of these ideas and categories still shouldn't be actively discussed. This part of the process should impose a sense of order and discipline on the ideas that have been spilled on-screen. The discussion should focus on the hows and whys of clustering the ideas rather than whether or not the cluster itself is a good idea.

By carefully connecting, grouping, and editing, the screen will begin to display an outline structure or a map of the various idea clusters. People will be able to see how these clusters relate to one another.

At this point, DeKoven believes it's a good idea for the technographer to print out this new outline of ideas, hand a copy to each participant, and take a break. That gives people a change of pace and a chance to look at what they've done. (Of course, this is only an option. The group may decide to plunge ahead.)

Correct. This is the final—and usually the most tumultuous—phase of the computer-augmented brainstorming process. This is where people should discuss and argue the merits of their ideas. This is also the point where you'll want to call up the original list of criteria to test against the idea clusters to see if they still pass muster.

Obviously, some ideas may prove impractical, and some of the original criteria listed may now seem less relevant. The point is that this checklist creates an immediate basis from which to discuss the merits of these ideas.

The role of the leader here is to make sure that everybody participates in expanding, modifying, altering, and exploring these clusters. Now is the time to extract the pros and cons for all these new ideas. This can be done by splitting the screen in half vertically and listing pro comments on one side and the con comments on the other. With the right software, you can further refine the pro and con lists by annotating them.

The idea is to push the group to constantly refine and polish the on-screen ideas and to look for ways to add value to them by reordering, restructuring, and commenting on them. Treat the document like a living, dynamic creation instead of a static presentation. Spatial representations of information can be as important as the words themselves.

Voting/Ranking. Some groups like the idea of being able to vote on or rank their ideas. One obvious way to do this is to use software that has a ranking/weighting function that lets people register their degree of enthusiasm or disenchantment. This can be an extremely good way to take the group's temperature. This technology, however, requires people to disclose their preferences openly. Technology exists that lets people vote privately.

Printout. By far the most important tangible product of computer-augmented meetings is the printout. The ability of a meeting to actually manufacture a document is key to the belief that the group's work is anything but ephemeral. The printout serves as a reference document, a part of the group's memory, a plan, and a tool that lays the groundwork for future collaborations and group efforts.

As a rule, it is vital to get the document printed out, photocopied, and distributed before the meeting participants leave. The fact that these people get to go back to their offices with hard copy—something they can show their colleagues, coworkers, and bosses—is an absolutely fundamental change in the whole brainstorming process. These minutes can be an antidote to the perception that meetings are a waste of time and produce nothing. What's more, the document serves as a way to create shared understandings with those who weren't at the meeting.

In fact, if a session isn't going to generate a document that can be shown to relevant third parties, then perhaps the meeting shouldn't be computer augmented. Indeed, if brainstorming can't generate a document worth distributing, perhaps it's not a meeting worth holding. One global consulting firm, however, took a different tack. The meeting was recorded on Lotus Notes—and then pasted on the firm's global Notes network. No hard copy—but the brainstorming was instantly transformed into a firmwide computer bulletin board open for public inspection and comment.

It's not unfair to recall the cliché that "a camel is a horse designed by a committee." Computer-augmented brainstorming may indeed prove to be a way to build bigger and better camels. When these tools are used properly, however, they increase the chances of designing out the humps. For example, the checklist can exert a discipline on the creative process. Similarly, participants can—if they choose—see how much they are gold plating ideas or drifting into self-indulgence. The point is that the computer-augmented environments greatly improve the odds for successful brainstorming sessions. Instead of just tossing out ideas for consideration, the shared space of the computer screen offers a medium where the best ideas can grow.

AGENDAS

The brainstorming begins with a blank screen. It's just as easy to begin with an agenda.

Of course, every single book and guide about meetings stresses the importance of agendas. In the real world, agendas are about as rare as the white rhino and about as useful. Frequently, by the time the meeting gets held, key items on the agenda have been superseded by events. Who hasn't been in meetings where someone spends a lot of time trying to prove that the agenda isn't appropriate?

That's the beauty of the computer-augmented environment. An agenda can be prepared in advance and displayed for all to see. Then, if circumstances require, it can be updated, modified, enhanced, or improved. Even if the people walking into the room haven't bothered to glance at the agenda beforehand, they get to see what will be discussed.

Participants should bring to these agenda-driven meetings an understanding that they will treat the agenda like a spine and grow muscle, sinew, and flesh around it.

There are a variety of ways to focus the discussion. The agenda can be treated as individual items to be handled separately or as a coherent whole that will be amended and annotated. Each approach stimulates a different texture of discussion. The former yields very focused conversations; the latter finds people constantly trying to tie one part of the discussion to other parts of the agenda. The group or the group leader has to decide which approach is best.

Within the framework of the agenda, the "collect, connect, and correct" process works exceedingly well. However, the more explicit the agenda items, the more they become constraints and the less of a brainstorming session the meeting becomes.

GROUP WRITING

Writing a short story or a novel is not the optimal way to use a computer-augmented environment. But when groups have to come up with mission statements, reports, or documentation, the computer-augmented environment is ideal. In this mode, documents are less created than assembled collectively.

It's best not to begin a group writing session with a blank screen. Experience dictates that an outline or actual draft of the document offer the best jumping-off point. Indeed, the practice seems most successful when it resembles group editing more than group writing.

The downside is that this is an extremely time-consuming method. The good news is that organizations—such as GM and McKinsey & Company—have discovered that they can get an awful lot done in a comparatively short period of time because people don't need to spend weeks revising drafts. The key to the success of this approach is to make sure that the right people are in the room when the document is drafted—or that the right people can quickly review the draft the group generates. A classic example of this is lawyers working out the details of a contract.

BUDGET

While text is the medium of reports, spreadsheets are the medium of budgets. Computer-augmented environments are ideal for budget reviews. Displaying a spreadsheet to a group and then changing the budget assumptions and outcomes interactively is an enormously effective way to convey the financial dynamics of a project.

The strength of this approach is that with split-screen capability, it is easy to compare various budget projections. What's more, one can simultaneously annotate the spreadsheet with comments explaining extraordinary situations or exploring key budget assumptions in depth.

Using the spreadsheet as a conversational template creates a different conversation than collaborations around a text. There are a lot more what-if questions and significant playing with assumptions.

Inevitably, the discussions grow most heated around the key assumptions used to generate the spreadsheet projections. The virtue of this is that the group becomes keenly aware of just what the spreadsheet is taking for granted. The downside is that these discussions are often so heated that the portion of the group that loses out insists on appending a minority dissent to the final budget document. Very few budget arguments using this technology, it seems, end up achieving a consensus.

PROJECT SCHEDULES

In the same way that the spreadsheet is a good collaborative template for budgets, project-management/calendar software is a superb template for collaborating on project schedules.

Instead of beginning with a blank screen, the people in this meeting begin with a calendar/scheduler and discuss realistic target dates, map them out, and comment publicly on what it takes to hit the milestones.

One key aspect of these meetings is that people become aware of just how interdependent they are. The shared screen clearly delineates critical paths for projects, and this often encourages people to communicate with one another in greater detail than they had in the past. People figure out ways to work together to shave time off the project or add additional value at key steps.

The software lets people isolate critical junctures in the schedule or look at the schedule as a whole. What's more, it becomes easy to play what-if scenarios and see how a missed day or two will affect the entire project.

Another virtue of this approach is that people can make contingency plans for unanticipated events or expected slippage. This makes people feel even more comfortable about completing the project because they feel as if even the unexpected is being taken into consideration.

For all intents and purposes, the group is simulating the process of completing the project. This injects a scheduling discipline that simply talking about the project can't achieve. The shared space makes public all the key assumptions—and fears—associated with getting the work done on time. Indeed, the discussion quickly shifts from the hypothetical scenario to the concrete.

However, one of the major drawbacks to this collaborative approach to project management is that many people are reluctant to commit publicly to a schedule in front of their bosses and their peers. The public aspect of signing off on a document that will become part of the project record can be very unpalatable. Nevertheless, if the right people are in the room, no one can leave one of these meetings more confused than when they went in.

NEGOTIATION

For a contract negotiation or an arbitration, the shared space can be an excellent tool to list the areas of agreement, disagreement, and solutions for several parties.

It is best if negotiators rely on an impartial facilitator to draw out and map on the screen these areas of agreement and disagreement. Splitting the screen is one way to delineate these areas. But there are other ways that the shared space can be used to augment the negotiation. For example, the participants can weight their feelings on proposed options or positions they have, using scales like these:

> **Like....../ ..../ ..../ ..../ ....Dislike**
> **Fair.........../ ..../ ..../ ..../ ..../ ....Unfair**

These semantic differential techniques offer an easy way to draw out the positions of the parties. Obviously, if they feel equally strong about every point, they either aren't particularly rational or are playing games. These tools can help flush out the games.

What's more, depending upon how adeptly the facilitator handles the negotiations, the output is a document that both sides believe fairly represents their positions. The document can be printed out then and there.

SALES PITCH

Salespeople who are interested in collaborating with their customers instead of just pitching them might explore portable computer-augmented media.

As mentioned earlier, instead of presenting a sales pitch, a salesperson using a portable computer with a large display screen would encourage the prospect to describe his preferences. Presumably, the salesperson would have a sales template displayed on-screen that detailed how the customer could customize the product and the order to fit his needs.

The idea is that the salesperson would gain insight into the customer's priorities and the customer would learn just how the salesperson's product could be tailored. In essence, the technology makes it easier for the salesperson and the client to create a shared understanding, not just complete a sale. Both the salesperson and the client come away knowing more about their own needs, not to mention each other's.

Clearly, computer-augmented environments for collaboration can be both a medium for compromise and a medium for creation. There is a real risk of homogenizing all the disparate points of view into a porridge document that has substance but no flavor. And yet we all run these same risks when we pick up the phone, read a memo, or go to a meeting. This technology isn't a panacea, but it's not a placebo either. It creates environments where the design and constraints encourage people to add their individual spice to a group collaboration.

TECHNOLOGY

The decision as to what technology to use depends entirely on the purpose of the meeting. That can best be determined, says Rob Fulop, who has conducted scores of these collaborations, by answering the question, *"What is the takeaway from the meeting?"* That answer will suggest the appropriate software that will, in turn, dictate the appropriate hardware.

For graphic flexibility and the ease of shifting from application to application, Apple's Macintosh computer is a superb machine to augment meetings and small group collaborations.

Microsoft's Windows system for personal computers promises to make data and applications transport significantly easier.

Whichever platform one chooses, a skilled operator of the software is obviously necessary. The meeting leader should also have a grasp of what the software can or cannot do—even if he or she is not personally a "power user." Also, a laser printer is the best device to generate the hardcopy minutes/transcripts/summaries of the meeting. One cannot overstress the importance of a concrete product as both a tangible result and a mechanism to focus the group's attention and concerns.

DISPLAY

For meetings of two to four people, it is not usually necessary to use a screen projector. For groups larger than five, a projector to enlarge the shared space of the screen becomes important. The Limelight projector works very well. Similarly, there are a number of "data pads" that link the computer screen to an overhead projector —the pad is laid on the projector as if it were an ordinary transparency. Kodak's Datashow light pad is one example of such a product. However, these technologies are constantly changing and *Presentation Products* magazine continuously reviews screen projectors at all levels of quality. It might be advisable to rent this gear for the first three or four meetings until you feel comfortable with lighting levels, ease of setup, and performance.

Obviously, questions about whether to set up formal meeting rooms armored with this technology or simply create a flexible set of technologies that can turn any office into a computer-augmented meetings environment is a matter of choice, aspirations and budget.

Design for Collaboration

ORGANIZATIONS THAT CARE ABOUT CREATING EFFECTIVE COLLABO-
rations have to begin with an honest answer to a straightforward
question: Are you framing the problem/opportunity in a way that
incites and encourages collaboration?

DESIGN FOR COLLABORATION

The Big Problems—figuring out how to build a heavier-than-air
flying machine, discovering the secret structure of life itself, curing
AIDS—are inherently so inspiring that people will do whatever is
necessary to participate in their solution. Like a powerful magnetic
field or a cognitive pheromone, a Big Problem draws talented people to it and forces them to subordinate their egos to the challenge
at hand. Nothing builds creative community faster than a Big Problem. That's why monumental egotists like Picasso, Watson, Crick,
Heisenberg, and Pauli were all willing to enlist in the enterprise of
collaboration.

Not all problems are Big Problems, but every problem can be
framed in a way that increases its appeal. Wilbur and Orville Wright
wanted to build the first heavier-than-air flying machine. Braque
and Picasso collaborated to create a new perspective in visual art.
The quantum physicists struggled to capture the essences of matter
and energy. Watson and Crick were racing to discover the secret
structure of life itself. These are unambiguous Big Problems. They
matter.

Consequently, they inspire mutual creativity and make it easier for talented individuals to subordinate their egos to the challenge at hand. These are the kinds of problems that invite the sharing of ideas, intense conversations, and the playful co-creation of models and prototypes. Like a powerful magnetic field or a cognitive pheromone, these problems inherently get people to align themselves collaboratively to the task. They build creative community. In effect, these problems make collaboration make sense. To be sure, creative collaboration isn't the only option but—given the enormity of the challenge—it seems to be the best option.

The single most important issue confronting the leadership of collaborative organizations, then, is how to pose problems and opportunities in forms that will elicit and inspire a collaborative response.

Unfortunately, most leader/managers are extraordinarily lazy and shortsighted when it comes to the creative framing of organizational challenges. Where's the incentive to collaborate in a management challenge to cut the budget by 15 percent in twelve months? Where's the collaborative challenge in reorganizing to slash the head count by 20 percent? What new insights need to be co-created here? What vital information must be shared to accomplish these feats? Rather than inspire collaboration, these challenges seem deliberately designed to provoke the sort of political infighting and parochialism that explicitly dictate against collaboration. That's leadership? That's management?

Yet that is what organizations call for even as they bleat about the importance of "teamwork" and "our people are our most important resource." Putting aside the blatant hypocrisy, the point here is that we can't realistically expect people to collaborate if we thrust them into situations where collaboration is likely to be inimical to their interests. A Churchill can ask a nation to sacrifice for a greater good; a corporation can ask its employees to tighten their belts to better cope with difficult times—but unless the challenge is framed in such a way that it makes more sense to collaborate than to go at it alone, where is the leadership? Where is the vision? Where is the sense of a collective future?

Rather than seek a bean counter's 15 percent cut in costs, management might challenge employees to come up with ways for the organization to reduce waste or scrap. This has worked very well in the context of Japan's Quality Circles, where the goal was never an explicit cost target but rather the relentless *kaizen* of ongoing process improvement. Similarly, instead of asking a new product team to boost a product's performance level by, say, a third, why not ask them to redesign the product using a particular new computer-aided design system or a new material?

The issue is not one of ridding management of quantitative goals; on the contrary, numerical targets frequently inspire tremendous collaborative efforts. The issue really is: Are we designing problems —are we creating challenges—that invite people from different parts of the organization to collaborate and share in ways that they haven't before?

If we are not, then we are failing in our essential responsibilities as managers and leaders. Our lack of ingenuity and creativity—our lack of leadership initiative—makes the collaborative creation of value just that much more difficult. Now, perhaps, the task at hand isn't one that really demands a great deal of collaboration. If that's the case, let's have the decency and honesty not to trumpet the importance of collaboration in getting that job done. But if we genuinely believe that a complex problem or a unique opportunity requires a collaborative approach, let's have the courage and integrity to put it before the organization in a way that will make people immediately recognize that collaboration is the best way to go.

Warning: Collaboration often falls victim to organizational politics. The surest sign of this is when managers start talking about collaboration in the context of "buy-in"—that is, the idea that managers go around the organization and seek support—or buying in— for their initiatives and call it collaboration.

In reality, that's using collaboration as a false front for coalition building and alliance forging. *If we get Marketing to buy in to this, then we can go to Manufacturing and they won't be able to reject us without going to the executive VP.* While it is undeniably true that "collaboration" has a rich history in politics (see Quisling and Vichy France), the risk an organization runs by falsifying the concept is that *collaboration* is transformed from a word linked to the creation of value to a word used to describe internal politicking.

In effect, collaboration comes to be seen as a political tool rather than a genuine approach to encourage new kinds of creative relationships. It is, of course, naive to believe one can divorce value creation from organizational politics. But by the same token, it is even more cynical and dishonest to promote collaboration as something it's not. That breeds the kind of cynicism and dishonesty that undermines collaborative culture.

DELEGATION VS. COLLABORATION

Framing the collaborative challenge is only the first essential step to promoting collaborative interactions. Managers have to grasp that managing for collaboration demands nontraditional responses to complexity. Typically, one of the best compliments a manager can hear during a review is that he or she is a "good delegator." Indeed, most managers are evaluated by how well they delegate tasks to their subordinates in the face of a complex problem. The instinctive reaction to confronting complexity—a reaction that is intellectually reinforced by prestigious business schools on both coasts—is to crack that complexity into its component parts and parcel them out to the appropriate individuals or "teams." The task of reassembling —or synthesizing—those pieces into an integrated solution is thus left to the manager. What usually happens, of course, is that these pieces don't fit and that the manager ends up redelegating the tasks all over again. In essence, managers are designing their problems for delegation, not collaboration.

Designing for delegation and designing for collaboration are simply two different tasks. Instead of asking "How can we break down the complexity into more manageable parts?" managers must ask themselves, "What kind of relationships and interactions can we create around this problem to solve it?" Think in terms of managing the complexity of the opportunity through relationships rather than the deconstruction of the problem.

To be sure, the two are not mutually exclusive: one can simplify a problem in a manner that respects the collaborators who will ultimately tackle it. Of course, the most talented managers know their personnel well enough to know what kind of collaborative delegation makes sense. They intrinsically know how to strike the appropriate balance. But the thrust of the collaborative organization must be to recognize that the traditional model of delegation—whether to individuals, departments, or teams—fundamentally misses the point. Just as problems must be framed to invite collaboration, managers and their workers must crack those problems into chunks that respect the collaborative challenge. Traditional delegation merely leaves us with the pieces of the puzzle; the task of putting them all together—the task of integration—is too frequently defined as "we solved our piece; that's *their* problem." Or the manager's problem.

Designing for collaboration means just that: managers must champion collaboration as a value that must be respected throughout the entire value-creating process.

DESIGNING COLLABORATIVE TEAMS

At this point, an interesting array of organizational design options presents itself. Should the organization simply assign people to collaborate on the problem/opportunity? Should the organization state the problem/opportunity to be addressed and wait for people to enlist? Or should there be one or two core people who go out and recruit the collaborative team for the task? Or should the organization count on bottom-up collaborations to set the direction for the firm?

Many companies offer a mixture of these approaches. At a company like 3M, for example, bottom-up collaborations have traditionally been engines for innovation. Indeed, 3M explicitly encourages bottom-up innovations from its technical ranks. The story of Post-it notes offers the classic 3M paradigm/parable for bottom-up collaboration. Two 3M technologists—one with a need for a hymnal bookmark and the other a polymer chemist with a tacky adhesive—collaborated to create sticky yellow pads that transformed the office. There were no grand strategic plans or McKinsey & Company consulting reports to launch a line of sticky paper.

At the same time, the Minneapolis-St. Paul–based global giant also outlines market themes of interest and encourages interested people to enlist in the effort. 3M takes the C. K. Prahalad and Gary Hamel concepts of "core competencies" quite seriously. "Adhesives" and "abrasives," for example, are considered to be among 3M core competencies. Consequently, the company organizes top-down teams to identify new markets to better apply those competencies. 3M is a company that has committed to both top-down and bottom-up collaborative initiatives.

Tracy Kidder's book *The Soul of a New Machine* offers an excellent example of how Data General (then a major competitor in minicomputers) used a charismatic technical leader to recruit a crack team from across the company for a special development project. That same approach was used by Ford in the development of the Taurus and by Chrysler in its recent development of the Neon.

Of course, most companies simply assign people to teams and expect those selected to be ready, willing, and able to collaborate. The belief is that any group of people within the organization can be assembled into a team where the whole is greater than the sum of the parts. If top management knows its people well, that belief may well be justified.

It's often impossible to know whether the "top-down" or "bottom-up" or "middle-down and across" approach is most appropriate. However, the issue of how collaborative teams are designed will likely prove to be one of the most significant management challenges for organizations over the next decade. Which approach is most compatible with the culture of the organization? Which approach makes the most sense for the tasks at hand? Reconciling those conflicts will be integral to creating productive collaborative environments. The design of collaborative teams may be the key to creating and sustaining the core competencies that provide a competitive edge.

COLLABORATIVE RULES/HEURISTICS

But how can an individual or a work group be confident that they are effectively collaborating? The following is a set of questions and guidelines to check.

WHERE'S THE SHARED SPACE?

The first question that has to be asked is *Where's the Shared Space?* If there isn't some sort of shared space—if there isn't a clear, explicit place where individuals can jointly create value—a yellow pad, a white board, a computer screen, a prototype, etc.—then the chances are you aren't collaborating. In much the same way, if you are in a room with no tables, nothing to drink, and nothing to eat, you probably aren't having lunch. It takes shared space to create shared understandings. Yes, collaboration begins with a problem to be solved or an opportunity to be addressed, but the act of collaboration begins within a shared space.

BUILD MODELS

Collaboration is literally an act of co-creation. Building models, mock-ups, prototypes, etc., together—either within the shared space or *as* the shared space—is at the heart of creative collaboration.

How many experiments did Watson and Crick perform on the way to discovering the double helix? The answer is absolutely *none!* Drawing primarily on chemical and crystallographic data generated by others, Watson and Crick did little but talk and build metal models of helices. Single helices, double helices, triple helices—the point is that their collaboration was in large part managed by the models that they built. This is true for virtually all effective collaborations. To be sure, they had a sophisticated grasp of the data they were modeling, but the key to their success was their ability to collaboratively transform the data into tangible models that made sense.

What is being built? How is it being built? Who is collaborating to build it? From physics to molecular biology to aviation to software development—any knowledge-intensive endeavor—these are the questions constantly being asked. We see endless streams of model building and experimentation. The collaborative community is *always* a model-building community.

WHEN IN DOUBT, BUILD ANOTHER MODEL!

The message here is not simply to build many iterations of the model but to recognize that variety can be an essential spice of collaboration. The unfortunate trap most organizations fall into, however, is the notion that there is a model that is the right way—the only way—to go. In other words, they marry themselves to a monopoly model.

A classic example of this was Detroit's historic infatuation with clay models for automobile design. Those intricate, elaborate, and expensive clay models sculpted by America's Big Three body designers didn't readily lend themselves to easy modification or rapid iteration. Quite the contrary: the efforts required to craft them made them more like untouchable works of art than malleable platforms for creative interaction. "American automobile companies didn't have an iterative culture," observes industrial designer David Kelley. "Clay . . . was like God's tablets. . . . It just didn't integrate with the functional side."

"As the model-making material changes, the design process changes," says industrial designer Michael Barry. For example, "Hewlett-Packard used to do its calculator modeling in cardboard, which explained why all their calculators featured angles and edges. When the company switched to foam, you saw calculators that had a softer and more rounded look. . . . Foam lends itself to certain kinds of subtleties."

Similarly, software prototyped in one computer language requires different thought processes than does that same software modeled in another. Videotaping a performance yields a different aesthetic than does filming it. Computer sketches are palpably different from sketches drawn by hand.

The diversity and mix of models—as well as the development budgets associated with them—could be said to represent the organization's prototype "portfolio." Just as an investment portfolio reveals the risk/reward equation that reveals the investor's expectations, the model portfolio yields insight into the organization's own innovation/market expectations. Models are as much media for managing risks as for exploring opportunities. They can be treated as an insurance policy or as an option on the future. That's why a collaborative organization facing doubt or uncertainty should build another model.

INVENT WORDS

Charms, gluons, quarks, muons, introns, exons . . . Before physicists and molecular biologists invented these words, they didn't really exist. Once they were introduced—and the validity of the ideas that sparked them was demonstrated—everyone in the field began using them.

One of the surest signs that innovation and change are going on is the emergence of new vocabulary to describe them. Indeed, one of the surest signs an organization has that a new idea is catching on is that it starts hearing the words used to describe the idea coming back to the people who introduced it in the first place. There is power in words. There is influence in managing the vocabulary of the organization.

One of the quickest ways to create a collaborative community is to create its own language. Hospitals have their own vocabularies; so do airline cockpits and other communities of expert practice. The risk, of course, is that this vocabulary degenerates into obscurantist jargon, that it becomes a mechanism to exclude rather than a medium to communicate ideas. But with that risk in mind, one of the smartest things a collaborative team can do to generate excitement and curiosity is to create a few good, colorful, and descriptive phrases to capture the innovations they're creating and the problems they're solving.

USE LANGUAGE TO CREATE MODELS
USE MODELS TO CREATE LANGUAGE

Let's not divorce new words from shared space. Just as language can inspire people to build new models and representations, models can encourage new forms of expression. For example, industrial designer David Kelley recalls designing a toothpaste tube prototype for a giant consumer products company. One of the questions the prototype had to answer was what level of "suckback" the tube provided. Suckback, of course, is the way the tube "sucks back" the toothpaste after the user stops squeezing it. Prototyping enabled both designer and client to create a vocabulary to calibrate the desired level of suckback.

This is a cutesy—but illustrative—example of how language creation and model building can be mutually reinforcing parts of a creative collaboration. The words are essential to describing the phenomenon; the model is essential to giving meaningful context to the language.

Successful collaborators are always on the lookout for ways to connect their model-building collaborations with their creative vocabulary. They build meaning via models, via language, and via the vital relationship between them.

CHANGE THE SCENERY

A Shakespearean sonnet read by candlelight feels different than one read in the harsh glare of fluorescent illumination. The rhymes and meter may be exactly the same, but the poetic experience is probably not.

Similarly, the shared space at the office that everyone goes to every day will evoke different conversations than will a shared space nestled in a mountain retreat. The issues and images may be precisely the same, but the collaborative experience around and within the shared space most probably is not.

There is a reason why most successful collaborative communities collaborate over a wide range of both formal and informal environments. Different environments offer literally different perspectives on both the shared spaces and the people who contribute to them.

The quantum physicists went sailing and mountain climbing together not just because they enjoyed sailing and mountain climbing. Werner Heisenberg recalled that some of the most insightful conversations he had with Niels Bohr happened during their walks together. Changing locations changes the views. The same words and ideas articulated in a different place become part of a different context. Different contexts lead to new opportunities for creating shared understandings.

Indeed, the best change of scenery is really a change of shared space. In intense collaborations, the grooves of consistency can frequently degenerate into ruts. Collaboration doesn't—and shouldn't

—take place only in the assigned office. Effective collaborators create a variety of informal and formal environments in which to share their thoughts, ideas, and understandings.

WHAT ARE THE INCENTIVE STRUCTURES?
WHAT ARE THE DISINCENTIVE STRUCTURES?

What you reward you get more of; what you punish you get less of. If the Nobel Prize was awarded to individuals only instead of to collaborators as well, isn't it possible that that would be a disincentive to certain kinds of collaboration? After all, it wasn't Watson *or* Crick who won the Nobel—it was Watson *and* Crick (along with Maurice Wilkins). It's both foolish and hypocritical to expect fruitful collaborative relationships if the organization doesn't recognize or reward them—or, still worse, actively undermines them.

The classic example of this is organizations that champion the ethic of teams and teamwork. But when you ask them how people in the organization are compensated, they tell you that individuals are given bonuses, that individuals are given job reviews. One Texas-based Fortune 500 company talked about how difficult it was to get even 20 percent of compensation on a team-performance basis. "People think it's unfair," said one executive.

However, if an organization's reward systems reflect the practices that the organization considers valuable, the absence of collaborative incentives clearly signals that the organization pays only lip service to collaboration. They literally refuse to pay for it. If "The Boss" claims credit—and is rewarded—for the performance of "His Team," what kind of message is communicated to the people who actually did the work? This inability—or unwillingness—to create and align incentives with collaborative practice assures that changing the organization's values becomes that much more difficult.

Organizations that care about collaboration have to reward it: team performance must be recognized and rewarded at least as much as individual performance. Individuals who share information and ideas across traditional boundaries must be mutually recognized. Peer-evaluation techniques must play a part in annual reviews. Instead of individual job reviews dominating the evaluation process, the performance of the work group must be evaluated.

Managers must be evaluated on the quality of the collaborative relationships they support, not just on what individuals they groom.

In effect, the organization has to use its incentive systems to make collaboration an expected, integral part of the firm's behavior. Is it any wonder that individual-intensive reward systems like those of Salomon Brothers and Kidder, Peabody led to scandal, while more team-oriented investment banks—notably Morgan Stanley and Goldman Sachs—have managed to avoid this sort of illicit entrepreneurship? The reality is that the financial service firms that both value and reward collaboration are generally regarded as better places to work. What's more, they generate enviable profits as well.

There is a rich tradition of collaboration in the sciences. That's not because science is "naturally" collaborative. The most prestigious prizes reward collaboration; publications respect collaboration; and the academy expects its scientific leaders to foster collaborative communications. The culture and reward systems are inextricably linked. They both encourage collaboration. Organizations that want to reap the benefits of creative collaboration should act accordingly.

TRY TO VIEW YOUR CLIENTS AND COLLEAGUES AS MEDIA WHO CAN AMPLIFY YOUR ABILITIES, NOT JUST AS CREATURES WHO REQUIRE YOU TO COMPROMISE WHO YOU ARE.

Too many people go into a potentially collaborative relationship reeking with the prejudice that collaboration requires you to sacrifice who you are and what you want. To be sure, there is always some element of adjustment and compromise in any human relationship. But it may well be healthier—and more realistic—to recognize that collaboration can enable you to accomplish things that you could not accomplish on your own. Collaboration becomes a tool—like a computer or a telephone—that enables you to get more done. A successful collaboration is mutually productive even as it may be mutually exploitative.

If egotists like a Braque and a Watson and a Heisenberg can willingly go into a collaboration with the expectation that the costs will not outweigh the benefits, isn't it rather silly for less talented mortals to obsess about the interpersonal traumas that might ensue?

While it's understandable that some might fear a (temporary) loss of their individuality, the collaborative leader will take care to point out the individual benefits too. This is what the best football and basketball coaches do: they point out that the value of the individual and the value of the relationship are both essential to getting the job done. Managers must manage relationships, not just individuals.

The attitude is essential: good collaborators amplify who you are and what you can do; the compromises are secondary. Indeed, if the costs of collaboration outweigh the benefits, the odds are you shouldn't be collaborating anyway.

YOU DON'T NEED TO COLLABORATE TO TURN OUT THE LIGHTS. Collaboration is not a panacea. It is not the best approach for all organizational problems, opportunities, and challenges. Sometimes simply doing a better job of coordination is enough. After all, we don't need to collaborate to turn out the lights. We don't need to collaborate to answer the phone. Just as organizations shouldn't try to cram every situation into the maw of their bureaucracies, they shouldn't feel compelled to turn every challenge into a collaborative exercise. Smart organizations—and smart managers—will know when collaboration is the appropriate organizational medium to manage uncertainty. They will know because they'll recognize that a new shared understanding—a new shared discovery—will have to occur if the challenge is to be successfully met. If that isn't the case, there isn't a case for collaboration.

Bibliography

Barnard, Chester I. *The Functions of the Executive*. Cambridge, MA: Harvard University Press, 1937.

Bateson, Gregory. *Mind and Nature*. New York: Bantam, 1980.

Becker, Franklin D. *Workspace: Creating Environments in Organizations*. New York: Praeger, 1985.

Behlmer, Rudy. *Inside Warner Bros. 1935–1951*. New York: Simon & Schuster, 1987.

Bell, Daniel. *The Coming of the Post-Industrial Society*. New York: Basic Books, 1983.

Berg, A. Scott. *Max Perkins: Editor of Genius*. New York: E. P. Dutton, 1978.

Bijker, Wiebe E., Hughes, Thomas P., and Trevor Pinch, eds. *The Social Construction of Technological Systems: New Directions in the Sociology and History of Technology*. Cambridge, MA: MIT Press, 1987.

Boettinger, Henry. *Moving Mountains: The Art and Craft of Letting Others See Things Your Way*. New York: Macmillan, 1969.

Boorstin, Daniel. *The Republic of Technology: Reflections on Our Future Community*. New York: Harper & Row, 1978.

Briggs, John. *Fire in the Crucible: The Self-Creation of Creativity and Genius*. Los Angeles: Jeremy P. Tarcher, 1990.

Bronowski, Jacob. *A Sense of the Future*. Cambridge, MA: MIT Press, 1977.

Brown, John Seely. *A Personal Perspective on Collaborative Tools*. Austin, TX: Computer-Supported Cooperative Work Conference, December 1986.

Brown, Kenneth A. *Inventors at Work*. Redmond, WA: Microsoft Press, 1988.

Bruner, Jerome. *In Search of Mind*. New York: Harper & Row, 1983.

Bush, Vannevar. "As We May Think." *Atlantic Monthly*, July 1945.

Callen, Anthea. *Techniques of the Impressionists*. Secaucus, NJ: Chartwell Books, 1982.

Campbell, Jeremy. *Grammatical Man: Information, Entropy, Language and Life*. New York: Simon & Schuster, 1982.

Carroll, John B., ed. *Language, Thought and Reality: Selected Writings of Benjamin Lee Whorf*. Cambridge, MA: MIT Press, 1956.

Cassell, Eric J., M.D. *Talking with Patients*. Cambridge, MA: MIT Press, 1985.

Cassirer, Ernst. *Language and Myth*, trans. Susanne K. Langer. New York: Dover, 1953.

Communications of the ACM. Association for Computing Machinery, Vol. 30, No. 1. New York: January 1987.

Corcoran, E. "Groupware." *Scientific American*, July 1988.

Cott, Jonathan. *Visions and Voices*. New York: Doubleday, 1987.

Crease, Robert, and Charles C. Mann. *The Second Creation: Makers of the Revolution in Twentieth-Century Physics*. New York: Macmillan, 1987.

Crick, Francis. *What Mad Pursuit*. New York: Basic Books, 1989.

Crouch, Tom. *The Bishop's Boys: A Life of Wilbur and Orville Wright*. New York: W. W. Norton, 1989.

Davis, Stanley M. *Future Perfect*. Reading, MA: Addison-Wesley, 1987.

Deal, T. E., and A. A. Kennedy. *Corporate Cultures: The Rites and Rituals of Corporate Life*. Reading, MA: Addison-Wesley, 1982.

DeGrace, Peter, and Leslie Halet Stahl. *Wicked Problems, Righteous Solutions: A Catalogue of Modern Software Engineering Paradigms*. Englewood Cliffs, NJ: Yourdon Press, 1990.

Delbanco, Nicholas. *Group Portrait*. London: Faber and Faber, 1984.

DeMarco, Tom, and Timothy Lister. *Peopleware: Productive Projects and Teams*. New York: Dorset House, 1987.

Ditlea, Steve. "Another World: Inside Artificial Reality." *PC Computing*, November 1989.

Donoghue, Denis. "Poetry and Sanity." *The New Republic*, March 6, 1989.

Douglas, Mary. *How Institutions Think.* Syracuse, NY: Syracuse University Press, 1986.

Doyle, Michael, and David Strauss. *How to Make Meetings Work.* New York: Jove, 1976.

Drucker, Peter F. *Adventures of a Bystander.* New York: Harper & Row, 1978.

————. *Management: Tasks, Responsibilities, Practices.* New York: Harper & Row, 1974.

————. *Technology, Management and Society.* New York: Harper & Row, 1970.

————. "The Coming of the New Organization." *Harvard Business Review*, January/February 1988.

Dyson, Esther. "Implementation Support: Beyond the Decision." *Release 1.O.*, August 17, 1988.

Eco, Umberto. *Travels in Hyperreality*, trans. William Weaver. New York: Harcourt Brace Jovanovich, 1986.

Ehn, Pelle. *Work-Oriented Design of Computer Artifacts.* Stockholm: Arbetslivscentrum, 1988.

Eisenstein, Elizabeth L. *The Printing Press as an Agent of Change.* New York: Cambridge University Press, 1979.

Ellis, Russel, and Dana Cuff, eds. *Architect's People.* New York: Oxford University Press, 1989.

Ellison, Harlan. *Partners in Wonder.* New York: Walker, 1971.

Ellul, Jacques. *The Technological Society*, trans. John Wilkinson. New York: Vintage, 1964.

Englebart, Douglas C., Watson, Richard W., and James C. Norton. "The Augmented Knowledge Workshop." *AFIPS Conference Proceedings*, Vol. 42, 1973.

Ferguson, Eugene S. *Engineering and the Mind's Eye.* Cambridge, MA: MIT Press, 1992.

Flores, Fernando, and Chauncey Bell. "A New Understanding of Managerial Work Improves System Design." *Computer Technology Review*, Fall 1984.

Florman, Samuel. *Blaming Technology: The Irrational Search for Scapegoats.* New York: St. Martin's Press, 1981.

Foster, Gregg. "Collaborative Systems and Multi-User Interfaces." University of California at Berkeley, Ph.D. Graduate Thesis, 1986.

French, A. P., and P. J. Kennedy, eds. *Niels Bohr: A Centenary Volume.* Cambridge, MA: Harvard University Press, 1985.

Friedhoff, Richard Mark, and William Benzon. *Visualization.* New York: Harry Abrams, 1989.

Galegher, Jolene, Kraut, Robert E., and Carmen Edigo, eds. *Intellectual Teamwork: Social and Technological Foundations of Cooperative Work.* Hillsdale, NJ: Lawrence Erlbaum Associates, 1990.

Gamow, George. *Thirty Years That Shook Physics: The Story of Quantum Theory.* New York: Doubleday, 1965.

Gardner, Howard. *The Mind's New Science: A History of the Cognitive Revolution.* New York: Basic Books, 1985.

Garson, Barbara. *The Electronic Sweatshop.* New York: Simon & Schuster, 1978.

Geneen, Harold, and Alvin Moscow. *Managing.* New York: Doubleday, 1984.

Gerstein, Marc S. *The Technology Connection: Strategy and Change in the Information Age.* Reading, MA: Addison-Wesley, 1987.

Giedion, Siegfried. *Mechanization Takes Command: A Contribution to Anonymous History.* New York: W. W. Norton, 1948.

Gilot, Françoise. *Life with Picasso.* New York: McGraw-Hill, 1964.

Goffman, Erving. *Behavior in Public Places: Notes on the Social Organization of Gatherings.* New York: Free Press, 1963.

Goffman, Erving. *Interaction Ritual.* New York: Doubleday, 1967.

———. *The Presentation of Self in Everyday Life.* New York: Doubleday, 1959.

Grabow, Stephen. *Christopher Alexander: The Search for a New Paradigm in Architecture.* Portland, OR: Oriel Press, 1984.

Greenbaum, Joan, and Morten Kyng. *Design at Work: Cooperative Design of Computer Systems.* Hillsdale, NJ: Lawrence Erlbaum Associates, 1991.

Greenberg, Saul, ed. *Computer-Supported Cooperative Work and Groupware.* San Diego, CA: Academic Press, 1991.

Gregory, Richard L. *Odd Perceptions.* London: Methuen, 1986.

Greif, Irene, ed. *Computer-Supported Cooperative Work: A Book of Readings.* San Mateo, CA: Morgan Kauffman Publishers, 1988.

Hagstrom, Warren O. *The Scientific Community.* Carbondale, IL: Southern Illinois University Press, 1965.

Hall, Edward T. *Beyond Culture.* New York: Doubleday, 1976.

———. *The Dance of Life: The Other Dimension of Time.* New York: Doubleday, 1983.

———. *The Hidden Dimension.* New York: Doubleday, 1966.

———. *The Silent Language.* New York: Doubleday, 1958.

Hall, Stephen. *Invisible Frontiers*. Boston: Atlantic Monthly Press, 1987.

Halprin, Lawrence. *The RSVP Cycles: Creative Processes in the Human Environment*. New York: George Braziller, 1969.

Handy, Charles. *Understanding Organizations*. London: Penguin, 1985.

Heidegger, Martin. *The Question Concerning Technology and Other Essays*, trans. William Lovitt. New York: Harper & Row, 1977.

Heim, Michael. *Electric Language: A Philosophical Study of Word Processing*. New Haven: Yale University Press, 1987.

Hirschhorn, Larry. *The Workplace Within: Psychodynamics of Organizational Life*. Cambridge, MA: MIT Press, 1988.

Homans, George. *The Human Group*. New York: Harcourt Brace Jovanovich 1950.

Howard, Robert. *Brave New Workplace*. New York: Viking Press, 1985.

Illich, Ivan. *Tools for Conviviality*. New York: Harper & Row, 1973.

Innis, Harold A. *The Bias of Communication*. Toronto: University of Toronto Press, 1964.

Innis, Harold A. *Empire and Communication*. Toronto: University of Toronto Press, 1972.

Janis, Irving. *Groupthink*, 2nd ed. Boston: Houghton Mifflin, 1982.

Johansen, Robert. *Groupware: Computer Support for Business Teams*. New York: Free Press, 1988.

Johansen, Robert, Vallee, Jacques, and Kathleen Vian. *Electronic Meetings*. Reading, MA: Addison-Wesley, 1979.

John-Steiner, Vera. *Notebooks of the Mind*. New York: Harper & Row, 1985.

Jones, David Richard. *Great Directors at Work*. Berkeley, CA: University of California Press, 1986.

Jones, Steven G. *CyberSociety: Computer-Mediated Communication and Community*. Thousand Oaks, CA: Sage Publications, 1995.

Judson, Horace Freeland. *The Eighth Day of Creation: The Makers of the Revolution in Biology*. New York: Simon & Schuster, 1979.

———. *The Search for Solutions*. Baltimore: Johns Hopkins University Press, 1987.

Kanigel, Robert. *Apprentice to Genius*. New York: Macmillan, 1986.

Keen, Peter G. W., and Michael Scott Morton. *Decision Support Systems*. Reading, MA: Addison-Wesley, 1978.

Keidel, Robert W. *Corporate Players: Designs for Working and Winning Together.* New York: John Wiley & Sons, 1988.

Kelly, John N. "Technology That Supports Meetings." *Patricia Seybold's Office Computing Report,* September 1988.

Kevles, Daniel. *The Physicists.* New York: Alfred A. Knopf, 1977.

Kidder, Tracy. *House.* Boston: Houghton Mifflin, 1985.

———. *Soul of a New Machine.* Boston: Atlantic Monthly Press, 1981.

Koestler, Arthur. *The Act of Creation.* New York: Macmillan, 1964.

Kuhn, Thomas S. *The Structure of Scientific Revolutions.* Chicago: University of Chicago Press, 1970.

Latour, Bruno. *Science in Action.* Cambridge, MA: Harvard University Press, 1987.

Leibenstein, Harvey. *Inside the Firm: The Inefficiencies of Hierarchy.* Cambridge, MA: Harvard University Press, 1987.

Levering, Robert. *A Great Place to Work.* New York: Random House, 1988.

Levine, Howard, and Howard Rheingold. *The Cognitive Connection: Thought and Language in Mind and Machine.* New York: Prentice-Hall, 1987.

Littlejohn, Stephen W. *Theories of Human Communication.* Belmont, CA: Wadworth Publishing, 1989.

Lussier, Robert. *Supervision: A Skill-Building Approach.* Homewood, IL: Richard D. Irwin, Inc., 1989.

Lynch, Kevin. *The Image of a City.* Cambridge, MA: MIT Press, 1960.

Malone, Michael S. *The Big Score: The Billion Dollar Story of Silicon Valley.* New York: Doubleday, 1985.

Malone, Thomas, et al. "Intelligent Information Sharing Systems." *Communications of the ACM,* May 1987.

Mayo, Elton. *The Human Problems of an Industrial Civilization.* New York: Macmillan, 1933.

McCaskey, Michael B. *The Executive Challenge: Managing Change and Ambiguity.* Boston: Pitman, 1982.

McLuhan, Marshall. *The Gutenberg Galaxy: The Making of Typographic Man.* Toronto: University of Toronto Press, 1962.

———. *Understanding Media: The Extensions of Man.* New York: New American Library, 1964.

Merton, Robert K. *On the Shoulders of Giants.* New York: Free Press, 1965.

Meyrowitz, Joshua. *No Sense of Place: The Impact of Electronic Media on Social Behavior.* New York: Oxford University Press, 1985.

Minsky, Marvin. *Society of Mind.* New York: Simon & Schuster, 1985.

Mintzberg, Harry. *Mintzberg on Management.* New York: Free Press, 1989.

Mitchell, C. Thomas. *Redefining Designing: From Form to Experience.* New York: Van Nostrand Reinhold, 1993.

Mumford, Louis. *Technics and Civilization.* New York: Harcourt Brace Jovanovich, 1934.

Nelson, Theodor. *Computer Lib/Dream Machines.* Self-published, 1974.

New York University Symposium. *Technological Support for Work Group Collaboration.* New York: May Center for Research on Information Systems, NYU, 1987.

Noble, David F. *America by Design: A Social History of Industrial Automation.* New York: Alfred A. Knopf, 1984.

———. *Forces of Production.* New York: Alfred A. Knopf, 1977.

Nonaka, Ikujiro. "Toward Up-Down-Middle Management." *Sloan Management Review,* Spring 1988.

Ong, Walter J. *Orality and Literacy: The Technologizing of the Word.* London: Methuen, 1982.

Platt, J. R. "Strong Inference." *Science,* October 16, 1964.

Perrow, Charles. *Complex Organizations.* New York: McGraw-Hill, 1986.

Peters, Tom, and Robert Waterman. *In Search of Excellence.* New York: Harper & Row, 1982.

Postman, Neil. *Amusing Ourselves to Death: Public Discourse in the Age of Show Business.* New York: Viking Penguin, 1985.

Proceedings of the Conference on Computer-Supported Cooperative Work, September 1988. Portland, OR: Association for Computing Machinery, 1988.

Proceedings of the 1986 Conference on Computer-Supported Work. Austin, TX: Conference Committee for CSCW, 1986.

Reich, Robert. "Entrepreneurship Reconsidered: The Team as Hero." *Harvard Business Review,* May/June 1987.

Rheingold, Howard. *Tools for Thought: The History and Future of Mind-Expanding Technology.* New York: Simon & Schuster, 1985.

Rhodes, Richard. *The Making of the Atomic Bomb.* New York: Simon & Schuster, 1986.

Rochell, Carlton C., and Christina Spellman. *Dreams Betrayed: Working in the Technological Age.* Lexington, MA: D. C. Heath, 1987.

Rogers, Everett M., and Rekha Agarwala-Rogers. *Communication in Organizations.* New York: Free Press, 1976.

Root-Bernstein, Robert Scott. *Discovering.* Cambridge, MA: Harvard University Press, 1989.

Rosenblum, Ralph, and Robert Karen. *When the Shooting Stops . . . The Cutting Begins: A Film Editor's Story.* New York: Da Capo Press, 1986.

Rybczynski, Witold. *Taming the Tiger: The Struggle to Control Technology.* New York: Viking Press, 1960.

Sagan, Carl. *The Dragons of Eden.* New York: Random House, 1977.

Schon, Donald A. *The Reflective Practitioner: How Professionals Think in Action.* New York: Basic Books, 1983.

Schrage, Michael. "Manager's Journal." *The Wall Street Journal,* December 7, 1987.

———. "The Personal Computer Column." *The Washington Post,* November 18, 1985.

Simon, Herbert A. *The New Science of Management Decision,* rev. ed. Englewood Cliffs, NJ: Prentice Hall, 1977.

———. *The Sciences of the Artificial,* 2nd ed. Cambridge, MA: MIT Press, 1981.

Smith, Adam. *Powers of Mind.* New York: Random House, 1975.

Sommer, Robert. *Personal Space: The Behavioral Basis of Design.* Englewood Cliffs, NJ: Prentice-Hall, 1969.

———. *The Mind's Eye: Imagery in Everyday Life.* New York: Delacorte Press, 1978.

Stefik, Mark, et al. "Beyond the Chalkboard." *Communications of the ACM,* January 1987.

Stefik, Mark, and John Seely Brown. "Toward Portable Ideas." *Communications of Xerox PARC.* Xerox Corporation, Palo Alto Research Center, 1988.

Steiner, Gary A. *The Creative Organization.* Chicago: University of Chicago Press, 1965.

Steiner, George. *After Babel: Aspects of Language and Translation.* New York: Oxford University Press, 1975.

Stent, Gunther. *Scientific Genius and Creativity.* San Francisco: W. H. Freeman, 1985.

Stockman, David. *The Triumph of Politics: Why the Reagan Revolution Failed.* New York: Harper & Row, 1986.

Stockton, William. "Trouble in the Cockpit." *New York Times Magazine,* March 27, 1988.

Strassman, Paul. *The Information Payoff.* New York: Basic Books, 1985.

Sundstrum, Eric. *Work Places.* New York: Cambridge University Press, 1986.

Taylor, Frederick W. *The Principles of Scientific Management.* New York: Harper & Row, 1915.

Terkel, Studs. *Working.* New York: Ballantine, 1974.

Thackara, John. *Design After Modernism.* London: Thames and Hudson, 1988.

The 3M Meeting Management Team. *How to Run Better Business Meetings.* New York: McGraw-Hill, 1987.

Thomas, Frank, and Ollie Johnston. *Disney Animation: The Illusion of Life.* New York: Abbeville Press, 1981.

Thomas, Lewis. *Lives of a Cell.* New York: Viking Penguin, 1974.

Toffler, Alvin. *Future Shock.* New York: Random House, 1970.

Turkle, Sherry. *The Second Self: Computers and the Human Spirit.* New York: Simon & Schuster, 1984.

Vygotsky, Lev. *Thought and Language.* Cambridge, MA: MIT Press, 1962.

Watson, James D. *The Double Helix.* New York: W. W. Norton, 1980.

Weiner, Philip, ed. *Charles S. Peirce: Selected Writings.* New York: Dover, 1958.

Weisberg, Robert W. *Creativity: Genius and Other Myths.* San Francisco: W. H. Freeman, 1986.

Weisbrod, Marvin R. *Productive Workplaces: Organizing and Managing for Dignity, Meaning, and Community.* San Francisco: Jossey-Bass, 1987.

Whitmeyer, Claude. *In the Company of Others: Making Community in the Modern World.* New York: Putnam Publishing Group, 1993.

Winner, Langdon. *Autonomous Technology: Technics-Out-of-Control as a Theme in Political Thought.* Cambridge, MA: MIT Press, 1977.

Winograd, Terry, and Fernando Flores. *Understanding Computers and Cognition.* Norwood, NJ: Ablex, 1986.

Winston, Brian. *Misunderstanding Media.* Cambridge, MA: Harvard University Press, 1986.

Wright, Orville. *How We Invented the Airplane: An Illustrated History.* New York: Dover, 1988.

Yates, JoAnne. *Control Through Communication: The Rise of System in American Management.* Baltimore: Johns Hopkins University Press, 1989.

Zuboff, Shoshana. *In the Age of the Smart Machine: The Future of Work and Power.* New York: Basic Books, 1988.

Permissions

CURRENCY

DOUBLEDAY

Since 1989, Currency Doubleday
has published books on business by
Scientists, Scholars, Artists,
Philosophers, Theologians,
Storytellers, and Practitioners who
challenge readers to make a
difference, not just a living.

CURRENCY DOUBLEDAY BOOKS

The Art of the Long View: Planning the Future in an Uncertain World by Peter Schwartz

Schwartz, one of the world's leading futurists, gives you the tools for scenario planning, originally developed with Royal Dutch/Shell, to help your company plan for the future.

0-385-26731-2 / U.S. $24.00 / CAN. $30.00 / Hardcover / 258 pages

---

The Art of Worldly Wisdom by Baltasar Gracián, translated by Christopher Maurer

Follow the timeless advice of seventeenth-century Jesuit scholar Baltasar Gracián. Each of the elegantly crafted maxims in this *New York Times* bestseller offers valuable insight on the art of living and the practice of achieving.

0-385-42131-1 / U.S. $15.00 / CAN. $20.00 / Hardcover / 182 pages

---

Control Your Destiny or Someone Else Will: How Jack Welch Is Making General Electric the World's Most Competitive Company by Noel M. Tichy and Stratford Sherman

"Thinking of starting a revolution at your company? Before you do, read Noel M. Tichy and Stratford Sherman's book." —*The Wall Street Journal*

Includes a handbook for revolutionaries.

0-385-24883-0 / U.S. $27.00 / CAN. $35.00 / Hardcover / 384 pages

---

The Fifth Discipline: The Art and Practice of the Learning Organization by Peter M. Senge

This pathbreaking book on building "learning organizations" provides the tools and methods for freeing organizations of their "learning disabilities." A bestseller since 1990, this book has become the organizational bible at AT&T, Ford, Procter & Gamble, and Apple.

0-385-26094-6 / U.S. $27.50 / CAN. $35.00 / Hardcover / 424 pages

Also available as a Currency paperback

0-385-26095-4 / U.S. $18.50 / CAN. $24.50

The Fifth Discipline Fieldbook by Peter M. Senge, Art Kleiner, Charlotte Roberts, Rick Ross, and Bryan Smith

This is a participative book of tools and techniques based on Peter M. Senge's bestselling *The Fifth Discipline*. It is a workbook with exercises for both individuals and teams, a sourcebook for approaches and ideas, and a wisdom book of stories told by and about the people who are successfully putting the five disciplines into practice.

0-385-47256-0 / U.S. $29.95 / CAN. $38.95 / Paperback / 576 pages

---

First Comes Love, Then Comes Money: How Unmarried Couples Can Use Investments, Tax Planning, Insurance, and Wills to Gain Financial Protection Denied by Law by Larry M. Elkin

You may be in danger of losing your financial security if you are living together but unmarried. CPA Larry M. Elkin shows you how to protect yourself from certain inequities in U.S. law.

0-385-47172-6 / U.S. $22.95 / CAN. $28.95 / Hardcover / 288 pages

---

The Heart Aroused: Poetry and the Preservation of the Soul in Corporate America by David Whyte

The Heart Aroused proposes a new way to transform the practical need to work into an opportunity for spiritual nourishment. It uses the texts of classic poetry to unlock the secrets of how to live a full life at work.

0-385-42350-0 / U.S. $22.50 / CAN. $29.95 / Hardcover / 320 pages

CURRENCY DOUBLEDAY BOOKS

AVAILABLE AT YOUR LOCAL BOOKSTORE. OR YOU MAY USE THIS COUPON TO ORDER DIRECT.

ISBN	TITLE AND AUTHOR	PRICE	QTY.	TOTAL
26731-2	**The Art of the Long View** by Peter Schwartz	U.S. $24.00 /CAN. $30.00	x __ =	_____
42131-1	**The Art of Worldly Wisdom** by Baltasar Gracián, translated by Christopher Maurer	U.S. $15.00 /CAN. $20.00	x __ =	_____
24883-0	**Control Your Destiny or Someone Else Will** by Noel M. Tichy and Stratford Sherman	U.S. $27.00 /CAN. $35.00	x __ =	_____
26094-6	**The Fifth Discipline** by Peter M. Senge	U.S. $27.50 /CAN. $35.00	x __ =	_____
26095-4	*Also available as a Currency paperback*	U.S. $18.50 /CAN. $24.50	x __ =	_____
47256-0	**The Fifth Discipline Fieldbook** by Peter M. Senge, Art Kleiner, Charlotte Roberts, Rick Ross, and Bryan Smith	U.S. $29.95 /CAN. $38.95	x __ =	_____
47172-6	**First Comes Love, Then Comes Money** by Larry M. Elkin	U.S. $22.95 /CAN. $28.95	x __ =	_____
42350-0	**The Heart Aroused** by David Whyte	U.S. $22.50 /CAN. $29.95	x __ =	_____
26496-8	**Leadership Is an Art** by Max De Pree	U.S. $21.00 /CAN. $26.00	x __ =	_____
42018-8	**Leadership Jazz** by Max De Pree	U.S. $20.00 /CAN. $25.00	x __ =	_____
26241-8	**Money and the Meaning of Life** by Jacob Needleman	U.S. $21.00 /CAN. $26.00	x __ =	_____
26242-6	*Also available as a Currency paperback*	U.S. $15.00 /CAN. $20.00	x __ =	_____
42528-7	**The One to One Future** by Don Peppers and Martha Rogers	U.S. $22.00 /CAN. $27.50	x __ =	_____
42555-4	**The Real Heroes of Business and Not a CEO Among Them** by Bill Fromm and Len Schlesinger	U.S. $22.50 /CAN. $29.95	x __ =	_____
42056-0	**The Republic of Tea** by Mel Ziegler, Patricia Ziegler, and Bill Rosenzweig	U.S. $22.50 /CAN. $28.00	x __ =	_____
42057-9	*Also available as a Currency paperback*	U.S. $15.00 /CAN. $20.00	x __ =	_____
47485-7	**Warfighting** *The U.S. Marine Corps Book of Strategy*	U.S. $17.50 /CAN. $22.50	x __ =	_____
41703-9	**The West Point Way of Leadership** by Colonel (Ret.) Larry Donnithorne	U.S. $20.00 /CAN. $26.00	x __ =	_____

Parcel Post shipping and handling . . . . . . (add $2.50 per order; allow 4–6 weeks for delivery) _____
UPS shipping and handling . . . . (add $4.50 per order; allow 2–3 weeks for delivery) _____

TOTAL: _____

Please send me the titles I have indicated above. I am enclosing $_____.
Send check or money order (no CODs or cash, please). Make check payable to Doubleday
Consumer Services. Prices and availability are subject to change without notice.

Name: _____

Address: _____ Apt. #: _____

City: _____ State: _____ Zip: _____

Send completed coupon and payment to:
Doubleday Consumer Services
Dept. DR9
2451 South Wolf Road
Des Plaines, IL 60018

DR9–10/94